Sylvia Plath's Fiction

Sylvia Plath's Fiction

A Critical Study

Luke Ferretter

Edinburgh University Press

For Mackie

© Luke Ferretter, 2010

Edinburgh University Press Ltd
22 George Square, Edinburgh

www.euppublishing.com

Typeset in 10.5/13 Adobe Sabon
by Servis Filmsetting Ltd, Stockport, Cheshire, and
printed and bound in Great Britain by
CPI Antony Rowe, Chippenham and Eastbourne

A CIP record for this book is available from the British Library

ISBN 978 0 7486 2509 3 (hardback)

The right of Luke Ferretter
to be identified as author of this work
has been asserted in accordance with
the Copyright, Designs and Patents Act 1988.

Contents

Abbreviations

The following abbreviations have been used in this book for works by Sylvia Plath:

BJ   *The Bell Jar* (London: Faber and Faber, 1963)
CCS   *Collected Children's Stories* (London: Faber and Faber, 2001)
CP   *Collected Poems* (London: Faber and Faber, 1981)
J   *The Journals of Sylvia Plath, 1950–1962*, ed. Karen V. Kukil (London: Faber and Faber, 2000)
JPBD *Johnny Panic and the Bible of Dreams, and Other Prose Writings*, 2nd edn. (London: Faber and Faber, 1979)
LH   *Letters Home* (London: Faber and Faber, 1975)

Acknowledgements

I was enabled to begin work on this book by a Sesqui Postdoctoral Research Fellowship from the University of Sydney. Adrian Mitchell as Head of School and Tony Miller as chair of department supported my research there in every way. My thanks also to Penny Gay. Dan Gunn generously welcomed me to the University of Maine at Farmington, and my time there was immensely productive thanks to him. My thanks to Nancy Walters and the inter-library loan staff at Mantor library, who got me arcane materials with speed and good humour. At Baylor University, my department chairs, Maurice Hunt and Dianna Vitanza, have supported my research in every way. I am especially grateful for funding to participate in several conferences in Britain and America, which have significantly contributed to this project. I have been enabled to travel to the archives of Sylvia Plath's work at Indiana University, Smith College and Emory University by the awards of two summer sabbaticals from the Faculty of Arts and Sciences and by a grant from the University Research Committee. My thanks to my research assistants, Laura Schrock, who was more a collaborator than an assistant, and Emily Sgarlata.

One of the great blessings of working on this book has been the friendship of Karen Kukil, who has enabled and advanced my research in more ways than I can count. My thanks to Martin Antonetti and the staff of the Mortimer Rare Book Room at Smith College for help with every request. Peter Steinberg has shared his encyclopaedic knowledge of all things Sylvia Plath on many occasions, to my great benefit. I have learned a great deal from conversations with Sally Bayley, Tracy Brain, Bill Buckley, Nephie Christodoulides, Kathleen Connors, Jo Gill, Langdon Hammer, Anita Helle, Richard Larschan, Robin Peel and Linda Wagner-Martin. Heather Clark, Langdon Hammer and Peter Steinberg and have generously shared their work in progress with me. I have very much appreciated the generosity with which Perry Norton,

Philip McCurdy and Marcia Brown Stern have shared their recollections and thoughts on Sylvia Plath's life and work. Tristin Skyler and Julia Stiles kindly discussed their vision for their film version of *The Bell Jar*. My thanks to Stephen Enniss at the Manuscripts, Archives and Rare Books Library at Emory University for sharing his time and expertise with me and to Kathy Shoemaker for her help with all my requests. Breon Mitchell and the staff of the Lilly Library, Indiana University have given me every possible assistance, both during and after my visits to the Library. My thanks to Polly Armstrong at the Department of Special Collections at Stanford University.

I could not wish for a better editor than Jackie Jones at Edinburgh University Press. Her constant understanding, knowledge, patience and support have brought this book to press in its final form. I count myself extremely fortunate to have worked with such a fine editor. My thanks also to Nicci Cloke at Faber.

I would not have been able to write this book without my beloved wife, Jen. I owe her everything. I thank my parents for their constant support of my work, and my parents-in-law for their generous and unstinting help.

Finally, I acknowledge with respect and appreciation the work of Sylvia Plath.

Works by Aurelia Plath are reproduced by kind permission of Susan Plath Winston, © Estate of Aurelia S. Plath.

Works by Nathaniel Tarn are reproduced by kind permission of the author.

Materials from the Lilly Library are reproduced courtesy of The Lilly Library, Indiana University, Bloomington, Indiana.

Materials from the Department of Special Collections at Stanford University are reproduced courtesy of the Department of Special Collections and University Archives, Stanford University Libraries.

Materials from the Manuscript, Archives, and Rare Book Library, Emory University are reproduced with permission.

Excerpts from *The Bell Jar* by Sylvia Plath copyright © 1971 Harper & Row, Publishers, Inc. Reprinted by permission of HarperCollins Publishers.

Excerpts from *Johnny Panic and the Bible of Dreams* by Sylvia Plath copyright 1952, 1953, 1954, 1955, 1956, 1957, 1960, 1961, 1962, 1963 by Sylvia Plath. Copyright © 1977, 1979 by Ted Hughes. Reprinted by permission of HarperCollins Publishers.

Excerpts from *The Collected Poems of Sylvia Plath*, edited by Ted Hughes copyright © 1960, 1965, 1971, 1981 by the Estate of Sylvia

Introduction

There are two major ways of thinking about Sylvia Plath's work in contemporary criticism. One way, dominant since the publication of *Ariel*, is to think of this work as a progression towards the greatest poetry of Plath's career, the poems of 1962 and 1963. Plath herself said that these poems 'will make my name' (*LH* 468), and critics continue to think of her work, in Nancy Hargrove's words, as a 'journey toward *Ariel*'.[1] Tim Kendall writes of her 1954–55 poems, 'Were they not produced by the author of *Ariel*, the poems would hardly merit attention'.[2] In the introduction to their collection of Plath's visual art, *Eye Rhymes*, Kathleen Connors and Sally Bayley describe the contributors' interest in Plath's early work as 'an attempt to answer the question, How did Plath arrive at *Ariel*?'[3] During the last decade or so, another way of thinking about Plath's work has also begun to emerge, which can best described, in the title of Tracy Brain's study, as an investigation of 'the other Sylvia Plath'.[4] This kind of approach is exemplified in studies like those of Al Strangeways on Plath's intellectual work, of Robin Peel on her politics, of the contributors to *Eye Rhymes* on her visual art and of the contributors to Anita Helle's collection *The Unraveling Archive* on Plath's unpublished materials, as well as Brain's work on her environmentalism, national identity and literary influences.[5] These studies do not suggest that *Ariel* is not Plath finest work. Rather, they are interested in her large and diverse body of work as a whole, and focus their attention on less frequently discussed texts within this body of work, in order to build up a complete picture of the kind of thinker and writer that Plath was.

This is the approach I take in this book. Whilst *Ariel* is Plath's single greatest achievement, in my view, it is the achievement of a woman who wrote a great number of works in a great number of genres, indeed whose creativity was not limited to the written word, but who sketched, painted, made collages, decorated her furniture, indeed simply could not stop creating in whatever medium was to hand. Plath's large and multi-generic *oeuvre* is worth knowing and understanding as a whole. That is the principle behind this book, a study of Sylvia Plath's fiction. Plath spent her entire creative life, from before her teenage years to the last weeks of her life, working on some form of fiction. Ted Hughes described her 'ambition to write stories' as 'the most visible burden of her life'.[6] Plath wrote some seventy short stories and worked on three novels. There is to date no detailed study of these works. There are student guides to *The Bell Jar*, and there is Pat Macpherson's sociological discussion, *Reflecting on The Bell Jar*. We lack a comprehensive study, however, of Plath's lifelong work as a writer of fiction. This book is that study. Its aim is to provide a clear and comprehensive sense of the place of fiction in her life and work as a writer. In my opinion this fiction is altogether worth reading, enjoying and understanding in its own right. There is no question that it is a crucial and central part of Plath's complete and complex creative work.

Short Stories

There was no time in Plath's life, from the time she was a teenager, during which she was not writing fiction. This lifelong body of work can be considered in the following chronological groups.

1. Juvenilia (1946–50)

It is difficult to give a precise number of the stories of Plath's that survive from this period, since there is a fluid continuum of manuscripts, from notes for plots, through unfinished stories and character sketches, to completed typescripts. Six stories survive from 1946, written when Plath was just thirteen, and in some cases fourteen, years old.[7] There are also four incomplete works held at Smith College, which are undated and incomplete, but clearly early works, as the juvenile handwriting of some of them suggests.[8] The most interesting of Plath's stories from this period is the twenty-two page fairy story, 'Stardust', in which the young heroine, Nancy, walks up a staircase of snowflakes in the sky to an ice palace, and encounters a series of magical characters. The underwater imagery in the story – Nancy follows the fairy beneath the ocean to visit the Queen of Sea – is a precursor of the image of the better world under water that Plath would develop in her mature poetry. In Ted Hughes' children's story 'Billy Hook and the Three Souvenirs' the motif of a child walking up a staircase in the sky to a palace where the fairy queen lives remains.[9] Plath was already beginning to publish these early stories:

'Victory' appears in the *Wellesley Townsman* and 'A Morning in the Agora' in *The Phillipian*, the literary magazine of the Alice L. Phillips Junior High School.

The second period of Plath's early fiction spans her last three years at high school, during which she was in Wilbury Crockett's English class. Seven stories dating from 1948, eight from 1949 and four from 1950 survive, as well as an undated monologue called 'Watch My Line', whose style and content suggest that it also belongs to this period.[10] These stories are most interesting for the ways in which they prefigure the concerns of Plath's mature work. As Linda Wagner-Martin writes, 'The pervasive themes of Plath's fictional *oeuvre* appear here in miniature'.[11] In 'The Dark River', from 1949, a woman tells the narrator about a strange river which has come between her and everyone she has loved. When she was young she had been sure that her desires would all be fulfilled, but she has come to realise that the dark river that fascinates her will always prevent her from true relationship with others. At the end of the text, the woman who tells the narrator her story fades into the narrator's own imagination, which has been playing upon the real river in front of her.[12] In this early story, Plath sets up a powerful symbol of an inexplicable break in relationship between the heroine and those around her. 'East Wind', from the same year, develops this symbolism. The heroine is called Miss Minton, and her story ends in a similar way to that of her namesake in Plath's later story 'Sunday at the Mintons'. She follows a mysterious child, as fascinated by him as the heroine of 'The Dark River' is by the river, and the wind blows her hat into the river in her own city. She leans over a bridge and looks down, tempted to end her dull, disappointing life for ever. As with Elizabeth Minton, she imagines the ecstasy of floating out over the water, borne up by the air. She almost decides to throw herself over but, again like Elizabeth Minton, her joyful and aggressive fantasies turn out to be no more than fantasies. Ashamed of her excessive desires, she steps back from the edge.[13] This story prefigures the symbolism of mature poems like 'Full Fathom Five' and 'Lorelei', in which the speakers are attracted by the better world to be found, through drowning, under water. Plath's later concerns with gender roles are also evident in a story like 'The Visitor', from 1948, in which the question of whether a woman should choose marriage and family or a creative career is explored.

2. College Stories to 1953 (1950–53)

Plath took several creative writing courses at Smith College. In her sophomore year she took Eng 220a and 220b, Practical Writing. In her junior year, she took Eng 347a Style and Form, with Robert Gorham Davis. In her senior year, she took Eng 347a Short Story Writing with Alfred Kazin, and Eng 41b Poetry with Alfred Young Fisher. For the first four of these courses she produced a considerable body of fiction. The fiction she wrote for these courses, as well as that which she wrote on her own time, underwent a marked change in maturity after her breakdown in the summer of 1953 and her recovery in McLean hospital during the autumn. When she returned to Smith in Spring 1954, she was beginning to develop her mature fictional voices and styles. Before the summer of 1953, she wrote one truly fine story, 'Sunday at the Mintons', in April 1952. In addition, by my count, there remain twelve more works of fiction which Plath wrote between entering Smith in September 1950 and June 1953, as well as two that are now lost and fragments of a further two that have survived on the verso of other documents.[14] Three of these stories, 'Den of Lions', 'The Perfect Setup' and 'Initiation', were published in *Seventeen*.[15] In the best of them, such as 'The Perfect Setup', 'Brief Encounter' and 'The Estonian', Plath was beginning to develop some of her mature themes, dealing with the complex and difficult emotions that exist under the surface communications of social life. These stories are also notable for their diversity. 'Marcia Ventura and the Ninth Kingdom', from December 1952, is a futuristic moral allegory. 'Dialogue', from January 1953, is a seventeen-page philosophical exchange between two college students about a range of subjects from love to identity to ethics. 'I Lied for Love', from April 1953, is a long romance about a farmer's daughter who is misguidedly seduced by a wealthy boy but, after his death leaves her a fallen woman, ends up with the honest farmworker who has loved her all along.

3. College Stories (1954–55)

Following her return to Smith in February 1954, Plath began to develop her mature fictional styles. In this period she wrote, by my count, ten stories, almost all of which are significant works in themselves. The stories published in *Johnny Panic and the Bible of Dreams, and Other Prose Writings*, which include five of this group, are ordered thematically rather than chronologically, and sometimes dated by publication rather than by composition. I list the stories from this period here in the closest possible approximation to their chronological order, along with the most precise dates that it is possible to establish:

'Among the Bumblebees' (September–December 1954)
'In the Mountains' (September–December 1954)

'Superman and Paula Brown's New Snowsuit' (September–December 1954)
'The Day Mr Prescott Died' (29 January 1955)
'Tongues of Stone' (29 January 1955)
'The Smoky Blue Piano' (15 January 1955)
'Home Is Where the Heart Is' (26–29 January 1955)
'Tomorrow Begins Today' (26–29 January 1955)
'The Christmas Heart' (29 January–12 September, 1955)
'Platinum Summer' (July – c. 9 August, 1955).

The first five of these were written for Plath's short story class during the Fall 1954 semester. 'The Day Mr Prescott Died' and 'Tongues of Stone' were rewritten shortly before 29 January 1955 (*LH* 155). 'The Smoky Blue Piano' was probably written during the Christmas vacation of 1954–55 and then rewritten by 15 January 1955.[16] Plath told her mother on 29 January 1955 that she had written 'Home is Where the Heart Is' and 'Tomorrow Begins Today' 'in the last three days' (*LH* 155). She first referred to the story that became 'The Christmas Heart' on 29 January 1955 (*LH* 155) and finished it by the time she left America for Cambridge on 12 September. She referred to working on 'Platinum Summer' on 28 July, 1955, and had finished a draft by 9 August 1955, telling her mother that day that she would perfect and revise one or two passages and then submit the final copy.[17] 'The Smoky Blue Piano', 'The Christmas Heart' and 'Platinum Summer' are all romances written for the women's magazine market. 'Home is Where the Heart Is' and 'Tomorrow Begins Today' are stories with a moral message written as such for a contest run by the Christophers, a Christian organisation (*LH* 155).

4. Cambridge Stories (1956–57)

From her writing honeymoon in Spain in July and August 1956, through her second year as a Fulbright scholar in Cambridge, and then in her second writers' vacation in July and August 1957 on Cape Cod, Plath again produced a considerable body of mature fiction. Much of this now exists only in fragments, preserved on the verso of Ted Hughes' papers at Emory University, and some has been lost. This is a list, in the best possible chronological order and with the most precise possible dates, of these stories. (F) indicates that the story exists in fragmentary form. (L) indicates that the story, although completed by Plath, is currently lost.

'The Matisse Chapel' (F) (17 January–19 February 1956)
'The Black Bull' (F) (22 July–21 August 1956)

'Remember the Stick Man' (F) (22 July–21 August 1956)
'That Widow Mangada' (22 July–21 August 1956)
'Afternoon in Hardcastle Crags' (F) (post-September 1956)
'The Invisible Man' (F) (8–12 October 1956)
'The Wishing Box' (8–12 October 1956)
'All the Dead Dears' (September–October 1956)
'The Fabulous Room-Mate' (L) (10 August 1956–18 March 1957)
'The Laundromat Affair' (F) (9 January–18 March 1957)
'The Trouble-Making Mother' (L) (18–24 July 1957)
'Operation Valentine' (F) (18 July–5 August 1957)

'The Matisse Chapel' is a story based on Plath's visit to the Matisse chapel in Vence in Southern France with Richard Sassoon during her first Christmas vacation at Cambridge. On 17 January 1956, she told her mother she had sketched out the plot of the story (*LH* 208).[18] By 19 February she had submitted it to the *New Yorker* (*J* 201), which rejected it. During her writing honeymoon in Spain, Plath wrote 'The Black Bull', 'Remember the Stick Man' and 'That Widow Mangada'. On 16 October 1956, Plath told her mother that she had written some of her finest stories that week, including 'The Invisible Man' (*LH* 278), and that Hughes had criticised these stories in London the previous weekend, 13 and 14 October, which means that they must have been finished by Friday, 12 October. In a letter of 9 October to Plath, Hughes referred to an idea of Plath's about a story whose heroine cannot dream, indicating that she has told him in her letter of the previous day that she was writing 'The Wishing Box'.[19] 'All the Dead Dears', based on Plath's experience of meeting Hughes' family in Yorkshire in September 1956, was planned during that visit (*J* 579), and is probably one of the several stories Plath completed by 12 October. 'Afternoon in Hardcastle Crags' is also based on this visit to Yorkshire. The single page that survives deals with similar events to those in the first part of the poem 'The Snowman on the Moor'. The heroine, Olwyn, has stormed out of the hero's mother's house onto the moors, angry with the hero, Gerald, who spends his time composing poetry and listening to Beethoven. Olwyn reflects ruefully on her husband's brilliant mind and daydreams about his future fame.[20]

'The Laundromat Affair' and 'Operation Valentine' were written for the women's magazine market. Plath was working on the first of these in January 1957 (*LH* 290) and submitted it to the *Ladies' Home Journal* on 18 March (*LH* 303). They told her that they would reconsider the story if she revised the ending, which she did by 9 August (*LH* 312; *J* 295). 'Operation Valentine' is the story Plath refers to in her journals as a story about a mother's helper (*J* 288); she submitted it to the *Ladies' Home Journal* on 5 August (*LH* 326). The two lost stories from this period are 'The Fabulous Room-Mate' and 'The Trouble-Making Mother'. The first of these, begun in August 1956, contrasted the lives of the heroine and her room-mate, a character based on Nancy Hunter, Plath's own room-mate at Smith and Harvard Summer School in 1954 and 1955.[21] Plath continued to work on the story during the Christmas vacation of 1956–57, describing it as one of her 'love stories' aimed at the women's magazine market (*LH* 290). She submitted it to the *Ladies' Home Journal*, along with 'The Laundromat Affair', on 18 March 1957 (*LH* 303). 'The Trouble-Making Mother' was completed by 24 July 1957, when Plath called it her only well-written story in several years (*J* 291). She submitted it to the *Saturday Evening Post*, which rejected it (*J* 295), with plans then to submit it to *McCall's*, *Ladies Home Journal*, *Good Housekeeping* and *Woman's Day* (*J* 291). The story was autobiographically based, set over the course of a single day, during which there are several 'flashbacks triggered by telephone calls' (*J* 290). It is based on the 'Ira and Gordon crisis' of summer 1954, and emphasises the relationship between the heroine and her mother (*J* 287). Initially, Plath had planned to have the heroine dye her hair platinum blonde in order to distinguish herself from her mother (*J* 288). The relationship between the heroine and her psychiatrist, based on Plath's own therapist, Ruth Beuscher, is also a significant part of the story, and the first draft of the story ended with a long dialogue between the two (*J* 291).

5. Boston and Yaddo (1958–59)

This is the period in which Plath wrote most of her best short fiction. The period really begins in Northampton, in the summer of 1958, after Plath had finished her year as an instructor at Smith. Once this year was done, despite recording in her journals more or less constant frustration with her inability to write fiction to her satisfaction, Plath wrote a considerable body of short fiction, which includes some of her very finest stories. These are the most detailed dates for them that it is possible to establish. (F) indicates that the story, although completed, exists only as a fragment. (L) indicates that, although completed, it is now lost.

'Mrs McFague and the Corn Vase Girl' (F) (21 August 1957– c. 19 July 1958)
'Mrs Cherry's Kitchen' (26 January 1958)
'Stone Boy with Dolphin' (c. March 1958)
'The Bird in the House' (L) (19 July–27 September 1958)

'DAR Park' (F) (2 August 1958)
'Two Fat Girls on Beacon Hill' (F) (c. September 1958–June 1959)
'Johnny Panic and the Bible of Dreams' (16 December 1958)
'The Fifteen-Dollar Eagle' (pre-28 December 1958)
'The Shadow' (31 December 1958–7 January 1959)
'Sweetie Pie and the Gutter Men' (3–18 May 1959)
'Above the Oxbow' (17–31 May 1959)
'The Daughters of Blossom Street' (17–31 May 1959)
'The It-Doesn't-Matter Suit' (August–September 1959)
'The Fifty-Ninth Bear' (16 September 1959)
'A Prospect of Cornucopia' (F) (25–28 September 1959)
'The Mummy' (F) (29 September–3 October 1959)
'The Beggars' (L) (pre-15 November 1959)

'Mrs McFague and the Corn Vase Girl' was inspired by a couple named the Spauldings, whom Plath met on Cape Cod during the summer of 1957. She made detailed notes on this couple, who lived in a mobile home and rented out cottages, which they seem to have built themselves, for the summer, although they did not have a house of their own (*J* 612–13, 615). On 21 August 1957, Plath sketched out the plot of the story. Mrs McFague, a 'solid, good-hearted Cape-Codder', who loves to talk, rents out one of her cabins to a young husband and wife, and gets to know them as she offers to drive them around (*J* 297). Although Mrs McFague lives simply, she owns a pair of valuable old corn vases. When another family pays an uninvited visit to her mobile home, the children pick up the valuable vases and the parents make no attempt to prevent them (*J* 297). On 20 January 1958, Plath worked out the ending. Tookie, the young wife, angrily tells one of the children to put down the vase she is playing with and in the ensuing argument it falls to the ground and breaks. The girl claims that Tookie struck her and the story ends on the question of who believes whom (*J* 313). In the extant pages, Plath narrates Mrs McFague's endless tales about her earlier life, including her memories of the 1906 San Francisco earthquake when she was a child. She is still talking by page 10.

On 27 September 1958, Plath was rewriting the draft of a story she had completed by 18 September, 'The Bird in the House' (*J* 423, 422), based on an incident in July in which she and Hughes had rescued a badly injured bird, which they had eventually had to gas. As she wrote down her idea for the story, she specified that the bird acts as a 'torment-ing spirit', which 'darkens and twists' the lives of the couple that save it (*J* 409). Only two pages of 'DAR Park' and one page of 'Two Fat Girls on Beacon Hill' survive. The latter story is undated, but was presumably written during the year Plath lived on Beacon Hill, Boston. In the page that remains, Plath wrote a fascinating and detailed description of the appearance and eating habits of one of the fat girls of the title. Her description of what the woman's life must be like behind closed doors, eating sweets and fried foods, which turn her body grotesquely over-weight and unhealthy, indicates that the story may have been, in part at least, a study in pathos.[22]

The dates I have given for the stories published in *Johnny Panic in the Bible of Dreams* derive from Plath's references to them at *J* 441 ('Johnny Panic and the Bible of Dreams'), *J* 453 ('The Fifteen-Dollar Eagle'), *J* 453, 457 ('The Shadow'), *J* 481, 482 ('Sweetie Pie and the Gutter Men'), *J* 486 ('Above the Oxbow', 'The Daughters of Blossom Street'), and *J* 501 ('The Fifty-Ninth Bear'). The dates I have given for the stories published in *Collected Children's Stories* derive from Plath's references to them at *J* 320 ('Mrs Cherry's Kitchen') and *J* 509, 527 ('The It-Doesn't-Matter-Suit'). 'A Prospect of Cornucopia' is based on the journey that Plath and Hughes took to the small, idyllic town of Cornucopia, Wisconsin, during their road trip across America in the summer of 1959. She was working on it on 25 September 1959 (*J* 507) and had completed it by 28 September, when she described its theme as the 'impossibility of perfect happiness' (*J* 510). The same day, she submitted it to the *Atlantic Monthly*, which rejected it the following May.[23] 'The Mummy' is a story Plath first conceived of on 29 September 1959 as a 'diatribe against the Dark Mother' (*J* 512). She described it as a 'monologue of a mad woman' (*J* 513), and when she completed it, which she had done by 3 October, she called it an expression of 'symbolic and horrid fantasies' (*J* 514). She submitted it the same day to *New World Writing*.[24] The single page that survives is fascinating. The narrator's mother exerts an unpleasant control over her, extracting against her will the story of the romantic encounter from which she has returned and giving her a playful but unwelcome lesson in feminine wiles. She may seem to be a loving mother, the narrator reflects, but she is in truth controlling and destructive.[25] The morning after Plath finished the story, she was astonished to find in Jung's *The Development of Personality* several examples of precisely the same ideas as those she had put in the story (*J* 514). Jung recounts a case in which three girls had a '*most devoted*' mother but dreamt for years about her as a 'witch or a danger-ous animal'. When, years later, she became insane, she 'exhibited a sort of lycanthropy in which she crawled about on all fours and imitated the grunting of pigs, the barking of dogs and the growling of bears'.[26] This case illustrates the 'infectious nature of . . . parents' complexes' on their children, so that even when no trace of such complexes can be seen in a parent's normal life, the child will somehow pick up on it. Plath felt that her plot and imagery in 'The Mummy' had illustrated precisely this. Jung mentions the archetype of the deadly, devouring mother, as exemplified in the tale of Little Red Riding Hood, and Plath too had used the 'image of the wolf' for Mummy (*J* 514).[27] Indeed, Plath had used the very same metaphor as Jung to describe the relationship of a 'supposedly loving' mother who 'manipulated' her child. In Plath's story, the mother had done so on the 'chessboard of her desire' (*J* 514); Jung spoke of ambitious mothers who live through their children as playing with them on the 'chessboard of [their] egotism'.[28] The final story that Plath completed during this period, 'The Beggars', is now lost. Plath had completed it by 12 November 1959, when she planned to submit it for publication (*J* 527). She later recorded her dissatisfaction with the story, calling it 'sentimental' and 'stiff', adding with frustration that it had had the potential to be dramatically successful (*J* 530). She was still submitting it for publication two years later, sending it to her British literary agent in October 1961.[29]

6. British Women's Stories (1960–62)

After she had moved to England in December 1959 and given birth to her first child in April 1960, Plath turned her hand again to writing women's magazine stories. On 28 November 1960, she told her mother that, although 'rusty' and 'awkward' at first, she had finished one women's magazine story, was at work on another and that she and Hughes had drafted the outline of a third (*LH* 401). Four women's magazine stories from this period survive, which can be dated as follows:

> 'The Lucky Stone' (28 November–24 December 1960)
> 'Day of Success' (30 January–31 August 1961)
> 'Shadow Girl' (1 September–13 October 1961)
> 'A Winter's Tale' (1 September–28 December 1961)

'The Lucky Stone' is the only women's magazine story Plath published in her lifetime. It is the second of the stories to which she referred on 28 November 1960 (*LH* 401), and she had completed it by 24 December when she told her mother that her literary agent, Jennifer Hassell, had submitted it to British women's magazines (*LH* 403). It was accepted by *My Weekly* and published as 'The Perfect Place' in the 28 October 1961 issue.[30] 'Day of Success' is based on an incident that occurred during the week of 1 February 1961.[31] Plath wrote the story at her Chalcot Square address, which means that it was completed by 31 August 1961, when she moved to Court Green. 'Shadow Girl' and 'A Winter's Tale' were both written at Court Green, and Plath's records of submissions show that she submitted the former to her agents on 13 October 1961, and the latter to *My Weekly* on 28 December.[32] *My Weekly* rejected both on 19 January 1962, saying that they were 'a bit less homely than we aim for'.[33] One more story from this period survives, 'Mothers', whose date is given as 1962 in *Johnny Panic and the Bible of Dreams, and Other Prose Writings*. Although it was published posthumously in *McCall's*, it is not a women's magazine story like those Plath was writing in 1960 and 1961, but more the kind of observational mood piece published by literary magazines like the *New Yorker*.

Novels

The Bell Jar, Plath's only published novel, was the second of the three novels on which she worked at length. The first of these, *Falcon Yard*, was based on her experiences as a student in Cambridge. Hughes mentioned in a letter to Plath's mother and her brother, Warren, in December 1956 that Sylvia was reading a novel about Cambridge, which was getting good reviews, and which he hoped would 'set her off' on her own such novel.[34] Throughout 1957 and for much of 1958 Plath worked on several drafts of this novel, but never completed it to her satisfaction. She sketched out the plot in February 1957. An American student goes to Cambridge to 'find herself', where she has several relationships with different kinds of men. There is the 'stolid Yale man critic Kraut-head', based on Garry Haupt and Gordon Lameyer, and the 'little thin sickly exotic wealthy' man, based on Richard Sassoon and Lou Healy. The centre of interest will be the 'big, blasting dangerous love', based on Plath's relationship with Hughes (*J* 268). Plath planned to make the detailed descriptions of scenes in Cambridge, Paris and Rome 'subtly symbolic' and to explore the question of the heroine's identity through a 'double', a character based on Nancy Hunter and Jane Baltzell (*J* 268). The following month, she told her mother that she '[grinds]' each day on the novel, which she intended to cover nine months of action, about a 'soul-search, American-girl-in-Cambridge, European vacations etc.'. She planned to see how the plot developed as she finished the first draft and then completely to revise it (*LH* 305). On 17 June 1957, Plath wrote that she had been through several draft titles for the novel, but that she and Hughes had both recently hit upon *Falcon Yard*, the place of their first meeting and so of the novel's 'central episode' (*LH* 318). The extant pages of this novel are from early drafts called *Hill of Leopards*, of which one page remains, and *Venus in the Seventh*, of which fourteen pages remain.[35] Both drafts can be dated between 25 February 1957, when Plath began work on the novel, and 15 July 1957, when she had changed the heroine's name to Judith Greenwood (*J* 284, 289). In both *Hill of Leopards* and *Venus in the Seventh*, she is called Jess Greenwood. On 12 January 1958, Plath also changed the hero's name from Ian to Leonard, and the heroine's name to Dody Ventura, noting that Dody is a 'foolish anagram' of Dido Merwin's name, of whom the heroine was a kind of 'caricature' (*J* 311). She has also decided to turn each chapter into a story in its own right (*J* 311). The first of these stories is 'Friday Night in Falcon Yard' (*J* 312–13, 315), the central chapter of the novel, based on Plath's first meeting with Hughes. She had finished a draft of this chapter by 22 January 1958 (*J* 318), and on 28 February planned to rewrite it as a story for the *Sewanee Review* (*J* 340). This revision becomes 'Stone Boy with Dolphin', which can thus be dated approximately to March 1958. Plath's undated story fragment 'Runaway', based on her experience on a runaway horse in Cambridge, may be another of these stories based on a chapter of the Cambridge novel.[36] Plath continued to work on the novel until at least May 1958 (*J* 366, 375, 379, 387), but by the following year she had given up on it, planning in May 1959 a novel with the same title, but with a completely different plot (*J* 483). In March 1959, she told Lynne Lawner that, in trying to write the novel, she had 'encountered a huge block in trying to have the material take off from what actually did happen'.[37]

Plath seems to have taken up *Falcon Yard* again, and to have updated the events of its semi-autobiographical plot, by the summer of 1962. In a typescript now in the Smith College archive, a series of draft notes for a talk she gave at the Wellesley College Club in 1976, Aurelia Plath describes her daughter telling her about this novel during her visit to Court Green from late June to early August 1962.[38] As she wrote these notes, Aurelia was consulting the journal she kept during the time of this visit. She recalled that Plath told her that she had completed one novel and almost completed a second in draft form. Plath told her mother that the second novel was 'autobiographically based' and Aurelia established that its subjects were the following:

> her student life at the University of Cambridge, her romance and marriage, the combination of married life and teaching at Smith, the Beacon Hill year following, the return to England – all ending with the birth of Frieda.

Plath had intended to dedicate this novel to Hughes, who was its hero, and to give it to him as a surprise gift on his birthday. She showed her mother the dedication page with the words 'To Ponter', her nickname for Hughes, and read her parts of the novel. On 10 July 1962, the day after Plath intercepted Hughes' lover Assia Wevill's telephone call, Aurelia wrote, she saw her daughter burn the manuscript of the novel in the courtyard of Court Green.

The Bell Jar was written between early April and late August 1961, mostly in the study of W. S. Merwin, Hughes' friend and neighbour in London. On 27 April Plath wrote to her friend Ann Davidow that she was more than a third of the way through the novel. She told Ann that she had been trying to write a novel for several years, but had always had writer's block at the idea. As she began dealing with Alfred A. Knopf, the American publishers of *The Colossus*, this block suddenly disappeared.[39] In what she described to her mother as a 'night of inspiration' she stayed up until the small hours planning the novel, and the following day began writing it each morning in Merwin's study (*LH* 418). These letters allow us to be fairly precise about the date at which Plath began *The Bell Jar*. Judith Jones of Knopf expressed the American publisher's interest in *The Colossus* in a letter dated 29 March 1961, to which Plath replied on 5 April. She told her mother that her night of inspiration occurred when Knopf's letter arrived, which was therefore either on or shortly before 5 April 1961. From that date on, she began to work on *The Bell Jar* seven mornings a week in Merwin's study (*LH* 418).[40] Hughes wrote to Aurelia and Warren Plath on 22 April that Sylvia had been working 'at a great pace' since she returned from hospital after her appendicectomy, which she did on 8 March, and that she had 'really broken through into something wonderful'.[41] He later recalled that she wrote the novel 'at high speed, and in great exhilaration'.[42] By late August 1961, after vacationing in France with the Merwins and then hosting her mother in London and Yorkshire, as well as house-hunting, Plath had finished the novel. She wrote in her 1958–59 journal notes, next to where she had written in December 1958, 'Why don't I write a novel?', 'I have! August 22, 1961: THE BELL JAR' (*J* 438, 696). Plath published the novel under the pen-name Victoria Lucas, which had also been the name of the heroine when she submitted it to Heinemann. Her editor there did not want the author's and the heroine's names to be the same, however, and asked Plath to change them. She agreed that this was a mistake, and in a letter of November 1961, gave him the name of Esther Greenwood for the heroine.[43]

Plath's third and last novel, 'provisionally entitled *Double Exposure*' (*JPBD* vii), was unfinished at her death. Her first working title for this novel was *The Interminable Loaf*. There is an entry on her week-per-view calendar for 10 August 1962 in which she told herself to start this project.[44] By 20 November 1962, she had changed the title to

Doubletake.[45] On 29 September 1962, Plath told her benefactress Olive Higgins Prouty that she worked on the novel in the very early mornings, between her own waking and that of her two children.[46] She added that the painful experiences about which she was writing would make a greater novelist out of her, one who understands and empathises with the humanity of her characters, as she was gaining the kind of wisdom that comes through suffering.[47] She told Warren and Margaret Plath that *Double Exposure*, like *The Bell Jar*, is a comic novel: it 'makes me laugh and laugh, and if I can laugh now it must be hellishly funny stuff' (*LH* 467). Al Alvarez recalls that Plath described the novel to him as 'the real thing', better than *The Bell Jar*.[48] Plath gave some indication in her letters of the subject matter of the novel. Like *The Bell Jar*, it would be loosely autobiographical, based on the recent break-up of her marriage. She wrote to her mother that she would 'commemorate' the pain caused by her husband leaving her in the novel (*LH* 471).[49] On 20 November 1962 she told Prouty, to whom she wanted to dedicate the novel, that she had decided on the title *Doubletake*, because it would explore the theme that seeing a thing for a second time shows up aspects of it that are invisible at first glance. The book would be about a woman who had adored her husband, but whom he leaves for another woman.[50] In the course of her work on her book *Chapters in a Mythology*, Judith Kroll saw an index card, now lost, on which Plath had written notes for an outline of this novel. On it Plath 'refers to the principals as "heroine", "rival", "husband", "rival's husband"'.[51] Hughes' sister Olwyn, who read the surviving manuscript, recalled a passage in which the character based on Plath was weeding onions with the character based on Wevill. It took place, she recalled, on the Sunday morning of the weekend based on the first visit of the Wevills to Court Green in May 1962. She adds that Wevill was vilified in the novel fragment, as she had been to an even greater extent in Plath's last journals.[52] Wevill told her friend Nathaniel Tarn about the novel a month after Plath's death, and he recorded her observations:

> The second novel includes the Wevills, under the name of the Goof-Hoppers (?) and shocked Assia by its portrait of David [Wevill] who is presented as detestable and contemptible. A. is of course the icy barren woman. In the novel, apart from SP who is full of poems, kicks and kids, there are only miserable sinners.[53]

In the series of notes of which this is part, Tarn several times adds a question mark in parentheses after something Wevill has told him, as here after Plath's fictional name for the Wevills, to indicate his scepticism that she has reported a fact correctly. Elizabeth Compton Sigmund, to whom *The Bell Jar* was dedicated, recalls that Plath wrote to her that she and her husband David were to appear in *Double Exposure* 'briefly, as angels'.[54] Plath continued to refer to writing or wanting to write this novel until 22 January 1963.[55] In 1979, Hughes wrote that Plath had left a typescript of 'some 130 pages' (*JPBD* vii), but in 1995 he spoke of just 'sixty, seventy pages'.[56] Olwyn Hughes also, in notes written c. 2003, recalls that the typescript may have consisted of the first two chapters of the novel, and that it did not exceed sixty pages.[57]

I have divided my discussion of these works into five chapters. In the first chapter, I discuss Plath's fiction as it is formed in and responds to the literary and popular works of fiction which constituted her creative milieu. In Chapter 2, I discuss the relationships between the concerns Plath was expressing in her poetry and her fiction during the different periods of her writing life, and the relationships between similar subjects or events that Plath expressed in both poetry and fiction. In Chapter 3, I examine the development of Plath's political views and the ways in which she expressed these in her fiction. In Chapters 4 and 5, I address the central concern of Plath's fiction, the lives of women in her society. Chapter 4 places Plath's views on and portrayals of women's lives within the context of the gender discourses within which she formed her views and wrote. This chapter focuses on *The Bell Jar*. In Chapter 5, I discuss the variety of ways in which Plath portrayed women's experience in the wide range of her short fiction. In this way, I aim to provide the reader with a clear and comprehensive understanding, based both on close readings of Plath's texts and on an understanding of them in their historical and cultural contexts, of the significant place that Plath's fiction plays in the vast, diverse and powerful body of work she has left us.

Chapter 1

Literary Contexts

I begin with an examination of the literary contexts in which Plath wrote and to which her fiction responds. She made numerous references in her journals to attempting to learn style, technique and even content from the writers, both literary and popular, whose work constituted her contemporary milieu. On 4 March 1957, for example, she wrote that she needed 'several masters' in writing her Cambridge novel (*J* 274). She considers D. H. Lawrence, but rejects him as too 'bare' and 'journalistic', except in *Women in Love*. She considers Henry James, but rejects him as too 'elaborate', 'calm' and 'well-mannered'. She thinks of Joyce Cary, noting that she herself has Cary's 'fresh, brazen colloquial voice'. Salinger has that voice too, but his style demands a first-person speaker, Plath reflects, which is 'too limiting' (*J* 275). Hughes recalls that she 'analysed stories by various popular writers, taking them apart and studying their machinery', looking for all that she could learn from each author.[1] In this chapter, I discuss the writers and texts that constituted the most significant influences on Plath as a fiction writer.

Virginia Woolf

Plath first read *Mrs Dalloway* in Wilbury Crockett's English class at high school. As a sophomore at Smith, she studied Woolf with Elizabeth Drew in Eng 211 Literature of the Nineteenth and Twentieth Centuries. Drew published several pieces of criticism of Woolf's work, and from them we can get a good idea of the kind of interpretation Plath heard in her lectures. Drew's position is made clearest in her early book *The Modern Novel*. There, three years before Woolf published *A Room of One's Own*, Drew takes a diametrically opposed view to Woolf's of the conditions in which women are able to write:

Under modern codes of social ethics woman is free. She has complete liberty of action to develop her personality as she will . . . and complete liberty of speech to show the truth of existence as it appears to her.[2]

As a result of this position on women's social conditions, Drew takes a consciously anti-feminist position in her criticism of women's writing. She concludes her chapter 'Is There a "Feminine" Fiction?' by arguing that, although there is 'distinction' in all the novels by women she has discussed, and even 'brilliance' in some, nevertheless:

When all is said, and in spite of the feminists with the queen bee in their bonnets, the fact remains that the creative genius of woman remains narrower than that of man, even in the novel.[3]

Feminist criticism is simply misguided, for Drew, a distortion of the facts of women's writing. As a result, her studies of Woolf never mention questions of gender politics. In her 1963 book *The Novel* she describes Woolf's 'metaphysical' vision in *To the Lighthouse*. She gives a humanistic account of the novel, as one of those which 'never concern themselves with "society" in any real way' and in which Woolf's aim is 'to represent what she feels as a central truth about human experience'.[4] Woolf, according to Drew, is interested in portraying the nature of reality, the 'central theme' of the book, and she does so through a system of 'complex and subtle symbolism', in which four main symbols – the sea, the lighthouse, Mrs Ramsay and Lily Briscoe's picture – are 'woven together into a central meaning, a revelation of what Virginia Woolf sees as the nature of life'.[5] She lectured on these symbols, and Plath remembered her lectures, annotating her copy of the text accordingly, emphasising the same passages Drew does and making notes on the themes and symbols to which Drew points in the margins of her text.[6] By the first mention of Mrs Ramsay's 'green shawl', for example, Plath notes that this symbolises Mrs Ramsay's fertile nature, an idea clearly derived from Drew, who writes of Mrs Ramsay as 'the creator of fertile human relationships . . . symbolised by her green shawl'.[7]

Plath's negotiation with Woolf as a writer began in earnest in 1957, when she was working on the draft of her Cambridge novel and on several short stories. In February, she bought several of Woolf's novels, along with *A Writer's Diary*, which she began to read straight away. She adored Woolf's diary, noting with pleasure that Woolf responded to rejections from publishers by cooking 'haddock and sausage'. Plath wrote that she felt 'linked . . . somehow' to the older writer (*J* 269). In March, she told her mother that reading *A Writer's Diary* was giving her strength as she worked through the rough draft of her Cambridge novel: 'I feel very akin to her, although my book reads more like a slick best-seller' (*LH* 305). The extant pages of Plath's Cambridge novel, although recognisably her own, indeed contain Woolfian passages. The passage in which Plath is perhaps most directly indebted to Woolf is one in which the narrator, Jess Greenwood, reflects, as she boards a plane back to England after her European vacation, on the complex nature of identity. No one on the plane knows who she is. She compares living with the all the other people in the world to sinking to the bottom of the sea: you leave a kind of dead shell or chrysalis of yourself with everyone who knows you, while you yourself sink into the unknown. All the men in her life, Jess reflects, such as Winthrop, the character based on Gordon Lameyer, whom she has just left at the airport, have such a dead shell of her in their minds. Like the dead bodies of the pharaohs, these shells may have no life in the present, but they have the power to come back and haunt at any time.[8] This concept of the disparity of the self, spread out amongst the different people to whom the heroine relates, is one which Plath learned from Woolf. She heavily underlined the passage from *Mrs Dalloway* on Clarissa's sense of belonging to all the people and places she had been:

> It was unsatisfactory, they agreed, how little one knew people. But, she said, sitting on the bus going up Shaftesbury Avenue, she felt herself everywhere; not 'here, here, here'; and she tapped the back of the seat; but everywhere.[9]

I have underlined here the text that Plath underlined in her own copy of the novel. She also underlined the next sentence but one: 'She was all that. So that, to know her, or any one, one must seek out the people who completed them; even the places', and noted in the margin that the text concerns the question of the self.[10] Plath's trope in *Venus in the Seventh* is recognisably her own – Woolf would not describe the pieces of one's self one leaves with all those one has met as dead things, since she thinks of this disparity as precisely the life of the self. Nevertheless, this multiple existence of a woman's identity across the people and places she has known is a concept Plath derived from Woolf. Even by the time she was writing *The Bell Jar*, confident of her own voice, a phrase like 'They were part of me. They were my landscape' (*BJ* 227), as Esther realises of all the events of her breakdown, can be traced back, through *Venus in the Seventh*, to Woolf.

In July 1957, Plath began to read the Woolf novels she bought in Cambridge, and to take up the conflicted relationship to Woolf as a literary foremother in which she would continue throughout her writing life. She wrote in her journal at this time, 'Virginia Woolf helps. Her novels make mine possible' (*J* 289). One way in which Woolf's novels make Plath's possible can be found in her annotations and underlinings in her copy of *Mrs Dalloway*, which she reread some time after February 1957, when she bought the book in Cambridge. These show that she was most interested in Woolf's characterisation of Clarissa. She underlined numerous long passages of Woolf's disparate and complex entry into Mrs Dalloway's consciousness, such as the fifth paragraph of the novel, 'Heaven only knows why one loves it so . . . '. Most of this paragraph on Mrs Dalloway's vision of London life is underlined and asterisked, and Plath doubly underlined the central phrase 'they love life'. Scarcely a passage of Woolf's intimate and complex characterisation of Mrs Dalloway, of her experience or her thoughts, is not underlined and asterisked, whether it be long passages or even single words, such as 'Like a nun withdrawing, or a child exploring a tower she went', or 'something very profound in her, which he had felt again this morning talking to her; an impenetrability'.[11] Plath was interested in everything about Mrs Dalloway, from her complex experience of time to her complex relationship with Sally Seton, and she underlined and asterisked all these passages at length. She heavily underlined Mrs Dalloway's feelings about her parties, and her feelings about Septimus Smith at the party. Plath was also interested in Woolf's characterisations of other female characters, underlining passages about Lady Bruton's obsession with emigration. She was clearly impressed by Woolf's exploration of women's complex experience of daily life. This is one of the first things Plath learnt from Woolf – the possibility of writing entirely from within the experience and consciousness of a woman, however different or un-literary that may be from the perspective of literary history. Plath wrote almost entirely about women, and it was in *Mrs Dalloway* above all that Woolf provided her with a model of how to do so.

Plath seems to have learned in a fairly uncomplicated manner from *Mrs Dalloway*. This is far less true of her relationship with *To the Lighthouse*. The second way in which Woolf's novels make Plath's possible is that Plath learned from Woolf, and above all from *To the Lighthouse*, a model of feminist writing, of writing fiction in protest against the gender norms of the society in which she and her characters live. Woolf's portrayal of Mr Ramsay, the great philosopher with a 'splendid mind', who is admired by the whole of society but whose relationship to the women and children in his life is one of 'tyranny', suffuses many of the male experts of Plath's fiction, highly regarded by society but of whose relationships to women she is deeply critical, from Henry in 'Sunday at the Mintons', through Harold in 'The Wishing Box', to Dr Gordon in *The Bell Jar*.[12] Indeed, Plath's key symbolic term for her father, 'colossus', can be found in Woolf's portrayal of her own father-figure in *To the Lighthouse*, as Mr Ramsay's 'remarkable boots' are described, in Lily Briscoe's view, as 'sculptured; colossal'.[13] The splendour of Mr Ramsay's mind allows him to denigrate the minds of women, as is case with all of Plath's similar characters. Perhaps the clearest debt is over the question of spatial thinking. Mr Ramsay can scarcely believe his daughter cannot locate points on a map. 'Half laughing' and 'half scolding', he demands that Cam point out east and west to him, but she cannot:

> He could not understand the state of mind of anyone, not absolutely imbecile, who did not know the points of the compass . . . He thought, women are always like that; the vagueness of their minds is hopeless.[14]

Henry Minton is scandalised in precisely the same way by Elizabeth's different, feminine mode of thinking from his own. He looks at her in 'dismay' when she tells him that she never knows the direction she is travelling on a map when she goes on a journey. Surely even he does not do that, she responds with irritation, an idea he clearly regards as so fantastic as to be 'open insolence'. He responds 'staunchly', a 'ruddy colour' appearing in his face, '"Of course I think where I'm going . . . I always trace out my route beforehand . . . and I take a map with me to follow as I travel"' (*JPBD* 146).

In *A Writer's Diary*, Woolf worried that *A Room of One's Own* had a 'shrill feminine tone' that her friends would dislike.[15] Plath underlined this phrase in her copy of the text. She learned above all from *To the Lighthouse* a model of feminist writing that could not be criticised in these terms. She learned, that is, to write fiction that articulates feminist criticism of the patriarchal society in which it is set, but which remains feminine in a socially acceptable sense. In *To the Lighthouse*, as in much of *A Room of One's Own*, Woolf does this with humour – with a dry, understated, ironic wit, a mode of feminist writing extremely influential on Plath's own. Lily Briscoe's vision of the kitchen table in a tree, subverting with its quotidian feminine nature and ridiculous position the importance of Mr Ramsay's philosophy, which she tries to understand with it, is an example. Indeed, Lily practises the technique directly. In response to Mr Tansley's view that 'Women can't write, women can't paint', she makes no angry retort, but decides to focus on her painting and all it means to her:

> Could she not hold fast to that, she asked herself, and not lose her temper, and nor argue; and if she wanted a little revenge take it by laughing at him?[16]

Not to lose her temper, and if she wants revenge, take it by laughing at him. This is how Woolf's humour works in *To the Lighthouse*, and it is how Plath's also works. Her understated juxtaposition of expert male views and feminist subversion of them, a frequent device of her fiction, descends directly from Woolf. An extreme example is the electric shock scene in *The Bell Jar*. Plath gives her memorable description of the horror of Esther's botched ECT, which she contrasts with Dr Gordon's inappropriately self-absorbed response. After the treatment, Dr Gordon asks her which college she attends, and when she tells him, his 'face lighted up with a slow, almost tropical smile'. '"Ah!"', he remembers fondly, '"They had a WAC station up there, didn't they, during the war?"' (*BJ* 139). Plath subverts Buddy Willard's sense of his own manhood in the same way, as Esther comments, when Buddy exposes himself to her in preparation for marriage, that it made her think of 'turkey neck and turkey gizzards' and that she 'felt very depressed' (*BJ* 64). Like Woolf in *To the Lighthouse*, Plath does not lose her temper, but takes her revenge on the patriarchal society in which she lives by laughing at the men who run it.

Despite this debt to *To the Lighthouse*, Plath's annotations and markings in her copy of the novel do not indicate that she made a conscious choice to pay close attention to its feminism. When Woolf portrays Mr Ramsay's emotional demands on his family, his authoritarianism, his children's violent responses to him and even the sexism of characters like Mr Tansley, Plath tends not to underline or mark these passages. For example, in the fourth paragraph of the novel, we hear about the suppressed violence James Ramsay bears towards his father, a theme Plath certainly identified with and learnt from *To the Lighthouse*:

> Had there been an axe handy, a poker, or any weapon that would have gashed a hole in his father's breast and killed him, there and then, James would have seized it.[17]

There is no question that Woolf's portrayal of this kind of emotional violence provided Plath, when she read it, with a model of how to portray this important concern of her own. Yet she did not mark the passage in her copy of the text. In the entire paragraph, highly resonant with the gender reflections that characterised Plath's own life and writing, Plath marked only the words 'lean as a knife, narrow as the blade of one', with which Woolf described Mr Ramsay's stance over his wife and son, noting in the margin next to this mark that this is a sign of the sterility of Mr Ramsay's masculine nature. Plath clearly had Drew's interpretation of the text in mind when she wrote this. Drew emphasised that 'Mr Ramsay stands as the symbol of the sterile, destructive barriers to relationship', whereas Mrs Ramsay 'is above all the creator of fertile human relationships', and indeed quotes the text Plath underlined in her discussion of this symbolism.[18] When Mr Ramsay's demand for emotional solace from his wife is described as a 'beak of brass', Plath noted in the margin that this concerns the difference between the generative nature of women and the sterile nature of men.[19] It is clear from a letter of 1953 from Dick Norton, whom she had been dating for two years, that Plath had discussed this interpretation of the Ramsays with him, as he agreed that Mrs Ramsay symbolises maternity and Mr Ramsay male sterility.[20] Norton also referred to reading Plath's anno-tated copy of *To the Lighthouse*, in which she had explained many of the symbols in the margin.[21]

Plath's relationship with *To the Lighthouse* is thus a conflicted one. It functions as one of the most influential texts on her fiction, yet she does not consciously acknowledge that influence in the margins of her text as she does with *Mrs Dalloway*. Her conflict with Woolf only grew as she continued to read the latter's novels in 1957 and afterwards. She responded in two ways to *The Waves*, which she read in Eastham in July 1957. On the one hand, she strongly disliked the 'endless sun, waves, birds' and criticised Woolf's 'unevenness of description' in the novel (*J* 286). On the other, she praised the 'hair-raising fineness' of its last section. These last pages immensely impressed Plath, but she could still write, 'I shall go better than she' (*J* 286). Here Plath begins her openly conflicted relationship with Woolf, dismissing all but the last fifty pages of Woolf's novel, and asserting that she will be able to write better fiction. Plath clarified what she meant by better in the next paragraph of the journal entry where she calls Woolf 'too ephemeral, needing the earth' (*J* 286). Two years later, she took a similar view of *The Years* (*J* 494). Woolf's fiction lacks the earth, for Plath – physicality, relation-ship, sex, children, all the materiality of life and family and relationships that she wants to write about.

Steven Axelrod argues that Plath's conflicted relationship to Woolf is played out above all in Plath's reading of *A Room of One's Own*, over the question of anger.[22] Plath's copy of *A Room of One's Own* is unmarked, and Axelrod sees in this lack of negotiation with the text a psychological rejection of the arguments contained within it, especially of the threatening argument that anger spoils women's writing. It is certainly difficult to know what to make of the fact that Plath made no marks or annotations in her copy of *A Room of One's Own*. It is dif-ficult to imagine her reading the book without energetically negotiating with its ideas in the margins of the text. She underlined almost all of the comments Woolf makes in *A Writer's Diary* about the book. I disagree with Axelrod's view, however, that Plath could not allow herself to pay close attention to the arguments within *A Room of One's Own* because they prohibited the kind of writing she wanted to do. Woolf only begins to write that women's fiction is spoiled by anger in the fourth chapter of the book and to introduce the theme at the very end of the third. There is much material in the first three chapters that would have resonated strongly with Plath before she encountered Woolf's claim that women's writing is distorted by anger. It is difficult to believe that Plath's imagination would not have been engaged by positive statements such as 'Women have served all these centuries as looking-glasses possessing the magic and delicious power of reflecting the figure of the man at twice its natural size', which appears thirty pages before Woolf writes about women and anger.[23] Furthermore, Woolf herself writes with understated anger before the fourth chapter, for example in the account of Oscar Browning, in precisely the way that Plath would learn from her.[24] Indeed, even after Woolf's claims about anger, she gives further prescriptive statements to women writers that Plath would not have found threatening. She tells them, 'You must illumine your own soul with its profundities and its shallows, and its vanities and its generosities'.[25] The woman writer must discuss the meaning of her beauty or her plainness, Woolf continues, and must deal with her relationship to the 'everchanging and turning world of gloves and shoes and stuffs swaying up and down among the faint scents that come through chemists' bottles down arcades of dress material over a floor of pseudo-marble'.[26] This is a prescription for precisely the kind of fiction Plath was able and willing to write. The marble façades of Madison Avenue in *The Bell Jar* are a direct descendant of the pseudo-marble floors of Bond Street that Woolf evokes here, in the passage in which Esther recalls how 'stupid' she was to 'buy all those uncomfortable, expensive clothes, hanging limp as fish in my closet' and how all her college accomplishments seemed to mean nothing among the 'slick marble and plate-glass fronts along Madison Avenue' (*BJ* 2).

Plath's central conflict in her complex relationship to Woolf, then, is less with *A Room of One's Own* than with *To the Lighthouse*. She learned the legitimacy in general and certain techniques in particular of feminist fiction from *To the Lighthouse*, but she did not say so consciously in the margin of her text. She had a complex relationship of acceptance and rejection of Woolf, but her most marked instance of rejection was not her denigration of the light, ephemeral qualities of *The Waves* and *The Years*, nor the absence of marks in *A Room of One's Own*, but her rigorously non-feminist annotation of *To the Lighthouse*. She learned a model of feminist fiction, of precisely the kind to which she was already committed to writing, from Woolf's novel, yet did not consciously tell herself as much in her copy of the text or in her comments on Woolf in general. This refusal to acknowledge the influence of the feminism of *To the Lighthouse*, I would suggest, derives from two sources. First, Plath had deeply interiorised Drew's consciously anti-feminist interpretation of the novel; and second, she was able to interiorise this interpretation so thoroughly because, verbally at least, Plath did not want to identify herself as a feminist. As Isobel Armstrong and Alan Sinfield write:

> Like other women in the 1950s, Plath puts down old-style feminists as 'blue-stockings'. Betty Friedan found this general attitude at Smith College in 1959; Sheila Rowbotham recalls that 'feminism' meant older women who wanted to stop you doing things.[27]

In her college journals, Plath thinks of activism like that of Lucretia Mott as a negative form of selflessness, like serving one's husband or society, as an avoidance of the responsibility of creating for oneself the life one wants (*J* 100). Despite not consciously reading Woolf's work as an example of the feminist fiction she herself learned to write from it, Plath's own fiction shows the extent to which she learned from Woolf. She did so in practice rather than in theory, and her debt to *To the Lighthouse* is as great as that to *Mrs Dalloway*. If the latter provided her with a model of writing women's lives, the former provided her with a model of doing so politically.

The *New Yorker*

The next body of texts I examine that constitutes a significant influence on Plath's fiction is the stories of the *New Yorker* magazine. Publication in the pages of the *New Yorker* was considered by many American writers in the 1950s to be a high point of literary achievement, and Plath harboured a lifelong ambition to publish both poetry and fiction there.[28] She succeeded in the former goal, her first poem accepted being 'Mussel Hunter at Rock Harbor' for the 9 August 1958 issue, but never in the latter. Nevertheless, many of her stories are consciously tailored to suit her perception of the magazine's requirements.

Thomas Leitch has pointed out that, although the concept of 'The *New Yorker* story' had become current by the 1930s, it is a paradoxical one since, on the one hand, 'there is, experts agree, no *New Yorker* school of short fiction', but, on the other, 'everyone with any interest in the short story . . . can recognise a *New Yorker* short story from twenty feet away'.[29] Whilst the fiction published in the magazine is, at any given time, too diverse to be reducible to a typical set of characteristics, there are certain dominant characteristics in many of the stories that readers, as Plath did, find recognisable. Leitch argues that chief amongst these is that *New Yorker* fiction defines itself against current norms in fiction, including, by the time Plath was reading the journal, those of its own earlier stories. 'The founding move of . . . the *New Yorker* short story is the disavowal that it is following the rules of the short story'.[30] The way in which this is most typically expressed in the generation of authors publishing after the Second World War, he argues, is a mode of writing which 'suggested that even the most banal incidents could reveal unsuspected depths under the proper handling'.[31] Ben Yagoda, critical of the conservatism of William Shawn, editor of the *New Yorker* from 1951–1987, writes that even amongst the most innovative writers published in the magazine in the 1950s, 'the volume of their stories was subdued, the characters polite and well-bred, the ironies subtle'.[32]

A good example of the kind of *New Yorker* story Plath admired, but whose style and sensibility are simply too different from hers for her to be able realistically to imitate, can be found in the work of Peter de Vries. In February 1956, Plath miserably compared her story 'The Matisse Chapel', which the *New Yorker* had just rejected, with de Vries' story 'Afternoon of a Faun', which had appeared earlier that month in the magazine. She hid it 'like a stillborn illegitimate baby', embarrassed by its 'bathos'. She writes that she 'shuddered' as she compared it to de Vries' 'scintillant' story (*J* 205). Here Plath's self-confidence temporarily deserts her. 'The Matisse Chapel', from what can be inferred from the extant pages of the story, is heavy in naturalistic observation of the French countryside in which it is set and in the details of the characters' lives. We hear the title of the heroine's Honours dissertation, for example. After the first two pages of this kind of detail, a page from later in the story records, in a fashion most closely influenced by D. H. Lawrence, a bitter quarrel between the two lovers about their behaviour in getting into the chapel. Richard is furious with Sally, saying that if she really loved him, she would have been happy that he had been able to see the chapel. Sally responds hotly that seeing it without her simply shows how egotistic he is and how little he loves her.[33] After having this story rejected by the *New Yorker* and then reading de Vries' story, Plath's confidence in her own voice wavers. She comments that 'there are ways and ways to have a love affair' (*J* 205), suggesting that de Vries tells his love story the right way, whereas she tells hers the wrong way. Plath even assumed de Vries' Wildean tone when she added, 'Above all one must not be serious about it', hardly a sentiment expressive of her own considered view.

De Vries' style is polished, witty and urbane. His stories are full of Wildean epigrams and aphorisms – especially 'Afternoon of Faun', which is about a young man who consciously enjoys affecting them

– and take a tone of aesthetic contempt for the American bourgeoisie and intelligentsia. '"Instead of coming to one's senses," I airily returned, "how much more delightful to let one's senses come to one"'; '"The books Mother cannot put down," I said, "are the ones I cannot pick up"'.[34] De Vries' story 'The Irony of All' contains some fine parodies of the bestsellers published by a hated neighbour of the narrator: 'They abound in lines like "Behind him he could hear Dumbrowski's heavy breathing" and "With a bellow of mingled rage and pain he came at him"'; 'the frequency of "You mean – ?" in his dialogues indicates that he is no pathfinder there, either'.[35] Plath was able to imitate something of this when she wrote about Philomena's Guinea's bestsellers in *The Bell Jar* (*BJ* 37–8), but, with this exception, de Vries' sensibility is so different from hers that it was fruitless for her to attempt to imitate his style. When she wrote a year later that the thought of Irwin Shaw, de Vries and the other 'witty, clever, serious, prolific ones' blocks her ability to write, she had still not found sufficient confidence in her own voice not to feel that she ought to imitate others in order to write for the *New Yorker* (*J* 275).

The influence of J. D. Salinger on *The Bell Jar* has been pointed out since the earliest reviews of the novel. In the *New York Times Book Review*, Robert Scholes described it as 'the kind of book Salinger's Franny might have written about herself ten years later, if she had spent those ten years in Hell'.[36] Charles Newman described Esther as a 'female Holden Caulfield' and Margaret Shook wrote two years later that the view that 'Sylvia Plath is the first woman to write in the Salinger vein' was becoming standard.[37] Linda Wagner-Martin has discussed *The Catcher in the Rye* as a precursor of *The Bell Jar*, and Alan Sinfield has examined the significance of the Glass stories Plath read in the *New Yorker*.[38] Here I want to add a discussion of the influence of another group of *New Yorker* writers on Plath, which, although less frequently noticed, is in my view even greater than that of Salinger. It is amongst the women writers for the *New Yorker* that Plath was able to find the most realistic models of the ways in which her gifts could be used in publishing stories for the magazine.

One such writer was Jean Stafford. In 1956, Plath mentioned her as one of four women she respected because they were professional writers who had also married and had a family (*LH* 208). In Newton Arvin's class at Smith, she studied Stafford's novel *Boston Adventure*, and she may also have heard about the author's life and work from Alfred Kazin, who was a friend of Stafford's.[39] In Boston, she socialised with Stafford's first husband, Robert Lowell. In June 1959, Plath was reading the collection *Stories*, by Jean Stafford and three other *New Yorker* writers, and praised the 'colour', 'warmth' and 'humour' of her work (J 496). She was reading Stafford's stories again three months later at Yaddo. She referred to 'The Interior Castle' in particular, which means that she was probably reading the volume *Children are Bored on Sunday* (J 508).[40] There are several aspects of Stafford's work that influenced Plath. First, Stafford frequently explores the physical and mental effects of emotional distress on her heroines. In 'The Warlock', published in the *New Yorker* in December 1955, the heroine's husband had been on the point of leaving her for another woman, and she reflects that she may have fallen ill in order to keep him from doing so:

> It was almost . . . as if her body had said to Mark, 'See, if you leave me for Martha, I will die!'[41]

In 'Beatrice Trueblood's Story', the heroine goes deaf in order to avoid marrying a man with whom she will quarrel, since she cannot bear the idea of quarrelling in marriage. 'My God, the mind is diabolical!' she says to the friend to whom she tells her story.[42] Stafford even puts into this story the idea that Plath would write into 'Johnny Panic and the Bible of Dreams', that Beatrice's neurotic life is somehow truer and more real to her than so-called normality. Just as the patients in Plath's story, of whom the narrator becomes one, do not want to be 'cured', so Beatrice becomes less happy at the end of her story when she marries a different man and her hearing returns. Her friend reflects at the end of the story that he had 'never seen a face so drained of joy, or even of the memory of joy'.[43] In 'A Country Love Story', the heroine is driven to madness by the emotional cruelty of her husband, who insists on his dominant role over her. As with Esther in *The Bell Jar*, Stafford's characters, required to maintain an outwardly feminine decorum, display their distress physically in the form of neurotic symptoms. Indeed, in many of her stories there is no reason discernible for these symptoms; they are simply the effects of being a woman in a patriarchal society. In 'The Echo and the Nemesis', the once-beautiful heroine cannot stop eating and is now immensely overweight. In 'Bad Characters', the young heroine cannot help herself from blurting out the insulting things she is thinking about people. In neither case do we know why they behave in these ways. Plath wrote precisely this sense of unexplained distress into many of her stories. We do not where Sadie's murderous desires in 'The Fifty-Ninth Bear' come from, or Alison's in 'Sweetie Pie and the Gutter Men'. These stories simply project a world in which such emotional violence is present just beneath the socially acceptable surface of the characters' lives. Stafford even uses the image of a bell jar in portraying this experience. In 'The Echo and the Nemesis', the woman who cannot stop eating projects her younger self onto an imaginary dead sister, of whom she says 'one wanted to put her under a glass bell to protect her'.[44] In 'The Warlock', the sinister doctor who contributes to the heroine's distress has 'a jade tree under a glass bell' on his desk.[45]

Not only did Stafford provide Plath with a model of fiction in which women's distress begins to show in the society which causes it, but she also portrayed the doctors who treat them as part of the problem. In 'A Country Love Story', it is her husband's doctor who prescribes the year in the country which leads to the heroine's breakdown. She knows that this will not be good for them but, 'with exaggerated patience' and a 'courtly but authoritative' manner, the doctor dismisses her objections.[46] Indeed, she reflects that 'there was a greater degree of understanding' between her husband and his doctor than between her husband and herself. In 'The Warlock', the doctor frightens the heroine and enjoys doing so, taking advantage of her weakness rather than alleviating it. Indeed, the operation from which she is convalescing had felt like a kind of murder to her: 'Some part of her mind . . . had been awake in the operating room, while the rest of her had been killed violently with ether'.[47] This passage is a precursor of Esther's ECT treatment, which feels to her as if she is being beaten and killed for an unknown crime. It is also a precursor of Esther's reflection upon Twilight Sleep, the medication given to the woman she sees giving birth in *The Bell Jar*, in which she knows that the pain relief doctors provide for women is in reality nothing of the kind. It is in 'The Interior Castle' above all that Plath finds the most detailed model of portraying the victimisation of a female patient at the hands of her socially respected doctors. Dr Nicholas, like Dr Gordon in *The Bell Jar*, is 'young, brilliant, and handsome'.[48] His agonising operation on the heroine's nose, although a work of genius, is an 'outrage' to her, to which she responds with 'hatred'. 'You are a thief', she tells him in her mind, as he talks patronisingly to her after the operation, 'You should be put to death'.[49] He even believes, as Buddy Willard would in an early draft of *The Bell Jar*, that her bouts of sinusitis are 'coincident with emotional crises'.[50] Plath's sense that the medical institution is a patriarchal one, which claims to heal women but which in reality contributes to their distress, is one she learned not only from her own experience but also from the fiction of Jean Stafford.

A third aspect of Stafford's stories which provided Plath with an example of the kind of fiction she could write for the *New Yorker* is the atmosphere of emotional blackmail in the family lives of her heroines. In 'The Liberation', Stafford portrays the web of manipulation, under the guise of family love, perpetrated on Polly Bay by the aunt and uncle with whom she lives. They 'played tricks upon her will' to make her go and live with them, just as they had used 'threats and sudden illnesses and cries of "Shame!"' to try to keep their own children at home. As a result, Polly's 'life had been like a dream of smothering'. As her aunt and uncle attempt to keep her from leaving home to get married, she realises that she is slowly 'being killed' by their emotional manipulations, although no one could give her the 'name of her disease'.[51] In 'In the Zoo', Stafford portrays the emotional violence done to two children by their outwardly pious 'Gran', who ruins the happiness of anyone or anything that enters her house. Although described as a woman of 'Christian goodness' to the orphaned children, she takes a perverse pleasure in seeing tricks, swindles and disappointments wherever she looks. In these 'mists of accusation and hidden plots', the children 'grew up like worms'. 'No one could have withstood the atmosphere in that house', the narrator reflects later, and Gran violates their innocent childhood pleasures with increasingly cruel hypocrisy as the story develops.[52] Characters like these are precursors of the 'loving and reproachful' Mrs Greenwood in *The Bell Jar* (*BJ* 166), who is a dutiful citizen and even a loving mother as far as the outside world is concerned, but in whose house and in relationship to whom her daughter simply cannot thrive. In 'The Mummy', Plath would also portray a 'supposedly loving' mother, who was in fact selfish and controlling (*J* 514). These mother figures who meet their daughters' material needs but give them none of the emotional sustenance they need are in part derived from the manipulative parent figures of Stafford's stories.

A second woman writer for the *New Yorker* whose work influenced Plath was Sylvia Townsend Warner. Plath read Warner's story 'The Quality of Mercy' in the 2 May 1959 issue of the *New Yorker* and commented on it the following day in her journal, calling it 'the usual flawlessly realised stuff with a pathos-or-bathos point'. She reflected that, with hard work, she herself could write for the magazine, although she was 'far from it' at present (*J* 481). Warner wrote prolifically for the *New Yorker* from the 1930s through the 1970s. In the late 1950s and early 1960s, whilst Plath was writing and submitting short stories to literary periodicals, she was publishing three or four stories a year. Warner's style is indeed highly polished. She writes beautiful, ironic vignettes, with a gentle, humanistic wit. One of the first things that may have struck Plath about Warner's stories was that they are almost always set in England. She writes about a considerable variety of British regions and classes. One of her stories, 'The Locum Tenens', which appeared in the *New Yorker* in March 1958, is set in Yorkshire, which would have particularly caught Plath's attention, since she herself had already written two stories set in Yorkshire, 'All the Dead Dears', and 'Afternoon in

Hardcastle Crags'. In 'The Locum Tenens', Warner depicts the speech and manners of the residents of the northern town in which the story is set, as well as the history, town planning and landscape of the region. Indeed, she writes a fine passage in which the eponymous locum sees, in a dream, the ancient landscape of the region looming through the modern town, 'not just in a crannied view at the end of Church Street' or 'desolately preserved in the bluff of rock and sickly turf above the goods yard', but everywhere, 'shouldering itself out of houses . . . , sombre through the neon lights of the picture house, rough underfoot though he trod on stone pavements'.[53] Warner's stories portray a wide variety of British life – she observes rich and poor, aristocrats and workers, children and adults, eccentrics of all kinds, as well as life in numerous regions of Britain – and writes about them in loving detail. Plath needed no encouragement to write fiction about places and events that she herself had experienced. She wrote numerous drafts of the novel based on her time in Cambridge and many short stories based on her experiences in England and Europe. 'Runaway' and 'Stone Boy With Dolphin' are set in Cambridge; 'The Black Bull' and 'That Widow Mangada' are set in Spain; and 'The Matisse Chapel' is based on her vacation in Vence. Warner's many stories of English experience encouraged Plath to believe that there was a market for stories based on her own experiences in England and Europe in the pages of the *New Yorker*.

Warner writes with a humane irony and this contributes to Plath's idea of a successful woman writer's style. 'Shadows of Death', for example, from 1959, is a gentle satire on the heroine's aristocratic mother and other local 'Goodies' who feel it their religious duty to visit the poor. Warner's satire is articulated with a stylistic device that Plath makes much use of in *The Bell Jar*, the juxtaposition of the childish innocence of the narrator at the time of the narrated events with her knowledge at the time of narration of adult society and its weaknesses. The heroine recounts her instruction by 'our leading Goodie' to read *The Imitation of Christ* to Mrs Darwin. First, she goes enthusiastically to find her copy of the book:

> This was not a success. I have since found that assents made with alacrity seldom are, when made to Goodies. They prefer one to sound as if the road would wind uphill all the way, and the shirt be hairy.[54]

She goes on to ask the Goodie at what point she had left off in reading to her neighbour, but the Goodie obviously does not remember:

> As though brushing off a fly in a Christian spirit, she said, 'Any chapter will do, I imagine.' . . . I realised I still had something to learn.[55]

This is precisely the way that Plath's juxtaposition of Esther's innocence at the time of the events she narrates with her greater knowledge at the time she narrates them works. Warner's style can be heard behind a passage in *The Bell Jar* like the one in which Esther does not know how to tip New York cab drivers. After telling us that her driver was so outraged by her tip that he began to shout at her and she had to run away in embarrassment, she comments, 'When I asked Doreen about this she said the tipping percentage might well have risen from ten to fifteen per cent since she was last in New York' (*BJ* 50–1). Warner even uses the short declarative sentences to carry the effect of this juxtaposition that Plath also uses with such a sure touch in her novel. The rhythm of Warner's sentences, 'This was not a success', or 'I realised I still had something to learn' from the above passage can be heard in sentences like, '"I'm very fond of balalaika music," I said' in *The Bell Jar* (*BJ* 76).

Although Plath comments specifically on Warner's perfectly crafted *New Yorker* style, in fact her prose modulates in and out of several styles, some of which also influenced Plath. Warner is a consciously literary writer, incorporating literary tradition into her sensibility. One of her heroines can say, for example, of the photograph of her great-uncle, 'Pensive, elegant, high-minded, he looks like a stanza in "In Memoriam"'.[56] Of the same character, she writes that his conversation would take such scandalous turns during rectory dinner parties that his wife would have to 'collect the attention of the female guests . . . and shepherd them away into the drawing room . . . saying confidentially, "You must forgive dear Augustine. You see, he is so steeped in the classics"'.[57] Educated literary humour like this provided Plath with the space to write in a similar vein in the college scenes in *The Bell Jar*. When Esther is annoyed with Buddy for dating Joan Gilling, she tells him that she too is waiting for a date. Not expecting this, Buddy asks who her date is:

> 'It's two,' I said, 'Peter the Hermit and Walter the Penniless' . . .
> Then I added, 'They're from Dartmouth.' (*BJ* 56)

Warner occasionally rises above the polished irony that fits so well into the pages of the *New Yorker* into a grander, more meditative style. 'Interval for Metaphysics', for example, is a Wordsworthian story about a child's development out of a stage in which words and things have a beautifully separate existence:

> The Word, till then a denominating aspect of the Thing, has suddenly become detached from it and is perceived as a glittering entity, transparent and unseizable as a jellyfish.[58]

Whilst Plath herself kept such metaphysical writing for her poetry, Warner nevertheless provided her with a model of writing that is highly educated and intellectually sophisticated, but also acceptable in the literary marketplace in which she aims to succeed.

A third *New Yorker* writer whom Plath resolved to read carefully and learn from whilst at Yaddo was Mavis Gallant (*J* 511). Gallant's prose style is also polished, urbane and understated. She has a gift for direct and striking imagery that Plath's best prose too exemplifies. 'Doris was proud of her education – a bundle of notions she trundled before her like a pram containing twins'.[59] The single most striking thing about Gallant's *New Yorker* stories from the late 1950s is that they create a world in which sexuality, often excessive or deviant, is a constant, submerged presence, breaking improperly into the world of social inter- actions that more typically constitute the material of a *New Yorker* story. Gallant's characters are often promiscuous, although they keep their socially prohibited actions and desires as hidden as possible. 'Jeux d'Été', for example, is a story about three wealthy girls and their chaper- one on holiday in Europe, in which the chaperone herself, although she attempts to maintain a façade of decency, leaves the girls for encounters with local men. On a date with a 'shabby gentleman from a tourist office', 'not the first to have asked for help with the English language', the chaperone reflects on her vacation:

> She also remembered how the bootboy in Florence had pointed to her bed, then her, then himself, then clasped his hands, and put his head against them . . . How kind he was, how kind they all were.[60]

In 'The Moabitess', there are hints of an improper relationship between the elderly spinster heroine and her father when she was a girl, and hints of adulterous relationships between the guests at the *pension* where the story is set. 'Her eyes, her fat little hands, her full lips, suggested she was the last person in the world to deny that side of life'.[61] In 'Bernadette', a poor French-Canadian maid gets pregnant by a man she does not know, one of many sexual advances she accepts without knowing why she does so. The story's disturbing power comes from the combination of innocence and corruption in Bernadette. As her wealthy liberal mistress questions the illiterate maid, Gallant writes:

> She stole a glance at Nora, and something about that oblique look suggested more than fear or evasiveness. A word came into Nora's mind: sly.[62]

The sexual encounters in Gallant's stories are never directly narrated, and in many stories there are only hints or suggestions that they even take place. The world of Gallant's stories, however, is rife with these hints and suggestions, one in which the massive continent of human sexuality lies just beneath the surface of the characters' socially acceptable interactions, constantly threatening indecently and improperly to break through.

Plath does not project such a world in her own fiction. Even in the sexual humour of *The Bell Jar*, there is no sense that sexuality is indecent or threatening. On the contrary, the novel is a defence of the value of female sexuality. Nevertheless, Gallant provides a model for Plath of a fictional world in which a level of intensely strong emotions exists beneath everyday life and constantly threatens to erupt into it. This is one of Plath's own most basic aesthetic insights. She was projecting this kind of world in high school stories such as 'The Dark River' and college stories such as 'Sunday at the Mintons'. It characterises her best stories, like 'The Fifty-Ninth Bear' and 'The Shadow'. What reading Gallant showed her was that, when properly crafted, this insight could produce stories that the *New Yorker* would publish.

Another element of Gallant's stories that would have resonated with Plath as a potential theme for marketable stories is that she frequently deals with the emotional distress of children and its effects in later life. Gallant's novel *Green Water, Green Sky* is one of the major precursors of *The Bell Jar*. When Plath read it at Yaddo, it strongly impressed her as the kind of novel that she herself could write. She wrote in her journal of her 'involvement' with Gallant, in particular with her 'novel on a daughter–mother relation, the daughter committing suicide'. A novel of her own, Plath reflects in the next sentence, 'brazen' and 'arrogant', as she considered Gallant's to be, would give her life as a writer the meaning for which she was looking (*J* 518). Gallant's novel is in four parts, three of which had been published as separate stories in the *New Yorker* during the summer of 1959.[63] Much of the stories that went into the novel focuses on the intense distress suffered by Florence, the young heroine, whose mother is divorced by her father and leads her without a home or sense of identity through various hotels and resorts in Europe. 'Green Water, Green Sky', which became the first part of the novel, is about a day in which Flor's cousin George's parents leave him for a day. Gallant describes the child's distress in intense and disturbing detail. She portrays his anxiety manifesting itself in neurotic behaviour. Flor breaks a necklace:

> And poor little George, suddenly anxious about what strangers might think – this new frantic little George ran here and there, picking up large lozenge-shaped beads from under people's feet.[64]

Gallant's story 'An Emergency Case' is about a boy whose parents have died in a car crash waking in hospital and refusing to face the fact that he is now an orphan. The other patients' refrain, '*Pauvre petit!*', in this story picks up the narrator's 'poor little George' in the later one – to be a child, in the world of Gallant's stories, is to be utterly wretched. Plath would write distress in a more coded manner into her stories. She usually does not narrate a traumatic childhood experience directly, but rather portrays the effects of what the reader must infer are unspoken, unresolved traumas in her characters. We do not know where the murderous fantasies of Sadie in 'The Fifty-Ninth Bear' or of Alison in 'Sweetie Pie and the Gutter Men', come from, only that the events that produced them must have been correspondingly traumatic. Nevertheless, Gallant's stories represented to Plath a model for the literary expression of the kind of intense and unresolved childhood emotions she herself put into her best works of fiction.

Gallant's long story 'August', which became the second part of the novel Plath read at Yaddo, is the story that influenced her the most. The central character, Flor, with her nervous breakdown, largely a result of her hatred of her mother, who tries to maintain social appearances and to raise a respectable daughter, deeply influenced Plath's portrayal of Esther in *The Bell Jar*. Gallant describes the symptoms of Flor's breakdown in considerable detail, many of which Plath would duplicate in *The Bell Jar*. Flor begins to lose her grip on language, as Esther does in Plath's novel, fixating on a certain phrase as the only one she can understand, ' . . . upon the beached verge of the salt flood . . . '. She does not speak these words, not even silently, but rather has the 'ringing impression of a faultless echo' of them in her head. Gallant writes, 'They were words out of the old days, when she could still read and relate every sentence to the sentence it followed.'[65] In a similar way, Esther finds herself unable to write properly as her distress intensifies, her handwriting regressing to large, childish letters which she cannot even keep in straight lines (*BJ* 125). Nor can she read with attention, except for the tabloids, whose short paragraphs and many pictures do not allow the words to 'wiggle about' on the page (*BJ* 131). Like Esther, Flor loses the ability to sleep and ceases to be able to distinguish between day and night, knowing only a constant longing for sleep. Gallant describes a symptom that Plath would ascribe to Hilda in *The Bell Jar*, looking at her reflection in shop windows to make sure she is still there. Flor is afraid she may become invisible and this fear causes her to dress in bright clothes and to 'steal glimpses of herself in shopwindows, an existence asserted in coral and red'.[66] In *The Bell Jar*, Hilda stares at her own reflection in the same way, 'as if to make sure . . . that she continued to exist' (*BJ* 96).

Perhaps the single most characteristic feature of the *New Yorker* stories of the middle and late 1950s that Plath sought to imitate in her own work is their frequent refusal of a traditional plot. Leitch's point about the paradox of the *New Yorker* story obtains here. There are stories which do have a plot, such as de Vries' 'Afternoon of a Faun', which has a clear beginning, middle and end, and even concludes with a proposal of marriage. Nevertheless, the stories are much more often emotionally charged vignettes in which potential events do not occur, or in which the events that do occur are not those that typically carry the weight of a story's plot. In Warner's story 'The Fifth of November', for example, there are only two events: one is that the lonely heroine lights a candle in an empty church; the second that the rector speaks to her, but that she does not reply. Almost nothing happens in the story, but these quasi-events are charged with the intense, inarticulate emotions which are the main focus of the story. Several of Plath's stories are shaped by this kind of eventlessness. 'Sweetie Pie and the Gutter Men', which she wrote for the *New Yorker*, is about the visit of one housewife to the home of another. The action consists almost entirely of their conversation, with the closest thing to an event being the extremely violent fantasies the hostess's child has about her doll, Sweetie Pie: 'I knock her down. I spank her and spank her. I bang her eyes in', to which Myra replies weakly, '"Good . . . You keep on doing that"' (*JPBD* 358). 'Above the Oxbow', too, consists only of the encounter between two hikers and the park ranger at the summit of a mountain, in which the girl feels that the fee for walking up the mountain is unfair. The events in the story are the emotions attached to these actions and interactions of little practical consequence.

> 'I can see the *par*king fee' . . . A fleck of saliva showed at the corner of her mouth . . . 'But to pay for *wal*king!' (*JPBD* 332)

The eventlessness of these stories is a mark of Plath's attempt to write in what she perceived to be the *New Yorker* style. She submitted 'Sweetie Pie and the Gutter Men' to the *New Yorker* and, although there is no record of where she submitted 'Above the Oxbow', it is clearly written to be a *New Yorker* story. The same is true of Plath's story 'The Fifteen Dollar Eagle'. Although eventually published in the *Sewanee Review*, it is written with a certain kind of *New Yorker* story in mind, that which has no plot at all. Warner's 'Wild Wales' is an example of this kind of story: it is simply a series of impressions of the adult narrator's childhood holidays in rural Wales, linked only by the occurrence of these impressions in the same place. Whilst 'The Fifteen Dollar Eagle' has a certain sense of climax to the series of episodes in the tattoo shop in that the last encounter is with the tattooist's wife, it is nevertheless entirely without a plot, structured simply as a series of impressions from the narrator's visit to the shop. Like 'Above the Oxbow', Plath wrote it as such in order for it to be a *New Yorker* story.

Women's Magazine Fiction

Plath was as ambitious to publish fiction in commercial women's magazines as she was to publish in the *New Yorker*.[67] The journal in which she harboured the greatest ambition to publish was her 'beloved' *Ladies' Home Journal* (*LH* 455, 433).[68] Whilst she was a high school student, an editor at *Seventeen* magazine advised her to read all the back issues of the magazine and learn to adapt her material to its style. Aurelia Plath commented, 'Sylvia did just that and never forgot the advice'.[69] In March 1953, after the *New Yorker* rejected one of her stories, Plath wrote, 'I must study the magazines the way I did *Seventeen*' (*LH* 107). Two years later, she was at work on the same project, writing that she was going to 'read magazines religiously (as every Writer's Manual advises)' and publish her story 'The Smoky Blue Piano' (*LH* 157). Plath bought and closely read numerous trade books and magazines for professional writers. Hughes recalls, in a draft introduction to *Johnny Panic and the Bible of Dreams*, that she read such volumes assiduously, impressed by the pragmatic model of writing they promoted and ambitious to achieve the kind of professional success they offered.[70] Some of these volumes are preserved in the Smith College archive, and Plath's heavy markings and marginalia indicate how seriously she took learning and practising the craft of the professional fiction writer. She bought *The Writer's Year Book* in 1952, 1954 and 1955, and seems to have subscribed to the monthly journal *The Writer* during her final year at Smith. *The Writer's Year Book* contains a section each year which gives details of the best markets for freelance writers, which Plath carefully annotated. In 1954, the *Ladies' Home Journal* entry reads:

> Most of the stories we like do not completely exclude from their reflection of life such qualities as love and hope and generosity and mercy and courage and self-sacrifice, such things as laughter and content.[71]

The journal does not care for 'fiction which excludes beauty in favour of ugliness; happiness in favour of misery; which has no room for such elements as movement, excitement, suspense'.[72] Plath underlined every one of the required qualities listed here and a made a note in the margin on the importance of laughter and love. She heavily underlined and starred *Good Housekeeping*'s entry, which reads:

Stories must have a strong narrative line, well-developed characters and quality in style; must be lucid and complete. Cheerful subject matter stands a better chance . . . Good love stories, good suspense stories and good humorous stories are always in demand.[73]

This section, on freelance markets, is introduced by a piece which includes the sentence, marked by Plath, 'It's essential to know the precise requirements of a magazine if you're trying to pinpoint a special piece'. *Good Housekeeping* recommends specific stories for prospective authors to look at as good examples of suitable short fiction. Plath took this advice seriously. In July 1955, she told her brother that she had checked numerous issues of the *Saturday Evening Post* specifically in order to write the kind of story which could be sold to such journals.[74] Later that month, she was reading magazines as she worked on 'Platinum Summer', intending to sell it to one of them.[75]

As with the *New Yorker*, there is no one typical kind of women's magazine story during the 1950s. There is a heavy emphasis on love stories, on stories about families and on marriage as the conclusion of the love stories. The stories are most frequently told from a woman's point of view, but there are also stories by men and from a man's point of view in the *Ladies' Home Journal*, *McCall's* and *Good Housekeeping* throughout the decade. After love, marriage and family, religion is the most frequent subject addressed, and there are some stories that deal with a character's religious life in the way that others do his or her love life.[76] As the decade goes on, formerly taboo subjects, like extramarital affairs, divorce and unwed pregnancy, become acceptable as subject-matter, although they are usually incorporated within the ideology of marriage. Politically, the stories as a whole are complex. Whilst the husbands inevitably talk down to their wives, telling them what to do and how to behave, and usually regard women in general as foolish, the heroines of the stories, whilst not directly protesting against these relationships, are usually in control of the men, who only give the appearance of being the head of the family. 'Men are soft, Ginger, unless we women do for them', as one character tells the heroine of a *Ladies' Home Journal* story.[77]

Plath's stories became more and more like the stories published in the magazines at which she was aiming throughout the years she wrote them. When she sent 'The Smoky Blue Piano' to the *Ladies' Home Journal* they rejected it, saying that although it did not fully meet their specifications, it was nevertheless an attractive story.[78] They disliked that it was told in the form of journal entries, but added that if Plath reworked it into a third-person narrative, without losing its 'nice sparkle', they would reconsider it (*LH* 150). She was encouraged by this and rewrote the story that same day. She thought the revised version was the 'best' story of this genre, 'written to meet certain specifications, while being true to my own humour and ideas', she had yet produced (*LH* 150–1). The *Journal* again rejected the story, however, with a phrase that preyed on Plath's mind and that she would repeat in reflections on her magazine writing, that it 'lacked an "indefinable something" that made a *Journal* piece' (*LH* 156).

There are several qualities that make 'The Smoky Blue Piano' untypical of a *Ladies' Home Journal* story of the mid-1950s and to which the fiction editor was referring with her phrase 'indefinable something'. In the first place, it is about two college girls, rooming together at Harvard Summer School, the right one of which ends up with the hero of the story. Although this is not an insurmountable obstacle, because the *Journal* published experimental stories and variations on its most popular themes, there are very few *Ladies' Home Journal* stories set in a college. Whilst there are college girl heroines, they tend to be home for the summer or portrayed in some other way within the wider context of their family. 'Marry I Must', from November 1957, is about two girls at college, but, unlike Plath's story, it ends in marriage and has a heroine who has been trying to get married throughout the story.[79] What constitutes the 'indefinable something' lacking in the college girl setting of Plath's story is that the heroines have ambitions and sensibilities which, whilst they include marriage, are not limited to it. The narrator's friend Lynn is more in control of her desires with respect to marriage than any character in a *Ladies' Home Journal* story. She is in control of every relationship she has been in with a man. Her current boyfriend, a graduate student at Harvard, is no different, but Lynn is not interested in marrying him until she has her PhD – she will not give up everything for love while she is still a college student with ambitions of her own.[80] Even this slight disparagement of marriage is not found among the heroines of *Ladies' Home Journal* stories. The only time such an attitude appears is at the beginning of a story, as the kind of mistaken attitude out of which the heroine progresses during the story.[81] But there is no such progression in Plath's story. This is the first indefinable something that it lacks with respect to the standards of the *Ladies' Home Journal* – a sufficiently unequivocal commitment to marriage. Plath's heroine wants a PhD first, and so does not quite fit in the pages of the *Ladies' Home Journal*.

In Plath's first group of women's magazine stories, 'The Smoky Blue Piano', 'Platinum Summer' and 'The Christmas Heart', the heroines are too much in control of themselves and their relationships to men to be *Ladies' Home Journal* heroines. In 'The Smoky Blue Piano', the heroine and her roommate discover they have an attractive male neighbour.

Indeed, in the first drafts of the story, he is described as precisely the sort of character whom the heroine of a women's magazine story would have as a neighbour. In those stories, however, in one way or another, the heroine is always lucky enough to have an encounter of some kind with this desirable man; she is too ladylike simply to pursue him. That is what Plath's heroines do, however: the narrator and her friend Lynn decide to go on the offensive that very night, turning up at his door with an excuse to meet him. Women's magazine stories of this period do not use concepts like going on the offensive to describe their heroines' pursuit of a man, at least not without a considerable amount of hedging it around with self-deprecating humour. That Plath's heroines simply see an attractive man and go after him, without amusingly feminine failures and faults that teach them the error of their ways, makes them too forward to be *Ladies' Home Journal* heroines. In 'Platinum Summer', the heroine's friend Happy approves of men's reaction to her dyed blonde hair – they are intrigued, and to be intrigued is just what men need, she asserts.[82] This confident and conscious control of men's desires by sexually independent women does not happen in *Ladies Home Journal* stories. Even in an unusual story, from May 1955, in which the college girl heroine learns that she can control men, she does so only in the context of chasing away an unwelcome suitor and of overcoming her too strong attraction to an older man of whom her parents disapprove.[83] She controls men only in order to behave correctly within the family. The independence of the heroines of 'The Smoky Blue Piano' and 'Platinum Summer' is a characteristic only of bad women in *Ladies' Home Journal* stories, through whom the hero sees in order to meet or stay with the good, more modest, heroine. 'The Ugliest Woman in Town', from April 1955, provides a good example of this stereotype. Netta, the glamorous would-be adulteress, thinks, 'I've always wanted Horton Dickey. And here I am right on the spot. I'll grab him fast and make a dash for Paris with him'.[84] A similar kind of independence in the good characters of Plath's first two women's magazine stories is the second 'indefinable something' that makes them not quite right for the *Ladies' Home Journal*.

'The Christmas Heart' differs in a third way from the typical women's magazine story of the 1950s. Plath submitted this story to the *Ladies' Home Journal*, which rejected it. From Cambridge, she asked her mother to send it to *McCall's*, *Woman's Home Companion*, *Good Housekeeping*, *Woman's Day* and *Everywoman's*.[85] None of the these journals published the story, and she was still submitting it to British women's magazines in 1961.[86] One of the reasons for which the journals would have rejected the story is that the moral of women's magazines stories is almost invariably one for their female readers, whereas the moral of Plath's story is directed at the men to whom those readers relate. It is the man who needs to change in her story, and this kind of feminist moral is rarely found in the women's magazine stories of the 1950s. The heroine of the story (a fictional version of Plath) believes that the hero (a fictional version of Dick Norton, during his time at Ray Brook sanatorium) professes to love her only because he has none of his usual distractions whilst on a rest cure for tuberculosis. She tells him that wanting to get married to avoid being alone is a destructive emotion, which surprises him. But this is how she has come to think of marriage whilst he has been away, she tells him, as a relationship between two equals, in which both grow together.[87] This lesson is one that the man in the story, rather the woman, learns throughout its action. The woman already knows how he should behave, and he comes to learn, thereby winning her affections. The heroine asks herself later if he has learned the value of empathy, just as she has learned the value of independence. The answer is yes, he has learned this quality, and so she decides to stay with him instead of ending their relationship as she had intended to do at the beginning of the story. She had intended to tell him that, though their relationship had at times been a strong one, it was no longer what she wanted. Plath captures the domestic, emotional morals of *Ladies' Home Journal* stories well as the doctor's wife, with whom the heroine is staying, tells her that learning to be loved can be harder than learning to love. But in a *Ladies' Home Journal* story, this moral would be learned by the heroine herself, not by the hero. This is the third 'indefinable something' that this story lacks – *Ladies' Home Journal* stories articulate morals for women, not men. In the world of these stories, men are usually fixed and unalterable, and the heroine's task is simply to find the right one. The feminist desire of Plath's heroine to *make* the right one, in a story in which the hero learns how to love the heroine in the way she wants, is not the material of a *Ladies' Home Journal* story.

Having pointed out some of the qualities for which Plath's stories may have been rejected from the women's magazines to which she submitted them, it must also be pointed out that, despite some of these differences from the kind of story typically published in these magazines, Plath was nevertheless fluent in their structure and style. As the *Ladies' Home Journal* put it, whilst they could not quite accept 'The Smoky Blue Piano', it nevertheless had a 'nice sparkle' which made it very close to the kind of story they published. Despite the independence of the heroine of 'Platinum Summer', her desires are nevertheless firmly centred on marriage, as is always the case with the heroines of women's magazine stories. As the heroine looks at the attractive hero, part of his attractiveness to her is how easily she can see a man like him in the kind of home they would share as a couple.[88] Not only does Lynn want ultimately to get married, but marriage is closely associated in her mind with the kind of home her husband will be able to provide. The film *The Tender Trap*, released the same year that Plath wrote 'Platinum Summer', portrays this kind of desire in a scene in which Debbie Reynolds' character finds the rake, played by Frank Sinatra, attractive for the first time when she sees him in a living room set at a furniture exhibition.[89] In 'Midnight of a Bridesmaid', published in the *Ladies' Home Journal* in March 1955, the narrator and heroine reflects passionately that 'girls and how they dress and how they do their hair' is not a frivolous matter, as men think. Rather, the girl in the red dress with the plunging neckline on the dance floor knows very well that 'it takes this dress to get that fellow to let her wash his clothes in that washing machine he's going to buy when they are married'.[90] She adds, to the man she loves:

> I laughed and swam and danced and played tennis when all in the world I wanted was to direct that energy toward running a house for you.[91]

Ladies' Home Journal heroines dream about marriage and a home, and Plath attributes these dreams to her heroines in exactly the right way.

Plath's second group of women's magazine stories, written between January and August 1957, remain only in fragmentary form, and only 'The Laundromat Affair' and 'Operation Valentine' are extant at all. 'The Fabulous Room-Mate' and 'The Trouble-Making Mother' are lost. These fragments, however, indicate that Plath was able successfully to temper her concerns to the requirements of the women's magazine market as she continued to work at writing fiction for this market. 'The Laundromat Affair' and 'Operation Valentine' seem to conform more closely to the women's magazine stories of the time than Plath's earlier stories. For example, the feminist ideas in 'The Laundromat Affair' are hedged around with precisely the right kind of self-deprecating humour. The story is about two people who meet at a laundromat through the thirteen-year-old narrator, whom Plath describes as a 'quiz-kid type' (*LH* 312). Seven pages into the story, the narrator is arguing feminism with the hero in the laundromat – they talk about a philosopher whose works disparage women. The girl fulminates about how the philosopher thinks of women as infantile, vain and in general as lesser beings, to which the hero gently responds that perhaps he had just never known a really good woman like her.[92] Here the feminist ideas are acceptably softened by being placed in the mouth of a child and by being spoken to a man who is already the hero of the love story without needing to change in line with them. Good men already understand feminism, the story suggests, in exactly the right way for the women's magazine market, and so women need not get too strident about or committed to feminist ideas in order to love those men. Plath is also able to couch her narrator's ideas in a humorous context, in which the hero is aware of how amusing it is for a girl to have such ideas. She tells him women are equal in every way to men, if not superior to them. She asks him if he would like to hear her own philosophy on the issue, at which he suddenly develops a fit of coughing, but after a moment he recovers and signals that he would indeed like to hear her philosophy. Here Plath catches the humorous style of many *Ladies' Home Journal* stories perfectly. These are often characterised by a rather saccharine domestic humour, in which men find women exasperating, illogical or impossible to understand, but nevertheless utterly adorable. 'The Heart Has its Reasons', published in March 1954, is a good example of this – indeed, the entire story is about nothing else than a man who has an illogical, impractical wife whom he learns simply to adore. We hear, for example, that he 'entered the kitchen on the day that an egg, left to boil dry, had exploded. He received most of it in the eye, mercifully closed'.[93] His wife, tenderly ministering to his eye, wonders if he is accident-prone:

> 'Accident-prone!' he had yelped.
> 'Some people are, you know. You ought to be more careful. Did you know that nine-tenths of all serious accidents occur in the home?'
> He said yes, he knew, and he wasn't too surprised.[94]

As Plath narrates that the hero of 'The Laundromat Affair' is suddenly troubled by a cough, she captures this kind of domestic humour perfectly. The idiom is especially appropriate in her story in that it makes an acceptably domesticated joke of the feminist ideas of the narrator, which in themselves would be too directly critical of gender roles for a *Ladies' Home Journal* story.

'Operation Valentine' too seems to be very fluent in the idiom of the women's magazine story. A story published in the *Ladies' Home Journal* in November 1957, 'Marry I Must', three months after Plath submitted her story, features a college girl who calls her plan to find a husband in college, which constitutes the whole action of the story, 'Operation Marry-I-Must'. Plath is clearly able to think in the *Ladies' Home Journal* manner at this stage. She has also thoroughly mastered the romance idiom. The heroine of the story, to whom the narrator introduces the hero, pretends scarcely to know him. She says without hesitating that he is simply her tennis instructor, but her eyes, which melt like a sunset, betray her emotions.[95] Here the narrative sympathy for a girl in love is both in content and style exactly the material of *Ladies' Home Journal* stories. The idea that the heroine cannot hide her love, although she tries to, indicating that love is what a woman ultimately is, along with the poetic image for this love, lacks absolutely no 'indefinable something' that makes a *Ladies' Home Journal* story: this is the essence of what makes such a story. Plath continues to strike this note as the story develops. The older narrator empathises with the heroine in love – she too knows that love is the essence of a woman – and she bends the rules somewhat, in an altogether acceptable way, in order to help a girl in love. Employed by Sassy's wealthy mother, who wants her steered in the direction of a suitably wealthy young man, the narrator agonises over Sassy's request to ask Gary, the mere tennis coach with whom she has fallen in love, to the beach with them. In the end, knowing what it is like to be in love for the first time, she gives in and invites him. This is exactly the right thing to do in terms of the value system of the *Ladies' Home Journal*. Whilst there are social codes to be observed – here, the narrator's duty to the heroine's mother, who may be expected to know best for her daughter – a woman in love is a higher value, and both narrator and heroine fully enforce this value.

Women's Madness Narratives

I next consider a group of texts that influenced *The Bell Jar* in particular. These are the texts Susan Hubert describes as 'madness narratives', intending to include with this term both autobiographical and fictional narratives.[96] Marilyn Yalom has written of the 'sub-genre of the psychiatric novel', rightly pointing to its 'distinctly female cast'.[97] In fact, the texts available to Plath that made it possible to turn her own experiences of mental breakdown and recovery into *The Bell Jar* are not only novels, but also cinematic, autobiographical and journalistic narratives. In June 1959, she noted in her journal that she had read the whole of the latest issue of *Cosmopolitan*, in which there were 'two mental-health articles'. Plath reflected that she should write such an article herself, dealing with a 'college girl suicide'. She thought of writing a story and 'a novel, even' on the subject, planning to read Mary Jane Ward's novel *The Snake Pit* and commenting on the 'increasing market for mental hospital stuff' (*J* 495). Contemporary reviews of *The Bell Jar* often mention its familiar subject matter. Anthony Burgess, in *The Observer*, spoke of 'what is fast becoming a stock theme among women writers', and wrote, 'We've met the situation before, but rarely so mature a fictional approach to it'.[98] *The Times* pointed out, 'The subject . . . has been treated in a not dissimilar way, though more sternly, in several recent novels'.[99] When

Harper & Row rejected the novel for publication in America in 1963, they gave as one of their reasons that 'there has been so much fiction in recent years dealing this area of experience'.[100] The influence of Robert Lowell's and Anne Sexton's poetic accounts of psychiatric treatment on Plath has been well documented. In this section, I focus on some of the narrative works that provided Plath with models of writing in *The Bell Jar* about her experience of breakdown and recovery.

The two articles Plath read in the June 1959 *Cosmopolitan* provided her with two very different sets of ideas about the possibilities for writing about mental health. One of them is the autobiographical account of the mental breakdown of an apparently successful woman, who has a good home, husband, children and career. She goes to an unsympathetic doctor, then to a more understanding one, spends some time in hospital, works through an affair her husband has whilst she is away, lives alone for a time and eventually takes her husband back. Many things about this narrative would have interested Plath as she considered writing about her own experiences of breakdown and recovery. In the first place, the heroine is clearly, as far as the face she shows to the outside world is concerned, a strong, successful woman. Like Plath, she has succeeded in having both a family and a career as a writer. Nevertheless, even such a strong character can begin her narrative, 'Seven years ago I wanted to die'.[101] There is a long passage on her visit to a psychiatrist, who, although 'highly thought of in his profession', simply fails to listen to her.[102] Although the visit to Dr Gordon in *The Bell Jar* is based on Plath's own experience, this *Cosmopolitan* article also provided Plath with a narrative frame in which to write that experience into her novel. The first doctor the author of the *Cosmopolitan* article sees is a 'smooth-faced, jargon-talking boy psychiatrist', just as Plath would portray Dr Gordon as 'young', 'good-looking' and 'conceited' (*BJ* 124). She too looks for a 'good psychiatrist who would make me really well', writing, 'This was my dream, to find a doctor who, like a magician would *make* me well', just as Esther hopes for a 'kind, ugly, intuitive man' who would understand her and gradually lead her back to being 'myself again' (*BJ* 123, 124).[103] The heroines of both narratives have their hope dashed, in a very similar way. The doctor's opening question in the *Cosmopolitan* article establishes his inability to relate to the author:

> 'I understand we're having a bad time, mmm-mmm?' he said in a fake soothing voice. 'Now tell me, by what means have you thought of taking your life?'[104]

In exactly the same way, Dr Gordon's opening question, '"Suppose you . . . tell me what you think is wrong"', makes Esther feel that he does not understand her, since it 'made it sound as if nothing was *really* wrong' (*BJ* 124). Patricia Blake, the author of the *Cosmopolitan* article, eventually found a good psychiatrist, just as Esther finds Dr Nolan, who helps her by listening to and understanding her. Under the care of these psychiatrists, both heroines benefit from ECT treatment and both heroines have them to thank for their recovery. Blake explicitly compares her good psychiatrist to a good parent, as Plath would with Dr Nolan: 'This is what a good parent must do for his children – share his light until the child has light of his own'.[105]

If this article gave Plath a framework for writing about her experience of mental illness and treatment, the second article she read in the magazine is an example of precisely the kind of cultural constriction from which Esther suffers in *The Bell Jar*. Entitled 'Psychiatry and Beauty', the article argues that mental health in women can be judged by the attention they pay to beauty and to personal appearance. This claim is supported by citations from doctors:

> It is not, as some women might fear, vanity to derive pleasure from being attractive. 'It's healthy,' says Dr Levine, 'to acknowledge your best points and do what you can to accentuate them.'[106]

What is true of the mentally ill women who are the subject of the article is also true, the author asserts, of all women:

> It is not only women in emotionally trying circumstances who can benefit from the wizardry of professional beauty care. Every woman can.[107]

Indeed, we hear more in the article about the psychologically uplifting effects of beauty treatment in healthy women than in the hospitalised women the article is ostensibly about. Although this message is a patriarchal one, linking women's value to their appearance for the male gaze, it is nevertheless one Plath writes into *The Bell Jar*. Esther ties her value, despite the conflict this causes her, closely to her appearance. Her breakdown begins with the symbolic discarding of her New York wardrobe from the roof of her hotel, and a sign of her illness, in Plath's novel just as in the *Cosmopolitan* article, is that she does not change her clothes or wash her hair for three weeks. Similarly, at the end of the novel, as she hopes to graduate from mental hospital back into society, Esther has smartened herself up. Her 'stocking seams' are 'straight', her shoes 'polished' and her 'red wool suit' as 'flamboyant as my plans' (*BJ* 233). The last phrase, indeed, invokes precisely the view articulated in the *Cosmopolitan* article, that a woman's appearance symbolises her inner state.

The *Cosmopolitan* article is contradictory, and Plath writes some of this contradiction into *The Bell Jar*. Having spent five pages extolling the psychological importance of beauty, the final page of the article suddenly switches tack and asserts that women must not attach too high a value to their looks. Despite have been counselled to do nothing else for five pages, we suddenly hear, 'For a woman to evaluate herself wholly in terms of her beauty is sheer folly, Dr Riss believes':[108]

> Women who are beset with this longing [for beauty] have the idea, admittedly not altogether baseless, that people regard personal beauty as proof of personal flawlessness.[109]

This attitude that the doctor now criticises is precisely the one that the article has expressed and supported with quotes from doctors at considerable length. Readers of the article are thus asked to tread a very fine line. Women must care about beauty, but not too much. You must want to be beautiful, otherwise you may be mentally ill, but nevertheless you must not want it too much, otherwise you may be mentally ill. Plath wrote precisely this double message into *The Bell Jar*, and portrayed its disastrous effects on Esther. Esther loves beauty and fashion, but its sheer emptiness and pointlessness is part of what causes her breakdown. The height of achievement for a college woman turns out not to be worth achieving. On the one hand, Esther is 'attracted . . . like a magnet' to the 'marvellous, elaborate decadence' of the girls at Doreen's society college, who match each one of their dresses to handbags made specially for the purpose (*BJ* 5). On the other, as she sees Hilda's exquisitely fashionable outfit, she cannot help thinking that the fashion she exemplifies so beautifully is ultimately 'full of nothing' (*BJ* 95). Hilda's mindlessly amoral attitude towards the execution of the Rosenbergs symbolises the mindlessly amoral nature of the fashion industry of which she is the ideal subject. Furthermore, just as the *Cosmopolitan* article offers its readers no way out of the contradiction it articulates, Plath's novel also remains within the same double bind. Although she portrays the damaging effects of the ideology of beauty and fashion on Esther, Plath also ends the novel with Esther as committed to personal appearance, and even to its symbolic value, as when the novel began. Linda Wagner-Martin has argued that 'Plath intended to create a thoroughly positive ending for Esther's narrative'.[110] Tim Kendall's assessment, however, is the better one: 'the destructive social systems remain in place at the end of the novel, and Esther has still not discovered a desirable identity for herself'.[111] The final scene, which seems to be the beginning of Esther's recovery, sees her as anxiously well dressed as in the early scenes which narrated the reasons for this breakdown, one of which was the all-importance of beauty and fashion for women. Just as in the article she read in *Cosmopolitan*, Plath portrays no way out of the contradictory ideologies of beauty and fashion, but only the damage that being caught in them does to their subjects.

One of the most popular novelists to write about mental illness in the 1950s was Shirley Jackson. In May 1953, Plath selected four writers whom she would like to interview for her forthcoming guest editor assignment at *Mademoiselle*. and Shirley Jackson was one of them (*LH* 114). Jackson wrote both literary fiction for *The New Yorker* and popular fiction for women's magazines, just as Plath herself aimed to do. Linda Wagner-Martin has pointed to the influence of Jackson's 1954 novel *The Bird's Nest*, on *The Bell Jar*.[112] More significant an influence, I would suggest, is Jackson's 1951 novel *Hangsaman*. This tells the story of an adolescent girl who lives in an impossible space within her own family, which gradually drives her to schizophrenic delusions as she leaves home for college. Perhaps most like *The Bell Jar*, Natalie, the heroine of *Hangsaman*, is required, by her family and by the society of which it is a part, to be normal. Her problem, like Esther's, is that she is not normal, nor does she want to be. As Plath would in her 1952 story 'Initiation', Jackson includes a scene in which the freshmen in Natalie's dorm undergo an initiation ceremony, the purpose of which is for each girl to prove that:

> she was not in any way eccentric, but a good, normal, healthy, American college girl, with ideals and ambitions and looking forward to a family of her own; she had merged.[113]

Plath describes her own experience of initiation into a sorority at high school in a similar way, as a process in which one entered the 'cherished Norm' and was 'tailored' to fit the 'Okay Image' (*JPBD* 24). Although Natalie fails the initiation, she continues throughout *Hangsaman*, just as Esther does throughout *The Bell Jar*, to try to appear as normal, as feminine and as ladylike as possible. Furthermore, Jackson generates a similar kind of comedy from her heroine trying and failing to conform to complicated sets of social rules as Plath would do with Esther. When she has cocktails with a young faculty wife, for example, she goes through an immensely elaborate thought process over the etiquette of cigarette lighting:

> It was difficult for Natalie to get up from the overstuffed chair and walk across to Elizabeth with a match, but it was unthinkable that Elizabeth should stand up from the couch and walk across to Natalie with a match.[114]

Natalie does not dare begin smoking until she has resolved the issue. She then thinks of lighting a cigarette only once Elizabeth has been smoking hers for a suitable period of time, 'taking one from her pocket with an absent-minded air, as one who smokes without thinking, and lighting it carelessly, holding the match a trifle too long while she talked'.[115] Plath uses precisely this kind of humour in relating Esther's difficulties with the etiquette of tipping or using finger bowls or ordering drinks (*BJ* 50–1, 38, 9–10). Jackson's novel ends, furthermore, like Plath's, on a thoroughly ambiguous note in terms of their heroines' recovery from breakdown and ability to live in the real world, with an assertion by the heroine that she is now able to live in the society that caused her breakdown in the first place, but with a conspicuous lack of evidence that she has acquired any resources with which to do so.

Hangsaman identifies Natalie's distress entirely as a matter of gender roles. Jackson, as Plath also would in *The Bell Jar*, identifies the institutions of marriage and the family as the most oppressive to her female characters:

> 'It all starts so nice,' Mrs Waite said, twisting her face into a horrible look of disgust. 'You think it's going to be so easy. You think it's going to be good.'[116]

Men will 'tell you lies', she tells Natalie, and 'make you believe them'. Then they will 'give you a little of what they promised, just a little, enough to keep you thinking you've got your hands on it', until one day you wake up to discover that you have been 'tricked, just like everyone else'.[117] Jackson even includes a scene that Plath would also write in *The Bell Jar*, in which Mrs Waite puts her creative talent and energies into domestic works that are utterly unappreciated by her family for whom she does them. In Jackson's novel it is Mrs Waite's Sunday casserole which, 'incredibly complex and delicate, would be devoured drunkenly . . . by inconsiderate and uncomplimentary people'.[118] In *The Bell Jar*, this becomes Mrs Willard's rug, which took her a long time to make and whose beautiful design impresses Esther, but which is used simply as a kitchen mat, so that it quickly becomes 'soiled and dull', like any other cheap mat (*BJ* 80). For Jackson, as for Plath, the only outlet provided by society for creative women is one in which their creations are instantly destroyed, when they are allowed at all, by the contemporary institutions of marriage and the family.

In 1959, whilst thinking about writing her own mental health story, Plath resolved to read Mary Jane Ward's novel *The Snake Pit*, about a woman's experience of treatment in and release from a mental hospital. She had seen the 1948 film of the novel, and wrote to Eddie Cohen from McLean in December 1953 that her own recent experiences reminded her closely of the 'deep impression' the film adaptation of *The Snake Pit* had made on her when she saw it some six years earlier (*LH* 132). The film was part of their cultural vocabulary – two years earlier Eddie had described the apartment he shared with his friends as the 'Snakepit'.[119] It is important to understand that Plath had seen the film before she had a similar set of experiences to those of its heroine. It is not the case that her own experiences of breakdown, treatment and recovery were simply the raw materials which she worked up into the aesthetic form of *The Bell Jar*. Rather, her own experience was, to an extent, already scripted by madness narratives like the film of *The Snake Pit*. This film may be the most formative influence of all on *The Bell Jar*, in that it provided Plath with a narrative framework not only for her novel but also for the very experience on which the novel is based. Perhaps the most striking aspect of the film is the portrayal of the heroine Virginia Cunningham's ECT treatment as an extremely frightening experience. The film won an Academy Award for Best Sound, and the music during the electric shock scenes is loud and scream-like, making it sound as if Virginia is screaming in pain, although in fact the unsettling experience of watching the scene is increased by the fact that a nurse stuffs a gag in her mouth just as she has plucked up the courage to demand a lawyer for what she thinks is a criminal punishment. This scene is preceded by one in which a line of anxious women wait for this punishment, with Virginia crying, 'I'm afraid, I'm terribly afraid'.[120] This was the scene which provided Plath with the most fundamental model for writing her account of electric shock treatment in *The Bell Jar*, because it also provided her with a model for understanding her own experience of such treatment.

There are many aspects of the novel *The Snake Pit* which Plath would use in *The Bell Jar*. Virginia is a likeable, ironic, socially observant narrator, as able to laugh at herself as she is at those around her, as Esther is in *The Bell Jar*. Like Esther, Virginia is constantly at pains to appear ladylike, normal and socially graceful, and like Plath, Ward derives a good deal of ironic humour from this device. In the first conversation of the novel, in which we gradually learn what Virginia has forgotten, that she is in hospital in the middle of her treatment, she makes polite and encouraging conversation to a fellow-patient whom she thinks is a failed writer who has begun talking to her in a New York park.

> 'I'm not so young,' said Virginia. 'I'm . . . ' How old am I? What year is this? What month? . . . Quickly she selected an age that was substantial and uncontroversial. 'I'm thirty-five,' she said.[121]

She worries about her appearance, her dress, accessories like her pocketbook, just as Esther does. She is also a sharp and critical observer of the ways in which others fit into, or fail to fit into, the system of social rules and mores, commenting on the poor looks or dress sense or manners of various nurses: 'she had a Dutch bob, always the favourite cut of square-faced, dark, fat women'.[122] As in *The Bell Jar*, this vein of humour derives from a serious social observation, that personal appearance is essential to a woman's survival, success and material life in contemporary society. As Virginia observes, 'When they lose their minds [men] look less lost than women'.[123] Whilst most of the men in the mental hospital could pass for normal in any crowd, she reflects, not one of the women could, because 'a woman without a pocketbook or a compact or a pair of gloves or a hat or even a handkerchief is a lost soul'.[124]

Ward strongly criticises the patriarchal structure of the treatment of mentally ill women. The doctors by whom Virginia is treated, in whom her husband trusts – indeed 'simply worshipped' – for much of the novel, are all convinced of their own expertise and pay little or no attention to Virginia herself, who, it turns out towards the end of the novel, has a clear and accurate idea of the social conditions that caused her to break down in the first place.[125] Ward emphasises that it is their place as men in a patriarchal society that allows and encourages Virginia's doctors to assume control of her life and mind as they do. She and her husband have a school friend who has recommended her doctor to them and who has always thought of himself as an expert, because as a man he is simply able to do so. Becoming a doctor, Virginia comments, has simply institutionalised and socially sanctioned his already existing view that he had a right to authority. 'Oh Charles, even then, had words to say, but no M.D. to back them up'.[126] She later adds, 'Charles and his thinking. He's always thinking. I wish he would have a shock treatment himself. That would stop him for a while'.[127] In her final interview, Virginia simply blurts out what was clearly the problem all along, and it is quite at variance both with her doctor's psychoanalytic diagnosis and with the biological assumption at work in the prescription of ECT treatment:

> 'I was tired . . . And I suppose I was scared about money. It was my fault, really, that Robert gave up his nice job at home, and so I kept trying to write something that would make up for it.' [128]

She was worried about her husband's long hours and lack of sleep and, as a new bride, she felt homesick. As with Esther in *The Bell Jar*, despite her doctors' use of ECT treatment, it turns out that Virginia's problems were caused by her social conditions and that these conditions are gender-specific. It is trying to live out the role prescribed by her society for a woman that causes her to break down.

Jennifer Dawson's novel *The Ha-Ha*, published in 1961, whilst Plath was writing *The Bell Jar*, is about a young woman in the latter stages of recovery from schizophrenia. As contemporary reviewers pointed out, it shares a great deal with Plath's work. Josephine, the heroine of Dawson's novel, has a mental breakdown whilst she is a student. She went to Somerville College, Oxford, just as Esther went to one of the top women's colleges in the United States. As in Plath's novel, Josephine's distress is traceable to her mother, who is unsympathetic to her daughter and part of her problem. She manipulates and plays self-indulgent games with her daughter over the question of her maturity, for example, as she tries to buy a dress when she is invited to a party:

> 'I shall soon be having a real all-rounder for a daughter', she said with a meaningful glint. 'I have a feeling that you will soon be meeting your match in the world, and I shall be seeing less of you.'[129]

Josephine admits to precisely the same death-wish Esther has towards Mrs Greenwood. After her mother dies, she says, 'I blurted out with vehemence at last, "I am glad! I am glad she's dead. The future can begin."'[130] Like Esther, Josephine hates her mother with a buried aggression that emerges as murderous fantasy. Indeed, after an 'accident' with the electric blanket, Josephine feels that she has actually killed her mother. 'It was as though my laughter had killed her'. This relationship to her mother's death is more complex than Esther's. Josephine struggles to admit her hatred of her mother to herself, whereas Esther simply fantasises about it, wanting to wring her mother's neck to stop her snoring (*BJ* 118–19). Nevertheless, both heroines feel aggression to the point of murder towards their mothers, and both blame their mothers for their illness.

As Esther would in *The Bell Jar*, Josephine experiences freedom from the strict code of sexual ethics for women as liberating. Although she receives little pleasure from her single sexual encounter with Alisdair, the male patient with whom she falls in love, the fact of a love affair, albeit temporary and one-sided, is the most meaningful experience she has:

> Something had presented itself to my mind hugely real, like a land sighted from the sea . . . I could stretch out and touch and share things. I could shout out across the disturbing world and someone would reply.[131]

Esther's experience of contraception as 'climbing to freedom' and becoming her 'own woman' (*BJ* 213) articulates a similar experience: however contrary to contemporary sexual ethics, sexual relationships free of the guilt imposed by these ethics are genuinely liberating for the heroines. Nevertheless, Dawson's novel ends, just as Plath's would, on a note of assertion by the heroine of future recovery for which we have seen no evidence in the narrative that precedes it.

An earlier British novel which recounts a descent into and out of schizophrenia is Antonia White's *Beyond the Glass*, published in 1954. Virginia Woolf had used the metaphor of a wall of glass to describe Septimus Smith's neurotic inability to feel after his friend's death – 'Beauty was behind a pane of glass . . . Even taste had no relish to him'. This metaphor for neurotic experience is a precursor of Esther's bell jar, to be inside which is to be 'blank and stopped as a dead baby' (*BJ* 227). Woolf even uses the image of the dead baby, speaking in *A Room of One's Own* of Fascist poetry as 'a horrid little abortion such as one sees in a glass jar in the museum'.[132] Other modernist women writers would use the same metaphor. H.D. wrote of an experience as of a 'bell-jar or half-globe as of transparent glass spread over my head like a diving-bell', so that she was 'immunised or insulated from the war disaster'.[133] In Anaïs Nin's story 'Under a Glass Bell', a metaphorical 'glass bell' covers the house in which three adult siblings live a strange, insular life. At the end of the story, Nin writes, 'The glass bell which separated them from the world was visible in the light. Would Jeanne see it? Would she smash it and be free?'[134] Antonia White uses a similar metaphor in *Beyond the Glass* of the heroine's experience of the neurosis that leads to schizophrenia. She sees herself as 'someone forever outside, forever looking in through a glass at the bright human world which had no place for her'.[135] Like Plath, White makes this metaphor central to the novel by using it as its title. In White's novel, as in Plath's, the heroine's madness is a response to the highly patriarchal society in which she lives, from her own family through to the social institutions with which she interacts.

Ted Hughes

Sylvia Plath and Ted Hughes both described the close working relationship they had during their marriage. Plath wrote to her mother in January 1957 that the two of them told each other everything, especially concerning what they were reading and what they were working on themselves.[136] Hughes wrote to his brother in May 1957 that the couple constantly 'repair each other's writings'. He called Plath 'one of the best critics I have ever met', and said that she 'understands my imagination perfectly'.[137] He said later, 'Our minds soon became two parts of one operation'.[138] After Plath's visit to Hughes' family in Yorkshire in September 1956 on their return from their honeymoon, Plath returned to Cambridge to finish the second year of her degree and Hughes stayed on in Yorkshire. The couple wrote to each other every day during that month, and Hughes quickly resumed an exercise they had done once before in Spain, sketching out the plot of a story for Plath to write up in full. Between October 3 and 22, he sent Plath the plots of twelve stories, ten of which are complete, one of which he rejected before he finished it, and one of which he invited her to finish. He wrote in the first letter, 'If I send one every day, by the end of the year we may have plots to last you for a while, five at least good'.[139]

The plots Hughes sent Plath show a keen understanding of the kind of writer she is. All but one or two could be stories by Plath. First, like almost all of Plath's stories, they are almost all about women. One plot, indeed, incorporates an episode in which an adolescent girl waits at home agonising over whether or not her date will arrive, a subject Plath had already written about in her story 'First Date'. In Hughes' plot sketch, a local thug, the boyfriend of a teenage shop girl, lets her know that he is interested in getting back together with her at a dance that night. The girl runs home, and Hughes sketches out a scene in which she is anxiously awaiting the arrival of her date, trying desperately to make sure that nothing will spoil the evening.[140] This is the sole subject of Plath's 'First Date'. The main interest of this story, indeed, consists in her portrayal of the intense emotions of the heroine, barely suppressed beneath a mask of feminine decorum. She is convinced she is going to throw up several times, and when her date finally arrives, she is practically hysterical in her polite assurance that he is not too late.[141] In Hughes' plot sketch, the heroine externalises precisely the kind of emotional violence that the heroine of Plath's story suppresses. In her anxiety to get ready for her date, she hits her grandmother and leaves her unconscious in order to go on the date. Plath's heroine is practically hysterical in her attempt to appear attractively feminine for her date, and the heroine of Hughes' plot sketch gets hysterical in exactly the same way as one thing after another goes wrong while she is hurrying to get ready.[142]

If Hughes knew that Plath was interested in exploring women's experience in fiction, he was also aware that she was interested in the differences in the ways men and women feel and think. One of his plots includes scope for her to explore these differences. In a story in which a rich but childless couple find an abandoned child, Hughes writes that the husband is concerned with what the law says regarding their taking the child home with them, whereas the wife is more emotional, outraged at the mother who could abandon it:

> His wife brings up every unreasonable reason for keeping the child and saying nothing, while the husband considers what shall be done formally.[143]

Perhaps the plot that would allow Plath the most scope for exploring the complexities of feminine experience is the one in which a reclusive woman finds a young man in her house. Although they scarcely talk, she cooks for him and he repairs things for her. They become more and more attached to each other, even to the point of sleeping together. One day the police come to the house to arrest him. When she goes to the city she discovers that has been charged with killing his wife. There is plenty of space for Plath to explore feminine desire in this situation. When the woman first sees the young man 'she makes him a meal', certainly something the heroine of a Plath story would do.[144] The heroine's conflicted desire for marriage is the space in the story in which Plath could explore some of her deepest concerns. She begins as a recluse and her house reflects her 'lone and lonely' life. The main focus of the story is on the woman's emotions while the young man is staying with her. She experiences 'wifely longings', and is 'desolate' when the police take him away, because her 'recluse instincts' have turned into 'wifely' ones. Plath is an expert at portraying both wifely longings and emotional conflicts, and this situation would allow her thoroughly to explore the details of both.

Although many of Hughes' plots are conceivable as stories by Plath, the most significant thing about them is that in fact she wrote none of them. Plath wrote a considerable number of poems from Hughes' suggestions, such as 'The Moon and the Yew Tree', 'Hanging Man', 'Sleep in the Mojave Desert' and 'On Deck'.[145] Heather Clark has argued that Plath and Hughes have a conflicted relationship to one another's work in the early years of their marriage.[146] This is borne out by Plath's fiction, in which she was sure enough of the kind of writer that she was to know that she did not want to express herself through the medium of Hughes' plots, however well suited to her concerns they might be. During the month in which Hughes was sending her these plots, Plath wrote several short stories. On 16 October, she wrote to her mother that she had written some of her finest short stories that week (*LH* 278). The best of all, she thought, was 'The Invisible Man', and it is clear from references in Hughes' letters that she was also writing 'The Wishing Box' and 'All the Dead Dears'.[147]

'The Wishing Box' is a very striking story in terms of Hughes' influence on Plath, in that it is about a young wife who protests against the influence of her husband who is trying to develop her imagination. The story articulates a sexual politics in which Plath protests at the way in which men represent their own abilities and tendencies as a standard, and denigrate women who do not or cannot meet it.[148] The heroine of 'The Wishing Box' is angry, not just that her husband has a richer imaginative life than hers but that he assumes that hers can and should be of the same kind and degree as his. She feels a 'strange jealousy' of the dreams he is always telling her about, spreading through her like a 'dark, malignant cancer' (*JPBD* 35). Harold's beautiful dreams are taken in part from Plath's experiences of Hughes'. Harold cherishes a recurring dream about a fox and an especially striking dream about a pike. He dreams of a 'white leopard with gold spots' standing astride a river, with a line of ants crossing the river over him, using him as a bridge, which Plath attributes a year later to Ian, the character based on Hughes, in her Cambridge novel (*JPBD* 36).[149] In 'The Wishing Box', Harold tries to help his wife to live as rich an imaginative life as he does himself. He is worried that she does not 'use [her] powers of imagination enough' and thinks that she should 'practise'. She should start, he advises, by 'shutting [her] eyes' (*JPBD* 39). Agnes obeys, but cannot see anything in particular. In the tone of one 'dealing with a malady that was, although distressing, not necessarily fatal', Harold tells her to imagine a goblet. With a great effort Agnes tries, but the goblet is so vaguely defined that she knows it will not meet Harold's standards. He asks her to specify its various features, in increasing detail, at which she eventually falls 'grimly silent'. Harold reassures her that if she will 'practise imagining different things like I've taught you' (*JPBD* 40), her imaginative life will improve. This is very similar advice to that which Hughes was giving Plath at the time. In a letter written between two daily plots, he writes:

> If you keep up a detailed vivid looking at things . . . , your dreams will go on improving . . . . Try writing them out each morning.[150]

If Hughes' daily plots influenced Plath's fiction writing, then, it was in this conflicted way, in the sexual politics of 'The Wishing Box'. It is not the content of the plots to which the story responds but to the fact of Hughes' writing them. Although they seem to be very appropriate and well chosen for Plath, her major fictional response to them is to reject the very idea of being told, even by a writer she believes is a genius, how to write. 'The Wishing Box' says directly what the sheer difference of the stories she wrote at the time Hughes was sending her daily plots to those plots says indirectly, that she knows who she is as a writer, and that she neither needs nor wants even the best writer in the world telling her otherwise.

Plath was closely involved with submitting Hughes' stories for publication during their marriage. She sent combinations of 'The Rain Horse', 'Snow', 'Sunday' and 'The Courting of Petty Quinnett' to *Harper's*, *The Atlantic Monthly*, *Mademoiselle*, *The London Magazine* and Faber, for the anthology *Introduction: Stories by New Writers*.[151] She also submitted 'The Caning' and 'Miss Mambrett and the Wet Cellar' to *The New Yorker* and the *Atlantic Monthly*.[152] On the whole, there is very little direct influence discernible from Hughes' stories on those Plath was writing at the same time, but there are two exceptions to this rule. This first is Plath's story 'The Invisible Man'. This was written in October 1956. Like those Hughes was writing at that time, it is a fable. The first draft of *How the Whale Became, and Other Stories*, which Plath typed and submitted to the Atlantic Monthly Press, was called *How the Donkey Became, and Other Fables*.[153] Hughes wrote to his sister, Olwyn, that he was pleased with these fables. He had no interest in writing in 'ordinary familiar prose style', he said, because he '[looks] at things in a completely moralising and stylised way'.[154] It is not only fables for children that Hughes was writing during the first year of his marriage to Plath. He told his sister in August 1956 that he was continuing to work on 'O'Kelly's Angel', which was also written 'in a kind of fable style'.[155] He wrote a second fable for adults, 'The Callum-Makers', in 1956, and published a third, 'Bartholomew Pygge, Esq.', in *Granta* in May 1957.[156] The fundamental generic characteristic of these stories is that the plot of each develops a central moral symbol. In 'Bartholomew Pygge, Esq.', it is the cruel factory owner's son, who is in reality a pig, and whose truly piggish nature becomes apparent at the end of the story as, although disguised as a person, he cannot resist pursuing a prize sow to her sty. 'O'Kelly's Angel' is about a man who captures an angel, puts it in a cage and charges a fee to see it, starting a religious war as a result. At the end of the story, the angel, which has remained tranquil and unseeing throughout, escapes from its cage during the fighting. The wounded men stop fighting, look at the bloody battlefield they have created, at the dead bodies and at the angel's empty cage:

Then they looked at the blue apex of heaven, which was darker now . . .
Then, finally, they looked at each other.[157]

Just as Hughes did in these stories, Plath developed a central moral symbol in 'The Invisible Man'. The hero, Oswald McQuail, is the all-American success story – popular, wealthy, good at sports, engaged to a sorority girl and about to enter his family's law practice. At this high point of his life as a college student, he starts to become invisible, but quickly realises that he is invisible only to himself, and that this must be kept to himself, even from his fiancée, Marilyn. He tries to respond morally to the situation with a positive frame of mind, and moral symbolism surrounds every new experience he has. His most disturbing experience of all, for example, is when he undresses at night, gradually revealing to himself, garment by garment, his own nonexistence. Oswald also finds comfort in his image in the mirror, which is still visible.[158] He exists more fully, he is more real, as his own image in the mirror than in himself, a symbol central to Plath's concerns with and portrayal of feminine experience. Pages 9–14 of the fifteen-page story are missing, and so the development of the second half of the plot is unclear, but at the end of the story Oswald's son has died, in some way because of Oswald's invisibility, and Oswald's visibility has returned. He tries to go back to his wife, but, although he is now visible to himself, he seems to her to be transparent. The story ends with her horror as she looks through him as if he were a ghost.[159] As in 'O'Kelly's Angel' and 'Bartholomew Pygge, Esq.', Plath's story develops and explores a motif heavy with moral symbolism. At a time in which Hughes' efforts in fiction were devoted largely to fables, Plath wrote her own American woman's fable, in which she questions with the story's central symbol the kind of success that consists in appearing successful in the eyes of others.

The only other place in Plath's fiction where there is a clear similarity to that of Hughes is the ending of 'The Fifty-Ninth Bear', which closely resembles the ending of Hughes' story 'The Harvesting'. Plath completed her story on 16 September 1959 (*J* 501), and Hughes also dates his story to 1959. Hughes' story is about an elderly farm manager, weakened by his hours in the sun, who is trying to shoot a hare. After twice passing out as his gun recoils against his shoulder, he chases the hare up a hill along with the dogs of the colliers working in the fields. In the twist at the end of the story, one of the dogs finishes off the exhausted man instead of the hare. He shouts 'louder than ever when he heard the sound that twisted from his throat, the unearthly thin scream'.[160] As the dog starts to attack him, it is as if he is 'picked up and flung' and he loses consciousness of everything but the 'vague, pummelling sensations far off in the blankness and silence of his body'.[161] Plath's story 'The Fifty-Ninth Bear' ends in a very similar way, with a twist in which the protagonist is killed by the bear he is trying to chase away from his campground. 'The darkness fisted and struck', his throat fills with 'thick, sweet honey' and 'as from a far and rapidly receding planet, he heard a shrill cry – of terror, or triumph, he could not tell' (*JPBD* 96). These passages are two of the most closely related that Plath and Hughes wrote. Both end their respective stories with an event of unexpected violence in which the hunter becomes the hunted and in which the protagonist is eaten alive. In both cases, the protagonist hears a final scream and in both cases his death is described as a process of moving far away from himself, so that he hears this scream from the receding world of his life. Hughes' figure of speech in which the dying man's scream is 'twisted from his throat' and he hears it as if it were someone else, not himself, uttering it, is a figure Plath picks up directly in *The Bell Jar*. After her botched ECT treatment, Esther remembers having been electrocuted before, an ordeal in which she did not scream but rather a scream was 'torn from my throat' and hovered in the air 'like a violently disembodied spirit' (*BJ* 139).

Chapter 2

Plath's Poetry and Fiction

There is a tradition in Plath criticism of interpreting the relationship between the texts on the recto and the verso of Plath's manuscript drafts. Plath wrote several poems in 1962, most of them *Ariel* poems, on the verso of her drafts of *The Bell Jar*.[1] Lynda Bundzten calls this 'back talking' to the text on the other side of the page, Susan van Dyne suggests 'a desire for sympathetic magic', and Tracy Brain speaks of the texts 'bleeding through the page'.[2] Although all these critics tacitly acknowledge as much, it must be clearly stated that interpretations of Plath's motivation in writing a given text on the verso of the draft of another are a matter of speculation. More reliable an investigation is one that has not yet been undertaken, that of the relationship between the poetry and the fiction that Plath wrote at the same time. There are few periods in Plath's life when she was not working on both kinds of text. In this chapter, I ask what light is shed on Plath's fiction by an examination of the poetry she was writing at the same time, and vice versa. I also examine the relationship between the works in which she explores similar concerns in both poetry and fiction.

Smith, 1954–55

Plath did a great deal of creative writing in her final three semesters at Smith, after her return, in February 1954, from McLean hospital. In the autumn 1954 semester, she took Alfred Kazin's course Eng 347a Short Story Writing, for which she wrote 'Among the Bumblebees', 'In the Mountains', 'Superman and Paula Brown's New Snowsuit', 'The Day Mr Prescott Died' and 'Tongues of Stone'.[3] Shortly after returning to Smith for her final semester in January 1955, she wrote 'Home Is Where the Heart Is' and 'Tomorrow Begins Today' for the Christophers contest, for which she won a $100 prize in April (*LH* 173). In the summer following her graduation, she wrote 'The Smoky Blue Piano' and 'Platinum Summer' for the women's magazine market, and by the time she left for Cambridge in September had completed 'The Christmas Heart'. She also wrote a considerable amount of poetry during this time. She took Alfred Young Fisher's course Eng 41b Poetry in the Spring 1955 semester, for which she submitted a collection of some sixty poems (*LH* 172), most of them written after her return to Smith in February 1954.[4]

Plath was putting quite different concerns into her fiction and into her poetry throughout this period. All five of the stories she wrote in Fall 1954 are autobiographical explorations of incidents and events from her childhood and young womanhood. This working over of her own experience is done very differently in her poetry at the time, in which she wrote many love poems, mostly about the pain of love, and several metaphysical meditations, particularly on the passage of time. Plath was putting her current experiences, of her love affairs with Richard Sassoon and others, into lyric poetry, but reserving for fiction her experiences of childhood and young womanhood. Indeed, whilst she focused most on the pain of love in her poetry, it is nevertheless in her fiction in particular that she expressed some of her most negative and painful experiences, thoughts and feelings.

'Superman and Paula Brown's New Snowsuit', based on an incident in Plath's own childhood (*LH* 148), is a story about the death of a child's sense of justice. There is no redemptive value in the story; its power derives precisely from the narrator's refusal to derive a moral or meaning from a situation of utter unhappiness. The young narrator is first disillusioned by a newsreel of Allied prisoners-of-war being tortured by their Japanese guards. However much she tries to think about Superman after seeing the film, she is never again able to dream of him avenging the injustices done to the prisoners-of-war. This disillusionment occurs not only at the social level but within the narrator's own family. She is blamed unfairly by the spoilt Paula Brown for pushing her into an oil spill and ruining the new snowsuit, and all the neighbours, as well as her own mother and the previously heroic Uncle Frank, believe Paula's lie, or at least compromise with it. They agree to buy Paula a new snowsuit, whatever the narrator says, 'just to make everybody happy' (*JPBD* 160). Plath ends the story with the child's sense of justice and goodness in the world being irrevocably destroyed. Lying in bed in the dark, she feels that there is nothing that can be trusted or relied on. All her childish images of heroes and justice have been 'wiped away, like . . . crude drawings', leaving only the blackness of the night. As Plath ends the story, 'That was the year the war began, and the real world, and the difference' (*JPBD* 160).

'Among the Bumblebees' ends with a similar refusal to find any redemptive value in a traumatic childhood experience. Alice Denway, the heroine, is a young girl who adores her father, but watches him dwindle with sickness from a strong man to an invalid. The story ends with a scene in which she visits him on his sickbed. She calls to him with her 'small pleading voice' (*JPBD* 265), but he is too ill to wake or hear. This is the last time she sees him. Although Alice is unaware of it at the time, the story concludes, 'there would be no one to walk with her' again as her father had done (*JPBD* 266). As in 'Superman and Paula Brown's New Snowsuit', the story finishes with a clear statement that the narrator's life is simply unredeemed. Things go bad and never get better: that is the moral of both stories. This was also the moral of 'Tongues of Stone', which Plath first wrote in autumn 1954 for Alfred Kazin. When she rewrote the story in January 1955 for *Mademoiselle*, Plath told her mother that Kazin had written to her about it, saying that she was a genuinely gifted artist but that art should 'give more joy' than 'Tongues of Stone'. She followed his suggestion and gave the story a new 'conclusion of dawn, instead of eternal night' (*LH* 156). In the story as Plath rewrote it, the heroine, in hospital after a suicide attempt, has managed to secrete two large pieces of broken glass in her shoes, with which she is going to try to kill herself again. That night, however, she has a positive reaction to her insulin treatment and feels better, for the first time since her suicide attempt. The story ends, as Plath wrote to her mother, with dawn instead of night. Lying in the dark, hearing the 'voice of the dawn', the heroine feels the 'everlasting rising of the sun' in her (*JPBD* 275). Clearly, the earlier version of the story ended either with the heroine's having acquired or having used the shards of glass. The story, as Kazin said, had no joy.

This joylessness, this refusal of redemption, is not a characteristic of Plath's poetry of the time. The most comparable poem she wrote during this period is 'Temper of Time', which stands out among her poetry of 1954–55 as unusually grim. The passage of time is a common theme in Plath's poetry during these years, but in this poem time is less a thief than a murderer. The poem ends with the character Kilroy, surrounded by evil omens, returning to his cottage, where he finds his family brutally murdered. The poem concludes: 'There's a hex on the cradle / And death in the pot' (*CP* 336). The image of a brutally murdered woman and children is unusually gruesome for Plath's poetry of the time, to say nothing of the cursed nature of the positive and nourishing sites of the cradle and the cooking pot. In her poetry during this period, Plath in interested in such subjects as love, time and the relationship between imagination and reality. 'On Looking into the Eyes of a Demon Lover' is a good example of the difference in the concerns of her poetry and fiction. In the first stanza, we hear that the lover's dark eyes turn everyone who looks into them into 'cripples' (*CP* 325). This image is one of comparable violence to the fantasies of the heroine of 'Tongues of Stone' – that her corrupt psyche would seep through her skin and cover it with a 'consuming leprosy' of scabs (*JPBD* 270) – or the experience of the heroine of 'Superman and Paula Brown's New Snowsuit' of seeing a newsreel of torture so gruesome that it makes her vomit (*JPBD* 156). In the stories, this violence remains throughout, and both end with the irreversible violence done to the child's sense of justice. In the poem, however, Plath forges a conceit in which the speaker is herself an ugly witch, so that her demon lover's eyes, which transform beautiful women into common animals, turn her into a beauty. She looks into his eyes, 'where beauties char', and 'found radiant Venus / reflected there' (*CP* 325). In the poem, Plath looks into the cruelty of the world, as she does in her fiction of the time, but she also forges some kind of redemption there in a way that she does not in the fiction. Something similar occurs in 'Lament', the poem in which Plath represents some of her feelings about the death of her father. In 'Among the Bumblebees', in which she works these same emotions into a story, that story is unremittingly negative. In the poem written at the same time, however, the ending is more ambiguous. Although the villanelle is entitled 'Lament', its final stanza is not as unequivocally negative as the final paragraph of the story:

> O ransack the winds and find another
> Man who can mangle the grin of kings. (*CP* 316)

The final two lines of this final quartet are the two refrains of the villanelle, occurring in each stanza of the poem, and so it is effectively these first two lines with which the ideas in the poem conclude. In the story about the death of the heroine's beekeeping father, she will never find anyone else to love her as he did; the poem about the same subject leaves this question open. The speaker calls for another man to fill the void in her life, and we do not know whether or not she will find one. In the story, the heroine is alone for the rest of her life; in the poem, she hopes not to be.

In her poetry of 1954–5, Plath is interested in the experience of pain, but it is primarily the complex pain of being in love, rather than the simply traumatic experiences of 'Among the Bumblebees', 'Superman and Paula Brown's New Snowsuit' and 'Tongues of Stone'. Even 'In the Mountains', which deals with the relationship between a young man and woman, deals with the difficulties of the young woman after her love for the man has passed. In the poem 'To a Jilted Lover', the speaker soliloquises about how angry she has made her lover after she has committed the slightest of faults. She will be stretched out on the 'rack' of the day until the sun is at its height, and he will see that she is 'still blazing' in this 'golden hell' (CP 310). Here, Plath expresses the pain her speaker feels at her lover's anger, even expressing it with the image of hell, suggesting it will not end. Nevertheless, despite the image of irredeemable pain, this remains a love poem, about the agonies the speaker goes through in love, which makes its emotional charge more complex than that of the stories. Plath is concerned with the experience of pain in her poetry but, in contrast to her fiction, it is the pains of love which her speakers go through. This means that the poems are much more complex in terms of the emotions with which they deal, the pleasure of the speaker's love relationship counterpointing the pain she also feels in this relationship. 'Circus in Three Rings', the poem that Plath thought of as sufficiently representative of her poems of this period to use it as the title of the collections she submitted to Fisher in April 1955 and to the Borestone Mountain poetry competition in July 1955, works in the same way. There Plath pictures her speaker in love as a beleaguered lion-tamer, under attack in a circus ring, protecting her 'perilous wounds' from the 'gnawings of love' (CP 322). In the first stanza, the speaker pictures her heart exploding in the circus tent in which her love affair takes place and its 'fragments' whirling in the air (CP 321). Plath imagines love as destruction and as being attacked in 'Circus in Three Rings'. In the final stanza, the speaker's lover is described as a 'demon', and the poem ends with an image of him as a magician who disappears 'with devilish ease' into 'smoke that sears my eyes' (CP 322). In her fiction of 1954–55, Plath explores traumatic experiences, based on her own, which remain unresolved; in her poetry, she prefers to explore the complex experiences, again based on her own, of love. Her love poems focus on the traumatic, excessive and violent emotions her speakers feel in love, but these are offset, in a way Plath simply does not use in her fiction, by the love in which they occur.

A third marked difference between Plath's poetry and fiction of this period concerns the politics of the relationships she writes about. Her stories deal with women who are in control of their relationships to men, strong characters who, even if they have to go through the detour of femininity to get what they want, know what they want and how to get it. In Plath's poetry, on the other hand, her women speakers and characters are much more controlled by the men they love, by their very passion for these men, and are much more the objects rather than the subjects of their feelings for them. Plath almost invariably used short fiction as a place in which women get what they want in love. This is by no means merely a result of the requirements of the women's magazine market, for which she wrote three stories in 1954–55. Not only did Plath choose to write fiction for this market as opposed to the kind of saccharine, domestic poetry published by the same magazines, but even in the stories written for other, more literary audiences, we see precisely the same gender relationships at work. In 'In the Mountains', written for Kazin's course, as well as 'Home Is Where the Heart Is' and 'Tomorrow Begins Today', written for the Christophers contest, the heroines are strong characters, making the relationships they want with the men in their lives. The heroines of Plath's women's magazine stories are in control of their relationships. Lynn in 'Platinum Summer' knows how to manage men; her friend Happy thinks that keeping men intrigued is just what they need. In 'The Smoky Blue Piano', Lynn is in control of every relationship she has been in with a man.[5] In all three of Plath's 1955 women's magazine stories, the plot consists in the heroine forging the relationship she wants with the hero. 'In the Mountains' too features a hero who is both physically and emotionally weaker than the heroine. Not only is he debilitated by tuberculosis, but he has come to need and depend on her during his convalescence in the mountains. When he tells the heroine that he has come to like black coffee, as she does, she is 'shocked' that someone once so 'proud' would 'acquiesce' in this way, and she cannot look at him (*JPBD* 168). 'Tomorrow Begins Today', like 'The Christmas Heart', is a story in which the heroine teaches the hero how to relate to her, making him into the kind of man to whom she wants to relate. Marcia, her arm broken in a car crash in which Pete was driving, can no longer edit the school newspaper, and she shows the previously irresponsible Pete that he can use his talents in reporting for the paper until her arm mends. He finds this hard to believe, but she gently encourages him. In a saccharine ending, Marcia tells Pete that he will later be able to tell people that he started out as a journalist because of an injury. He replies that, on the contrary, he will tell them that he started out because of her, whose values were an inspiration to him.[6]

Plath typed both 'Tomorrow Begins Today' and 'Home Is Where the Heart Is', the other story she wrote in January 1955 for the Christophers, and which also features a strong heroine who teaches herself a lesson in moral value, on the verso of drafts of her poem 'Bluebeard'. The poem and the stories on either side of the pages symbolise the difference between the ways in which Plath wrote about gender relationships in poetry and in fiction at the time. If her 1954–55 stories feature strong women, in control of their relationships to men, her 1954–55 poems are about women not only at the mercy of their passions for men, but often in danger of being attacked, killed and even eaten by them. The fairy-tale of Bluebeard, in whose terms the speaker of Plath's poem of that name thinks of her lover, exemplifies this. When he goes on a journey, Bluebeard leaves the keys to his castle to his new wife, forbidding her to use the one to his study. Overcome by curiosity, she enters the study and finds in it the dead bodies of his previous wives hanging on the walls. This is the figure the speaker of Plath's poem sees in her lover. He wants to love her, as Bluebeard does his new wife, but, also like Bluebeard, his love will be murder:

> in his eye's darkroom I can see
> my X-rayed heart, dissected body. (CP 305)

There is no question of managing men, as the heroine of 'Platinum Summer' does, in this poem. Nephie Christodoulides sees a victory for the speaker of the poem as she returns the key to the study to him.[7] Whilst the speaker does reject the relationship to her Bluebeard lover in this way, his love as such would nevertheless be fatal to her. In his very look, she sees his desire to 'dissect' her body. Her 'heart' is not a symbol of love to him, but the physical organ, detectible by X-ray, that he will cut up if she enters into a relationship with him. Love, for the female speaker of 'Bluebeard', is simply being butchered.

In 'To a Jilted Lover', the female speaker, having entered into a relationship with her lover, is out of control of this relationship. He is 'incandescent as a god' and she is at his mercy, of which he has little. His look 'chills' her 'to death', and she cannot hide from him anywhere, since 'moon and sun reflect his flame' (CP 309, 310). Plath ends this poem with the speaker 'still blazing in my golden hell'. If her lover is a god, he punishes her with eternal pain by sending her to hell. The speaker is altogether at the mercy of her all-powerful lover, whose inclination is to punish and hurt her. 'Circus in Three Rings' uses a similar metaphor – the circus acts which constitute the speaker's relationship to her lover take place in the tent of a 'drunken god' (CP 321). The lover himself appears in the poem as a 'demon of doom' (CP 322), searing the speaker's eyes with smoke, and the circus acts in which she is so hurt, and in which she is in danger of being devoured by lions, are metaphors for the relationship designed in this way by the god. The pain, the danger of being eaten alive that love constitutes for the speaker, are a situation over which she has little or no control – the work of a drunken, irrational god, who has created love to be the kind of relationship in which the female speaker suffers from wounds, gnawings and searing smoke. This poem is especially comparable to 'The Smoky Blue Piano', since both works are imaginative representations of the same relationship, Plath's to Lou Healy, her neighbour during her time at Harvard

Summer School in the summer of 1954. She writes in her journal that the poem was inspired by Healy, 'triggered by Lou, but written for Richard' (*J* 225). If in the poem the speaker is in danger of being destroyed by a demonic lover created by a drunken god, in the story based on the same relationship the heroine, after some clever manoeuvres with a master key, ends up with the hero of the story and acceptable dreams of marriage. Lou, the hero, asks her – not Lynn, who has been trying to date him – to dinner, and she imagines her wedding, where Lynn is a bridesmaid and the music is played on the piano of the story's title.[8]

'Terminal', another poem on the verso of which Plath types 'Home Is Where the Heart Is', is about a dream in which the male dreamer sees his lover served up to him to eat by the powers of hell:

for feast the sweetest meat of hell's chef d'oeuvres:
his own pale bride upon a flaming tray. (*CP* 328)

The comparison with the contemporary story on the verso of the drafts of this poem is instructive. Both take place in the kitchen. Initially, Mrs Arnold, the heroine of 'Home Is Where the Heart Is', feels unfulfilled by her life as a housewife and mother. Indeed, her home is described with one of the metaphors Plath uses for the lack of control the speakers of her poems feel in love, the circus in three rings. A request for help from her husband, however, stops her feeling sorry for herself, and she cooks a successful meal for his important dinner guest and thinks of ways to keep her three children happy at the same time. She had been thinking of entering a competition to win two weeks in Paris, but she realises at the end of the story that the most beautiful and exciting place she knows is her own home.[9] She takes control of her life, and becomes the mistress of her relationship to her husband and children. In the poem Plath had drafted on the other side of the typescript of this story, by contrast, the wife becomes not the mistress of her kitchen but the meat in it. The home in the poem is hell, and the woman is eaten by her husband in it. On the two sides of these pages, we can see how, at this period of her creative life, Plath was using fiction to portray women in control of their relationships to men, and poetry to explore the consciousness of women controlled by men, or at least by their passion for those men.

Cambridge, 1956–57

This remained true as Plath moved to Cambridge, and continued writing there. Her love poems of 1956 express the destructive power of love for their female speakers. In her story 'The Matisse Chapel', which she wrote in January or early February 1956, the character based on her lover Richard Sassoon is described as diabolical. When he gets angry with the character based on Plath herself, he seems to change from a man to a demon.[10] Many of the poems written during Plath's relationship to Sassoon describe the speaker's lover as a devil or a demon. He is a 'demon lover', a 'demon of doom', causing the speaker either to burn or be eaten in 'hell' (CP 325, 322, 310, 328). In the story 'The Matisse Chapel', however, although the character based on Sassoon is described as a devil, the heroine fights back against his cruelty in a way that none of the speakers of the poems do. In 'To a Jilted Lover', 'Circus in Three Rings' and 'Terminal', the demonic lover simply burns or eats his beloved. In the story, she answers back with equal vigour. Richard becomes demonic as he cruelly mocks Sally, telling her she is incapable of love, but she responds hotly that he is self-absorbed and egoistic. Indeed, in the argument the two characters have following this exchange, it is Sally who defines the outcome, taking her hand away from Richard's and refusing to relinquish her point of view.[11] Once again, as Plath creates imaginative works based on the same relationship, that with Sassoon, she writes poems in which her female speakers are overwhelmed by stronger, crueller men, but stories in which the heroines are stronger than those men.

One of the metaphysical themes that occupied Plath most often in her Cambridge poetry of 1956–57 is that of the relationship between the imagination and reality. Her poems 'Tale of a Tub', 'Recantation', 'November Graveyard', 'Black Rook in Rainy Weather', 'On the Difficulty of Conjuring up a Dryad', 'On the Plethora of Dryads' and 'Two Views of Withens' enact a complex exploration of the relative values of reality and its transformation by the creative imagination. This had also been a frequent concern in Smith poems such as 'Two Lovers and a Beachcomber by the Real Sea', 'A Sorcerer Bids Farewell to Seem', 'Moonsong at Morning', 'Metamorphoses of the Moon' and even a poem from as early as 1953, 'Admonitions'. In October 1956, she dealt with this concern for the first and only time in fictional form in the story 'The Wishing Box'. Plath's 1956–57 poems about the relative value of imagination and reality are complex, articulating several conflicting emotions at once. In 'Recantation', reality is simply preferred to the visionary powers of the occultist speaker. She chooses to 'forswear those freezing tricks of sight' and all her attempts to get beyond 'the flower in the blood' (CP 42). In 'Two Views of Withens', on the other hand, the speaker simply regrets that she sees only what is there and attaches greater value to her companion's vision, transformed by his imaginative powers. She sees only 'bare moor' and 'colorless weather', but he, 'luckier', can tell her of 'white pillars, a blue sky' and 'ghosts, kindly' (*CP* 72). Most of Plath's poems about imagination and reality, however, articulate within themselves the conflict between the desires expressed in these two poems. Both desires, for the truth of reality and for the trans-formative powers of the imagination, are expressed at once in a single poem. 'Tale of a Tub', for example, values the visionary power which transforms the world into a more beautiful place. The speaker at times simply loathes reality:

> the ridiculous nude flanks urge
> the fabrication of some cloth to cover
> such starkness. (*CP* 25)

Reality, especially that of the speaker's own body, is ridiculous to her. She describes it as a 'constant horror'. On the other hand, she values the honesty of seeing real things simply for what they are: 'the authentic sea . . . will pluck fantastic flesh down to the honest bone'. In this passage, reality is not ridiculous or horrific, but authentic and honest. This dual vision is summed up in the speaker's description of the bath tub in which she is speaking as both 'blank and true'. In 'November Graveyard', the same conflict remains; the speaker respects the reality of the world, yet desires the transformative powers of imaginative vision of that world, which makes being in it a richer experience. She speaks of the dead bodies in the graveyard in which she speaks as 'honest rot', and uses a similar metaphor of erosion to the one used in 'Tale of a Tub' to describe the truth of the death of these bodies, which '[pares] bone / Free of the fictive vein' (*CP* 56). On other hand, the blank reality of the scene is 'skinflint' and 'dour', and the speaker ends the poem by calling on the reader to view the scene through an effort of the imagination, making his eyes 'foist a vision dazzling on the wind'. She knows that there will be a certain unreality to this imaginative vision, but nevertheless she prefers it to the reality of 'blank, untenanted air' (*CP* 56).

This complexity also characterises 'The Wishing Box'. The main difference between Plath's expression of desire for the transformative vision of the imagination in the story and in the poems she wrote at the same time is that, in the poems, the relationship between imagination and reality is treated as a metaphysical question whereas in the story it is a political question. In the poems, the question of the relative truth of seeing the world simply as it is and seeing the world through the transformative vision of the imagination is dominant. In 'Tale of a Tub', although 'blank', the tub is 'true' (*CP* 25). 'November Graveyard' com-pares the 'honest' to the 'fictive' (*CP* 56); 'Recantation' speaks of 'those freezing tricks of sight' (*CP* 42); and 'On the Difficulty of Conjuring

Up a Dryad' describes the imagination as a 'counterfeit', which will 'hoodwink the honest earth' (*CP* 66). This question of the relative truth and falsity of reality and the imagination does not arise in 'The Wishing Box', however. The story revolves, rather, around the relative values of the perception of a husband and a wife. The question is less whose way of seeing is truer, but whose is more important. As Christina Britzolakis puts it, their 'marriage represents a battle for imaginative mastery'.[12] In 'The Wishing Box', Harold takes it for granted, and Agnes has no social resources on which to draw to contradict his assumption, that his way of seeing is better. The complexity we saw in the poems remains in the story. Although Agnes largely agrees that it is better to dream and to imagine as Harold does, the narrator of the story is less convinced. She several times emphasises how physically attractive Agnes is, and implies that Harold, despite the value of his imaginative visions, is wrong not to appreciate this more. We first see him looking with a glazed expression 'right through' the 'very attractive and tangible form' of Agnes in her pretty nightgown (*JPBD* 35). Whilst Agnes wishes she could dream and imagine as Harold does, and whilst she acknowledges that his dreams are beautiful, the narrator is less impressed. When Harold finally begins to listen to Agnes describe a vivid dream of her own, she writes that he began to notice for 'perhaps the first time' since they had been married how 'extraordinarily attractive' she looks each morning (*JPBD* 38). Exactly as in the poems, the relative value of imagination and reality is a complex issue in the story. On the one hand, Agnes wants to have an imaginative life as rich as Harold's; on the other, the narrator stands up for the value of her physical appearance on which Agnes takes pains as a young wife.

As this instance of the attractive appearance of the wife suggests, the complexity of the question in the story is, in contrast to the metaphysical question explored in the poems, political. The difference in the way Plath uses fiction and poetry to express the relationship between imagination and reality is fundamentally this: in her poetry she treats the two ways of looking at the world as ideas; in her story she puts those ideas into the heads of particular people living in a particular society. The story thus articulates less a conflict between the relative claims of simple and imaginative vision than a conflict between a husband and a wife within the contemporary institution of marriage. On the one hand, Agnes values without question the power of the imagination – she used to dream vividly when she was a child, and both she and Harold are 'visibly impressed' when she recounts such dreams (*JPBD* 38). She wishes she could dream as richly as her husband does, and tries both his and her own remedies to do so. However, Agnes wants to do so less because the imagination provides one with a richer experience of the world, and more because she wants to be her husband's equal and not his inferior. She feels 'left out' from the 'exhilarating' world in which Harold spends a considerable amount of his life. It begins to 'infuriate' her (*JPBD* 36). In the same way, although Agnes does have dreams of a kind, she is concerned that they are inferior to her husband's, and she is ashamed to mention them to him, afraid that they 'reflected too unflatteringly upon her powers of imagination' (*JPBD* 37). Power is the operative word here – Agnes does not want to be the less powerful partner in her marriage, even if the stakes are only the apparently innocuous powers of the imagination. It is as if there is an unspoken contest as to who is the greater artist in the marriage, and Agnes is determined not to lose.

It is in her playing this game of gender politics that the complexity of the ideas in the story consists and in which it differs from the complexity of the ideas in the poetry. Whereas the unresolved question in Plath's poetry on the relationship between reality and imagination was which way of seeing the world is better, the unresolved question in the story is who has the more power in the marriage. Whilst Agnes plays by Harold's rules, valuing dreams and doing exercises to develop her imagination, she loses; she cannot meet the standards he sets in his imaginative life. As the effort of trying to do so starts to take its toll, she begins to drink. This gives her precisely the power of shaping the real world to her satisfaction that is the stake of their contest. After drinking alcohol, she discovers with a 'malicious satisfaction' that Harold's face becomes so amorphous that she can 'change his features at will'. One day she gives him a 'pea-green complexion', another a 'Grecian nose' and another an 'eagle beak' (*JPBD* 41). Although descending into the stereotype of the alcoholic housewife, Agnes has, by precisely this self-destructive escape from her problem, solved it. When she drinks, she becomes precisely the kind of imaginative artist she was unable to be in her dream life. The fact that it is her husband's face on which she uses these transformative powers emphasises the political nature of imagination in the story – Plath stresses strongly that the imaginative powers of alcohol are a way in which Agnes gains power over husband. She becomes the one to shape him, rather than the one being shaped by him, as she practises his exercises or feels she ought to imitate his dreams. The story ends on this self-destructive note, pushed from Agnes' drinking to her suicide. Drinking becomes too passing a remedy for the emptiness she feels in comparison to Harold's dream life, and Agnes decides to end her misery with sleeping pills. Harold comes home from work, buoyed by a rich daydream he has had on the train, to find Agnes, dressed like a beautiful princess, by an empty box of pills. Her 'tranquil' face wears a 'secret smile of triumph', as if, in a place 'unattainable to mortal men', she is 'waltzing with the . . . red-caped prince of her early dreams' (*JPBD* 42–3). The question, who has won their battle over who is the greater artist, remains as unresolved as the question of which way of seeing is more valuable in the poems. Agnes has achieved a triumph, as her smile indicates and as the beauty of her appearance further suggests, but the triumph has come at the cost of her death. She can become the artistic equal of her husband only in death; there was no place for her as a wife on earth except as her husband's inferior. Furthermore, the narrator suggests a certain compromise even to the triumph she has won over her husband by dying in that she may, even after death, still be playing the game according to his rules, that is, dreaming as vividly as he does.

In considering the relationship of 'The Wishing Box' to the poetry Plath was writing at the same time, her 1956 poem 'The Shrike' is also important. Whereas the other poems I have mentioned explore the relationship between reality and imagination, as 'The Wishing Box' does, 'The Shrike' is a poetic account of the same kind of relationship – that of a wife angry at her husband's power to dream – portrayed in the story. In this poem, the speaker pictures herself as a shrike, also known as a 'butcher bird' because it impales its prey on thorns so that it can return to the carcass. Although, in most of her love poems of 1956, Plath's speakers feel butchered by their lovers, in 'The Shrike' it is the woman who plays the part of the butcher. After an account, similar to the fictional events of 'The Wishing Box', of the wife angrily shut out at night from her husband's dreams, Plath's poem ends at dawn. Then the wife, with her 'shrike-face', can 'peck open' his eyes, and devour the beautiful things and places where he spent the night in dreams:

> And with red beak
> Spike and suck out
> Last blood-drop of that truant heart. (*CP* 42)

We have seen that, in her Smith poems of 1954–55, Plath's women were much more at the mercy of the passion they felt for the men who dominated them than in her fiction of the time. 'The Shrike' does not conform to this rule. Although in the majority of her love poems of 1956 Plath's speakers are as victimised by their love for cruel men as in her Smith poems, in 'The Shrike' it is the woman who is about to kill and eat the man. 'The Shrike' can be read as a kind of revenge for the experience described in 'Pursuit' or 'The Glutton'. If the female speaker of 'Pursuit' is about to be cut up and eaten by her panther lover, so the female speaker of 'The Shrike' will in turn be the shrike who cuts up and eats her lover. Some of the complexity of 'The Wishing Box' remains in the poem. Despite the clear domination of the husband by the shrike wife, there is still a certain self-loathing in the way the poem's speaker continually describes herself as an animal, a stereotypical way of denigrating a woman. She has, she says of herself, 'taloned fingers' and a 'shrike-face' (*CP* 42). If, in the story, Agnes could only become her husband's equal in death, in the poem the wife can only wreak revenge on her husband by becoming the kind of monster – half-woman, half-animal – hated by patriarchal society and by herself. Whilst this complexity characterises 'The Shrike' as well as 'The Wishing Box', however, in the story the wife kills herself, whereas in the poem she kills her husband. By 1956, the rule that Plath writes stronger women in her fiction than in her poetry is beginning to break. The heroine of 'The Wishing Box' and the speaker of 'The Shrike' both articulate politically complex experiences. It is the speaker of the poem, however, rather than of the story, who avoids turning the aggression instilled by the conditions of her marriage in her society in on herself.

Falcon Yard, 1957–58

Throughout 1957 and for much of 1958 Plath was occupied with the several drafts and versions of her Cambridge novel. The central relationship in *Venus in the Seventh*, the draft of which most survives, is between Jess and Ian, the characters based on Plath and Hughes. Plath describes this relationship in similar ways to those she uses in her love poems of 1956, in which she expresses some of her feelings about this relationship in poetry. In the novel draft, Jess fully expects her relationship with Ian to be painful, but she tells herself to accept this love for what it is, something that will make her a stronger person, although certain to end with Ian smashing her to pieces and moving on to his next conquest. She has some reason for thinking in violent images about their relationship, since she seems to have been treated violently by him during their first sexual encounter, which had left her bruised all over. There is a scene in which Ian apologises for this, saying that he lost control.[13] This kind of violence is a marked theme of Plath's love poetry written during the time that this novel draft portrays a year later. In 'Pursuit', the lover is a panther whose love consists in killing and eating his lover. His 'rending teeth' are 'keen', and 'meat must glut his mouth's raw wound' (*CP* 22). Like Ian in *Venus in the Seventh*, this lover leaves 'charred and ravened women' in his path (*CP* 23). In both the novel draft and the poem, the violence wreaked on the woman by her lover is part of her attraction to him. In the novel, Jess has to some degree enjoyed their violent encounter. In the poem, the speaker says of the panther, 'His ardor snares me' and describes herself as 'appalled by secret want'. The same combination of the lover's violence with the speaker's love for him is articulated in 'The Queen's Complaint', where the poet says of the queen's lover that some 'fury urged him slay / Her antelope who meant him naught but good' (CP 28). In 'The Glutton', she fully develops the metaphor of the lover ripping apart and eating his beloved, to the point where submission to his hunger is the only ethic remaining to the attracted speaker: 'All merit's in being meat / Seasoned how he'd most approve' (CP 40).

There are two main differences in Plath's portrayal of the relationship based on her own with Hughes in her poetry and in the draft of her novel. First, it is in her poetry alone that she uses, and repeatedly uses, the metaphor of being eaten by her lover. In the novel, Ian is physically violent towards Jess, both in reality in their first sexual encounter and then in her fantasy life, in which she thinks of him walking all over her and smashing her to pieces. In the love poems of 1956, however, the speakers' lovers are not just violent towards them but cut them up and eat them. Plath uses the lyric form to delve much deeper into the fantasy life of the speakers of her love poems than she does in the novel. She allows Jess fantasies of violence in her relationship to Ian, but she penetrates another layer of the unconscious of her speakers when she portrays the same relationship in her poetry. Second, as we saw in her earlier fiction, the heroine of the novel, as of the story 'Stone Boy with Dolphin', which Plath worked up out of the novel's central chapter, is more in control of the relationship than the speakers of the poems. It is no longer a question of managing men, as in her earlier stories – Ian's violence is part of his attractiveness to Jess – but Jess nevertheless is confident in her power to be the one woman that Ian will not simply use and move on. Jess believes that she can even be the best and last of the women Ian goes through, that she is more than strong enough to beat any girl in a battle for his affections. Nowhere in the love poems based on this relationship does a speaker feel that she is strong enough in this way to match the violence of her lover. Even when the speaker is a queen, as in 'The Queen's Complaint', there is no question of her power being sufficient to master or tame her 'giant' lover. The poem ends with her kingdom having 'shrunk so small' (CP 29) in her eyes in comparison to her experience of the giant, so that she is less of a queen, since she rules over less, than she was before this experience. The beating in the love poems is all done by the lover; the speakers have no response except to receive his violent love; in the novel, by contrast, it is Jess who can beat any of Ian's other girls in the battle for his affections. She may not be able entirely to match Ian's violence – it is his other women rather than

Ian himself whom she beats – but she is strong enough to become his only love and to stop his conquest of one woman after another. She will make him unable to forget her.[14]

In 'Stone Boy with Dolphin', which Plath worked up into a story after February 1958, about a year after she was writing *Venus in the Seventh*, the heroine has become even stronger in her relationship to the hero. The story invites particular comparison to the poem 'Pursuit', in that Plath sets both against the background of Racine's *Phèdre*, which she was studying at the time of the events portrayed. In the story, Dody is typing a paper on the tragedy, and meets Leonard whilst looking for a relationship in which she will live as intensely as the play's characters: she wants to 'walk into *Phèdre*' and live out the passionate and tragic destiny of its heroine (*JPBD* 301). 'Pursuit' has a speaker for whom Dody's wish has been fulfilled, since the love of the panther it describes is prefaced with an epigraph from *Phèdre*: '*Dans le fond des forêts votre image me suit*'. Whilst in the poem it is the speaker who is being pursued by the panther, in the story it is Dody who pursues. She repeatedly reflects at the party where she has gone to meet Leonard that she is on a 'hunt' for him (*JPBD* 310). The repetition makes the situation clear: whereas in the poem the speaker is hunted by her lover, in the story it is she who hunts him. Furthermore, it is Dody who eats her beloved prey, in contrast to the speakers of the poems of 1956, who are eaten by their lovers. Leonard is as violent as Ian or the lovers of the poems. When he 'stamped' in answer to Dody's question, it seemed to her that the walls and the floor 'flew to kingdom come' (*JPBD* 312). Whereas the speakers of 'Pursuit', 'The Queen's Complaint' and 'The Glutton' are bitten and eaten by their lovers, in 'Stone Boy with Dolphin' it is Dody who bites and eats. Dody bites Leonard's cheek until she draws blood, 'laving the taste-buds of her tongue' (*JPBD* 312). Dody leaves the party with Leonard holding his handkerchief to his cheek to staunch the blood she has drawn. She imagines that she will become 'the girl who bit the boy', as mothers will say to their children (*JPBD* 314). Plath thinks of her heroine as a caricature of Dido, presumably meaning her new friend Dido Merwin. There could be no comparison to Virgil's heroine, since Dido's love destroyed her; she was precisely not the woman Jess in *Venus in the Seventh* imagines herself to be, who could stop her lover from using her and moving on. There is a progression in the strength of Plath's representation of the characters based on herself when she met Hughes. In the love poems of 1956, the speakers are killed and eaten by their lovers; in *Venus in the Seventh*, of 1957, Jess has strength enough to match her lover's violence; by the time Plath had worked this material up into its final form as 'Stone Boy with Dolphin' in 1958, it is Dody, the heroine, who hunts and eats her lover. As in her earlier stories, it is fiction in which Plath portrayed her female characters most in control of their relationships to men.

Although Plath does not delve as deeply into Jess's fantasy life concerning her relationship to Ian as she does with the speakers of her love poems, she does give Jess considerable expression concerning her self-image, which is as negative as Esther's at the beginning of *The Bell Jar*. Although Esther seems from the outside to be having the time of her life, inside she feels like a 'numb trolley-bus', 'dully' propelled by the chaos all around (*BJ* 2–3). Jess feels exactly the same way. Just as Esther has her photograph taken in the rooftop lounge of a New York hotel, Jess has her photograph taken on top of the bell tower in St. Mark's Square, Venice, knowing in just the same way how different the happy image she projects is from the emptiness she feels inside. She thinks of her mother looking at the picture, seeing a brilliant daughter with every opportunity in life, whereas in reality she feels utterly empty.[15] *Venus in the Seventh* differs from the later novel, however, in that Jess finds some kind of solution to this problem. Although we do not have the ending of *Venus in the Seventh*, in the pages we do have Jess finds the strength to move beyond her inner emptiness. As she returns to England, reflecting on the experiences she has gained in Europe, she feels as if the broken pieces of herself are being glued together again by a kind of inner force of development. This force is precisely what Esther lacks. Esther doubts that the bell jar has been lifted for ever at the end of her story; Jess is working through and beyond it. She even has a therapeutic technique she uses to help her do so, which she learned when she herself experienced what Esther went through, drawing up a list of ways to behave in future. Jess does this on her return to England, compiling a set of rules for how she will act amongst her Cambridge friends. This technique had worked for her in the period of utter despair she had experienced a few years earlier, an experience which explicitly relates Jess to Esther.[16] Jess's experience begins where Esther's leaves off, and whereas Esther has acquired no resources with which to move beyond the experience of the bell jar, Jess has done just that. She has learned during her breakdown how to keep living and finds that, a few years later, her technique still works.

In the poetry Plath was writing in 1957, at the same time as she was working on *Venus in the Seventh*, she expressed, through a series of images, a similar emotion to the inner deadness Jess feels in her novel. In 'The Thin People', the speaker sees the world withered and deadened by the presence of the ghostly 'thin people'. They make the 'tree boles flatten / And lose their good browns' (*CP* 65). Just by being in the world, they turn it 'thin as a wasp's nest'. In 'The Disquieting Muses', the figures placed around the speaker's crib have instilled in her a similar mood. When all the other girls danced and sang beautifully in a play, she was unable to 'lift a foot in the twinkle-dress / But, heavy-footed, stood aside' (CP 75). In the same way, the Muses keep the speaker from playing the piano with feeling. All her teachers notice that her 'touch' is 'oddly wooden in spite of . . . the hours of practicing'. In 'On the Decline of Oracles', the speaker has the gift of second sight, but even that seems useless to her, so blank is her mood: 'Worthless such vision to eyes gone dull' (CP 78). Plath is expressing a mood that can most simply be described as depression, in both her novel and the poems of 1957. She uses her novel, however, to portray her heroine's journey beyond these emotions; in the poems she creates a powerful effect by leaving the reader within them. Whereas in her earlier fiction Plath used the form of the short story to portray purely negative emotions, by the time she came to work on her first full-length novel, she was using fiction to describe a therapeutic journey through and beyond these emotions, which she used lyric poetry to portray in themselves.

Boston and Yaddo, 1958–59

During her year in Boston, from September 1958 to June 1959, Plath suffered from writer's block, and this can be seen in some of the poetry she produced in this period. She wrote a few very fine poems in Boston, such as 'Point Shirley', 'Suicide off Egg Rock' and 'Electra on Azalea Plath'. Nevertheless, in both the relatively small number of poems written during this year, and in the formal, exercise-like quality of many of them, the lack of the kind of inspiration, originality and fluency that characterised Plath's poetry from her return to Smith in 1954 to leaving Cambridge in 1957 can clearly be seen. The only poem in her corpus about the inadequacy of poetry, 'Poems, Potatoes', is one of the few she wrote in 1958 after her move to Boston. It is in this period, however, in which only a few of her best poems were written, that she began to write her best short stories. Tim Kendall points out that even these poems, written in a batch in early 1959, deal with material she would later transform into narrative form in *The Bell Jar*.[17]

As is frequently pointed out, Plath broke through her writer's block at Yaddo, where she and Hughes stayed from September to November 1959, with the seven poems of 'Poem for a Birthday'. It is here that, for the first time in poetry, she began to write about some of the experience of mental illness and treatment that she had put into fiction earlier that year in 'Johnny Panic and the Bible of Dreams'. The poems in

'Poem for a Birthday' which articulate this experience, 'The Stones' and 'Who', portray it in a very similar way to the story. Despite their difference in genre, the poems and the story articulate essentially the same message. In both cases, Plath remains utterly unconvinced of the value of the cure her speakers receive at the hands of the medical institution. In both the poems and the story, doctors work to effect a 'cure' in the speaker, as well as others, which is not really a cure at all, but a process of substituting the truth of the speaker's psychic life for a false appearance of social normality. In 'The Stones', Plath expresses this with the metaphor of the spare parts out of which the speaker is rebuilt. She speaks of the workmen in the hospital 'heating the pincers, hoisting the delicate hammers': 'a current agitates the wires', 'catgut stitches my fissures' (*CP* 137). There is no truth, no reality to the new, cured self which emerges from treatment in the hospital of 'The Stones'. Her real self had wanted to die – her 'head-stone' was 'quiet' and the 'stones of the belly' 'peaceable' – and the cure in the hospital of the poem puts together only the outward appearance of a real self, not a person but an automaton. 'I shall be good as new': Plath ends the poem with depressive irony, the positive phrase signifying the negative truth that 'as new' means 'not new', that the appearance of a new start to the speaker's life is in fact its absence. The doctors in 'Johnny Panic and the Bible of Dreams' function in the same way. In the first part of the story, whilst the narrator is still collecting the dreams of others, she takes a dim view of the psychiatric practices in whose context they have been recounted. She is a lover of dreams, unlike the doctors who merely use them for the 'worldly ends' of 'health and money' (*JPBD* 13). When a former patient is cured of his obsessional neurosis, she notes that the 'light' of fear has gone from his face, and that he leaves the hospital for the 'crass fate' of so-called 'health and happiness' (*JPBD* 14). When the narrator herself is submitted to ECT treatment at the end of the story, the mental patients incarcerated in the same room sing a devotional chant to the fear, portrayed in the figure of Johnny Panic, which is the truth of their mental life, before the doctors and nurses can silence them. In both poem and story, Plath values the truth of the real, if disturbed, mental life of her speakers. The speaker of 'The Stones' may have wanted to die; the speaker of 'Johnny Panic and the Bible of Dreams' may experience fear as the most fundamental emotion. Both, however, wish to remain true to their psychic experience and utterly reject society's claim to pathologise, diagnose and cure them.

The difference in the poem and the story consists in the contents of the psyche of the speakers which the doctors, and the society in whose name they act, presume to cure. In 'The Stones', as in many of Plath's poems written during this period, the fundamental desire of the speaker, pathologised by society but on whose truth she insists, is the peace of death. As the speaker of 'The Stones' describes her suicide attempt:

> I became a still pebble.
> The stones of the belly were peaceable,
>
> The head-stone quiet, jostled by nothing. (*CP* 136)

'Full Fathom Five' and 'Lorelei', two of Plath's finest poems from 1958, express the same desire. The first poem ends, 'This thick air is murderous. / I would breathe water' (*CP* 93). The second ends, as the speaker sees 'goddesses of peace' deep in the river, 'Stone, stone, ferry me down there' (*CP* 95). Indeed, 'The Burnt-Out Spa', the next poem Plath wrote at Yaddo after 'Poem for a Birthday', picks up on this metaphor of the peace of death to be found under water, as the speaker of the poem contrasts her reflection in the water beneath a bridge favourably with the reality it reflects. The woman beneath the water is 'gracious and austere', but the speaker cannot enter her world. 'The stream that hustles us' up in the real world, she concludes, 'neither nourishes nor heals' (*CP* 138). Whereas the speakers of Plath's poems experience this desire for the peace of death as their most fundamental emotion, in 'Johnny Panic and the Bible of Dreams' it is fear, for which Johnny Panic is the narrator's prosopopoeia, that she experiences in this way. The truth of the heroine of the story's mind is fear, whereas the truth of the speaker of the poems' mind is desire for death. This desire is consistent throughout the 1958-59 poems, but Plath portrays the psyche differently in her story. Even the desire for death is, in 'Johnny Panic and the Bible of Dreams', a result of the more fundamental emotion of fear. The 'twenty-storey leap', the 'rope at the throat': these are forms of the 'love' of Johnny Panic (*JPBD* 20). As Plath says at the beginning of the story, the entire 'world is run' by the Panic he represents (*JPBD* 3).

The story is thus more psychologically complex than the poetry. It makes sense for Plath to insist on the truth of her speakers' desire for peace, even if it is only the pathological desire for the peace of death, since peace is obviously desirable. It does not make so much sense, though, for the heroine of her story to insist on the truth of the fear which governs her mind and that of many others, since fear is obviously undesirable. Furthermore, fear is victorious at the end of the story in a way that the desire for death is not in 'The Stones' or in any other of the contemporary poems in which it is expressed. At the end of the poem, the speaker is left only with irony, mimicking the socially acceptable sentiment 'I shall be good as new', whilst clearly not meaning it. At the end of the story, on the other hand, the emotion of fear, as personified in the figure of Johnny Panic, wins. The doctors electrocute the narrator, hoping to eradicate fear from her mind, and replace it with their idea of health and happiness, but they fail. Their electric shock machine 'betrays' them (*JPBD* 20). Like Plath herself, the narrator gets a botched shock treatment, during which she remains conscious and in agony, which therefore has the result of increasing rather than eradicating her fear. Just as she thinks she is lost to normality, she sees Johnny Panic in a 'nimbus of arc lights' on the clinic ceiling. The shocks and flashes of the botched treatment are his 'Word', which 'charges and illumines the universe' (*JPBD* 20). Whereas the truest feelings of the speakers of the poems remain suppressed, leaving their speakers only with the frustrated desire for their expression ('Stone, stone, ferry me down there') or irony at the impossibility of this expression ('I shall be good as new'), in the story the truest feeling of the heroine is not suppressed but continues to be her most fundamental experience throughout the story. In 'The Stones', the desire for the peace of death is suppressed by the doctors; in 'Johnny Panic and the Bible of Dreams', fear remains, despite their best efforts. In the poetry a positive, if pathologically distorted, value (desire for peace) loses the battle for expression in society; in the story a negative value (fear) wins that battle. The poems accept the impossibility of living with the self-destructive emotions at the heart of the psyche; the story is a plea for doing just that.

The Bell Jar, 1961

From April to August 1961, and writing until the end of May in the study of W. S. Merwin, Ted Hughes' friend and neighbour in London, Plath devoted most of her writing time to *The Bell Jar*. The poems she wrote immediately preceding this work on her novel foreshadow in some detail the concerns she would express in that novel. Plath spent two weeks in late February and early March 1961 in St Pancras hospital following her appendicectomy, whose necessity had been hastened by a miscarriage in early February. The first poems she wrote after recovering from the surgery were the two poems based on her experience in hospital, 'In Plaster' and 'Tulips'. Both poems, with their hospital setting, prepare the way for Esther's experiences as a patient in the series of hospitals to which she is transferred in *The Bell Jar*. 'In Plaster', whose immediate inspiration was the patient in the bed next to Plath in a full-body plaster cast, foreshadows the idea of the double which runs throughout *The Bell Jar*. Just as Esther sees negative images of herself in Doreen and Joan Gilling, and sees herself as a negative image of Betsy, so the speaker of 'In Plaster' sees herself as a negative image of her plaster cast. The aggressive emotions that Esther feels throughout *The Bell Jar* are present in 'In Plaster', but the difference is that whereas Esther lives, for much of the novel, in a world in which she hates herself, in the poem the speaker lives in a relationship to the plaster cast in which it hates her. The aggression, that is, comes from another, from the outside world, rather than from within, as is the case in *The Bell Jar*. The speaker of 'In Plaster' says of her cast, 'Secretly, she began to hope I'd die' (*CP* 159). Furthermore, the speaker ends on a stronger, more self-assertive note than Esther ever manages. In the last stanza, she describes herself, in comparison to the pure white plaster cast, as 'ugly and hairy' (*CP* 160). Esther feels the same way in hospital when she looks at the 'stubble' all over her 'yellow' legs – 'disgusting and ugly' (*BJ* 166-7). Both Esther and the speaker of the poem are ugly and hairy, as well as having yellow skin that contrasts negatively with a white image of their less attractive bodies – pyjamas in Esther's case, the plaster cast in the poem. The speaker of the poem, however, musters more strength in this situation than Esther does: 'I may be ugly and hairy, / But . . . I'm collecting my strength; one day I shall manage without her' (*CP* 160). Her sense of her ugliness, and the powerlessness it symbolises in patriarchal society, is only temporary; soon she will be stronger than the more beautiful image of herself and destroy it. Esther does not feel this way: she does not cover up her legs, which look disgusting and ugly, because she thinks, '"That's what I am"' (*BJ* 167). She is overwhelmed with self-loathing in a way that the speaker of 'In Plaster' is not. The mental and moral strength to overcome her current negative self-image, with which the poem ends, is unavailable to Esther. When one compares the end of the novel to the end of the poem, the same contrast remains. Esther had expected to be 'sure and knowledgeable' after her experience in hospital, but in fact, she can see only 'question marks' (*BJ* 233). In Plath's work of 1954–55, which she does following her own return from mental hospital, the point at which Esther's story ends, the heroines of her fiction are stronger than the speakers of her poetry. This ceases to be the case as she begins work on *The Bell Jar*. Her first poem after returning home from hospital features a woman who finds the inner strength thoroughly to transcend her negative self-image as a patient, sick, weak and ugly, whereas in the work of fiction to which Plath proceeds, the heroine never finds such strength. Rather, she can only wonder whether and when the bell jar will 'descend again' (*BJ* 230).

In a letter to Aurelia and Warren Plath, Hughes associates the poem 'Tulips' with *The Bell Jar*. Since Sylvia returned from hospital, he writes, she has been working at high speed and has 'broken through into something wonderful – one poem about "Tulips" . . . is a tremendous piece'.[18] Between Plath's return from hospital on 8 March and the date of this letter, 22 April, Plath wrote just three poems, two of them on 18 March, and one on 28 March. Hughes' references to Plath's working at high speed and breaking through into something wonderful are, in part, references to *The Bell Jar*. Nevertheless, he is also able to connect this writing and this breakthrough to the poem 'Tulips', finished, like 'In Plaster', on 18 March. He was right to do so. Unlike the assertive speaker of 'In Plaster', the speaker of 'Tulips' finds great relief in the process of ceasing to be, just as Esther does in *The Bell Jar*. The tulips of the poem's title annoy the speaker precisely because she feels that their vivid colour is trying to pull her, like the doctors of 'The Stones' or 'Lady Lazarus', back into the world she is enjoying leaving. She begins, 'I am nobody', giving her life up to her nurses and doctors (*CP* 160). She ceases to be herself in her role as a patient, and she finds this process a relief from the burden of living in the world. The peace she feels in her hospital bed is an image of the peace of death. Her only desire is 'to lie with my hands turned up and be utterly empty' (*CP* 161). This is already an image of the speaker's own death, which she sees as a desirably 'free' state, an experience of 'peacefulness'. She goes on explicitly to compare the calm inertia she desires with death, conceived of as a kind of transcendental, even sacred, state:

> It is what the dead close on, finally; I imagine them
> Shutting their mouths on it, like a Communion tablet. (*CP* 161)

The speaker thinks of death itself, and of the process of relinquishing her life in the world, as a relief – as freedom, peace and, in the image of the communion wafer, a kind of ultimate consummation of her being with the universe, comparable to the union of the soul and God. This is how Esther will feel in the novel Plath writes a month or two later. The very first day after her return to the suburbs from her month in New York, she begins to feel harassed by the brightness of daylight in the same way that the speaker of 'Tulips' feels harassed by the brightness of the flowers in her room. She gets back into bed after waking up on the first morning, dragging the sheets over her head to 'shut out the light'. When that fails, she covers her head with a pillow and 'pretended it was night' (*BJ* 113). In both cases, the heroine wants to get away from the busy social world symbolised by the bright colour of the tulips and of the daylight, into a dark, still world that will ultimately be that of death. As Esther goes on to describe her place under the pillow as a 'bolt hole' where she tries also to block out the sound of the phone ringing, and goes eventually to answer it 'cursing' whatever friend, relative or stranger had sniffed out her homecoming (*BJ* 113), she repeats this first step on the weary journey out of life desired by the speaker of 'Tulips'.

Esther's agony is greater than that of the speaker of the poem, and Plath descends into territory much grimmer than she explores in the poem as she describes the details of Esther's plans and actions once she becomes consciously suicidal. Nevertheless what Esther seeks, in what will become a decision to commit suicide, is precisely what the speaker of 'Tulips' has already found, in the self-annihilation of becoming no more than a body in a hospital. She thinks that darkness is the 'most beautiful thing' she can imagine (*BJ* 141). In both the poem and the novel, it is brightness from which the heroine wants to get away into the restful peace of death. The similarity of the two characters' desires is cemented most firmly by Plath's use in both texts of the same series of images. In 'Tulips', the speaker says, 'The water went over my head. / I am a nun now, I have never been so pure' (*CP* 161). These are two of the images Plath uses to describe some of the most fundamental emotions she expresses in her work – the images of purity and of a world under water. She would repeat this trope of stripping away the layers of her speaker's external life until a kind of inner purity is reached in the later *Ariel* poems. In 'Fever 103°', the speaker is a 'pure acetylene / Virgin . . . (My selves dissolving, old whore petticoats)' (*CP* 232). In 'Getting There', the speaker says, 'From this skin / Of old bandages, boredoms, old faces / [I] Step to you . . . / Pure as a baby' (*CP* 249). Plath uses the same image, and with the same frequency, in *The Bell Jar*. When Esther skis out of control down Mount Pisgah, she passes through all her years of 'doubleness', 'smiles' and 'compromise' and enters her 'own past' (*BJ* 93). In both *The Bell Jar* and her late poetry, Plath uses this image of a journey, at some moment of crisis, back through all the external accretions of false appearances that make up the image of a person, to the pure self beneath. It is the journey Esther undergoes at the centre of *The Bell Jar*, as she tries to end her life. As the sleeping pills cause her to lose consciousness, a tide in her goes out, 'baring the pebbles and shells and all the tatty wreckage of my life', and then floods her with unconsciousness (*BJ* 163). This journey through the false appearances that make up the image of oneself to the hidden, true self beneath is also a journey from filth to purity. This is the case in both 'Tulips' and *The Bell Jar*. In the poem, the speaker says, 'I have never been so pure' (*CP* 161). In the novel, as Esther recuperates in a hot bath, she tells herself that all the experiences of the night with Doreen and Lenny Shepherd are 'dissolving' and 'turning into something pure' (*BJ* 19). By the time she finishes bathing, she feels 'pure and sweet as a new baby' (*BJ* 19).

There is a metaphoric chain in Plath's sensibility, in which the purity of a baby is the most desirable state and to which one returns by going back through or casting off the dirty self-images that make up one's personal history as an adult. *The Bell Jar* fully articulates this chain, and Plath began to express it in 'Tulips', written just two or three weeks before she began the novel. 'Tulips' is, in this sense, a precursor not just of the novel but of one of the most fundamental metaphors that underlies the *Ariel* poems.

The last poem Plath wrote before she began work on *The Bell Jar* is 'I Am Vertical', which she finished on 28 March, just a few days before the experience of seeing how to write the novel she described to Ann Davidow. This poem too prefigures some of the concerns she would deal with in the novel. The poem's speaker has little or no sense of her value or worth in the world and, like the speaker of 'Tulips', finds dying more attractive than living. In both poems, Plath explores the consciousness of the kind of heroine Esther will be in her novel, someone for whom death is a welcome relief. There is a progression in the three works, in which the desire for death becomes more explicit, and Plath had clearly begun to work out some of the thoughts and feelings in 'Tulips' and 'I Am Vertical' that she would explore most thoroughly in *The Bell Jar*. 'I am Vertical', as is often the case with Plath's poetry in comparison to her fiction, has a more metaphysical horizon than the immediate, personal experience described in the novel. The speaker sees death as a communion with the natural world. When she lies down, she is in 'open conversation' with the sky:

> And I shall be useful when I lie down finally:
> Then the trees may touch me for once, and the flowers have time for me.
>   (CP 162)

This communion with the natural world, which the speaker imagines she will achieve in death, and which she had felt too insignificant and insubstantial to achieve in life, is much grander and more universal than anything Esther imagines in *The Bell Jar*. Although Plath uses some of her most important imagery, that of the sea, in describing Esther's attempted suicide, her heroine seeks only individual peace. She takes the sleeping pills, curling up in her coat as if it were her 'own sweet shadow' (*BJ* 163). She may enter a better state, according to the imagery of the novel – that of a baby or of the world under the sea – but it is a purely personal state of peace and satisfaction. The sense of becoming one with the universe in a way she was unable to achieve in life expressed in 'I Am Vertical' remains absent from the personal narrative of the novel.

During the time she was writing *The Bell Jar*, Plath wrote four poems.

'Stars over the Dordogne' is one of her still-life poems, a piece of observation from her vacation with the Merwins in the Dordogne in July. The other three, 'Insomniac', 'Widow' and 'The Rival', are all explorations of ideas Plath was also working out at the time in her novel. Plath describes Esther's experience of insomnia in considerable detail in *The Bell Jar*, as one of the first and most distressing symptoms of her nervous breakdown. Whereas Plath wrote in 'Tulips' and 'I Am Vertical' about a desire for peace that would become a desire for death, in 'Insomniac', the speaker never gets to the thought of death as the solution to his problem in the way that Esther does in *The Bell Jar*. 'Insomniac', unusually in Plath's work, is about a male character. He feels the temporary peace produced by sleeping pills, something Esther is never portrayed as having experienced, as a state expressed in the same terms of desirability Plath uses in *The Bell Jar*, a state as pure as a baby. His life is 'baptized in no-life for a while', and he feels the 'sweet, drugged waking of a forgetful baby' (*CP* 163). For Esther, though, the supremely desirable state will become death, whereas it remains only sleep in the poem. In the poem, Plath keeps her male character in a constant state of insomnia; in the novel, she allows her female heroine a journey out of it towards death.

'Widow', dated 16 May 1961, whilst Plath was writing *The Bell Jar* seven mornings a week, has a similar relationship to the novel. Whilst there is nothing in the poem to enable us to say that it is directly about Plath's own mother, it is nevertheless about a woman in a similar situation to her mother, written whilst she was expecting her mother's month-long visit to England. Plath was writing about two women based on her mother at the same time – the character in the poem 'Widow' and Mrs Greenwood in *The Bell Jar*. There are two, related, differences in the portrayals of these characters in the poem and the novel. First, Plath uses the poetic form to express a far more bitter and one-sided hatred of the widow. In *The Bell Jar*, Esther tells Dr Nolan of her hatred of her widowed mother. Although many of Esther's descriptions of her mother are unflattering, she does not express this hatred in terms more aggressive than calling her 'anxious and sallow as a slice of lemon' (*BJ* 126). We know she feels this aggression towards her mother, as she fantasises about stopping her snoring by strangling her, but Esther does not express it as such; she simply states that she feels it. In the poem, on the other hand, the speaker gives vent to the kind of hatred that Esther says she feels: 'The bitter spider sits / . . . in the center of her loveless spokes. / Death is the dress she wears' (*CP* 164). The speaker of the poem curses the widow for her loveless life, accusing her of having murdered her husband and of hating him so much that she would murder him again if she could. For the rest of the poem, the widow is described in detail as the worst kind of woman in the lexicon of Plath's poetry, a woman who neither gives nor receives love. Plath uses the lyric form fully to express a set of emotions, hatred for a widowed woman similar to her mother, which she expresses in a more disparate and complex manner in her novel.

Second, Esther does not only state rather than give voice to her hatred of her mother in *The Bell Jar*. Rather, as Tracy Brain has pointed out, the portrayal of Mrs Greenwood is by no means as uniformly negative as it may at first sight appear.[19] Plath recognises as much as she describes the character in a letter to the novel's editor concerning libel issues. She lists the relations between the novel's characters and the real people on whom they are based, and says that whilst Mrs Greenwood is a fictional version of Mrs Plath, she writes nothing derogatory about her in the novel. She is a decent, upstanding person, whose daughter does not appreciate her.[20] Plath expresses a complex set of emotions towards this character, and this complexity characterises her portrayal of Mrs Greenwood in *The Bell Jar*. Whereas the widow of the poem is simply a negative character, hated by the poem's speaker, the widow of the novel is on the one hand a negative character, hated by the novel's narrator, but on the other someone with whom Plath allows us to sympathise. She is obviously a negative character: it is clear she has no idea how to help Esther, and that she continues to be part of the problem with which Esther needs help, when she says things like 'I knew you'd decide to be all right again' (*BJ* 140). Nevertheless, this is not the only side of her character that Plath allows us to see. Brain points largely to deleted passages which suggest Esther's unreliability as a narrator, but the complexity of the portrayal of Mrs Greenwood also remains clear in the final version.[21] Esther says irritably that her mother would never directly order her to do something, but would always 'reason with me sweetly, like one intelligent, mature person with another' (*BJ* 116). Although the reader's sympathies are always with Esther, here we can hardly condemn her mother for speaking to her reasonably, however much it irritates her. When Dr Gordon recommends ECT treatment for Esther to Mrs Greenwood, Esther threatens never to talk to her mother again unless she tells the truth. Mrs Greenwood replies, '"Don't I *always* tell you the truth?"' and 'burst into tears' (*BJ* 130). Here again, despite the reader's sympathy and identification with Esther, Plath also allows us to understand and sympathise with Mrs Greenwood's point of view. The novel allows Plath a more complex and nuanced portrayal of the character of Mrs Greenwood, whereas the poem allows her to explore a single, more intense emotion. As Plath puts it in 'A Comparison', a poem is 'concentrated, a closed fist', whereas a novel is 'relaxed, an open hand' (*JPBD* 45).

The poems Plath wrote after she completed *The Bell Jar* in August 1961 suggest that the experience of writing the novel was not a cathartic or therapeutic one. Linda Wagner-Martin has argued that 'writing *The Bell Jar* was a liberating experience for Plath', but there is no sense in the works written after she had transformed her early experiences of breakdown and recovery into the aesthetic form of the novel that the kind of emotions with which she deals in that novel have developed or changed.[22] There is no sense, as one reads Plath's poetry written before, during and after the composition of *The Bell Jar*, that completing the novel, whose plot appears to articulate a therapeutic journey, had any therapeutic effect on her sensibility. The first poem she finished after completing the novel is especially interesting in this respect. She had already visited Top Withens, the house in Yorkshire thought to be a model for Wuthering Heights, in September 1956, and written 'Two Views of Withens' about it. In September 1961, she completed a poem entitled 'Wuthering Heights'. Having finished her novel, Plath's next poem has the title of one of the greatest novels written by a woman. Some of the emotions Plath expressed in her novel remain unchanged in the poem she names after Emily Brontë's. *The Bell Jar* ends with Esther this side of the threshold of return to society and health, with only questions ahead of her and no answers. At one point in the planning of the novel, Plath had considered writing a coda after the novel's twenty chapters, consisting of two sections, the first concerning Esther's return to university and the second concerning her experiences during her final summer after university. Plath went to Harvard summer school between her junior and senior years, but it is clear from her plan that she intended Esther to have this experience after her senior year in college and for the novel to end with her about to leave for England.[23] Even had Plath written this coda, Esther would still have ended on the threshold of a new experience, going to England, where we would not see her arrive. In deciding not to write it, and thereby not to portray Esther's experiences after being released from hospital, Plath chose to emphasise the question marks with which Esther's story ends. It is precisely this note of question that she continued to sound in 'Wuthering Heights'. Tim Kendall locates this poem in the development of the relationship of Plath's landscape poetry to Emersonian philosophy.[24] It is less the courage Kendall sees in 'Wuthering Heights', however, than depression which characterises its speaker, a lack of energy and self-assertion in relation to the surrounding world. This emotion is as significant in relation to the novel Plath had just completed as it is to Romantic literary history. She did not take up poetry on the positive note that the structure of Esther's journey suggests she had finished the novel on. Rather, the poem sounds the kind of negative note that suggests that, if anything, Esther's bell jar has descended on the speaker of the poem. The landscape in which she writes is one symbolic of depression and of low energy – 'There is no life higher than the grasstops / Or the hearts of sheep' (*CP* 167). Indeed, the speaker feels that the moorland landscape is both trying to kill her and persuading her to kill herself. The wind wants to 'funnel my heat away' and the heather roots want her to 'whiten my bones among them' (*CP* 167). Most significantly of all, Plath repeats the trope of horizontal and vertical in this, the first poem she wrote after completing *The Bell Jar*, which she used first in 'I Am Vertical', the last poem she wrote before beginning the novel. In the first poem, the speaker says, 'I am Vertical / But I would rather be horizontal' (*CP* 162). In the latter, 'The sky leans on me, the one upright / Among all horizontals' (*CP* 168). Here we can see most clearly that, despite the therapeutic journey narrated in *The Bell Jar*, the writing of the novel consisted of no such therapeutic journey in Plath's sensibility. She was writing poems whose speakers are willingly persuaded to die by the world around them both directly before and directly after she writes the novel. The very first line of 'Wuthering Heights' is a death sentence – 'The horizons ring me like faggots' (*CP* 167). The image of the burning witch invoked here adds, precisely as was the case throughout *The Bell Jar*, the sense that being a woman, at least not the right kind of woman, is part of the crime for which the speaker has been sentenced to death.

Plath's last poem of 1961, 'The Babysitters', is comparable to *The Bell Jar* in that both works are revisitations of Plath's youth in the early 1950s from her maturity in the early 1960s. 'The Babysitters' is a complex poem. It has the structure of a nostalgic look at a happier time in the speaker's youth, but in fact the past is described in terms just as negative as those used for the present. The speaker and her friend row out to an island, which is 'deserted', 'stopped and awful as a photograph of somebody laughing / But ten years dead' (*CP* 175). Indeed, it is this complex structure that the poem shares above all with *The Bell Jar*, and which characterises both of Plath's contemporary portrayals of her youth in the 1950s. In both cases, the autobiographical story she tells in them is apparently simple, but the structure of both the poem and the novel indicate that this apparent simplicity is an illusion. It is impossible to say whether the emotional charge of the poem's final line, 'Everything has happened', is simply positive or simply negative. Is it a good or a bad thing for the speaker that everything has happened? It is both at once, and from the greater weight of the negative accounts of present and past in the rest of the poem, it feels that there is more negative than positive emotion in the mix. 'The Babysitters' as an autobiographical account of Plath's youth from 1961 has precisely the same complex set of emotions as the novel: both express the irreducibly complex ways in which Plath feels and writes about her past.[25] It was during the experience which Plath describes in 'The Babysitters', moreover, that she first encountered the metaphor of the bell jar. Several critics have discussed the significance of Philip Wylie's *Generation of Vipers*, from which the speaker's friend reads aloud in the poem. Plath's friend Marcia Brown, to whom the poem refers, has donated an extract from her journal to Smith College, in which she recalls reading aloud from the book to Plath on the day commemorated in the poem.[26] It is in this book that Plath encountered the image of the bell jar as a symbol of depression. Wylie speaks of his 'melancholia' at the state of contemporary culture, and writes that he feels 'as hollow as a pumped bell jar and as likely to shatter at the touch'.[27] Plath used the metaphor again in later correspondence with Marcia.[28] As she revisits in 'The Babysitters' the complex relationship to her own past which she had articulated the same year in her novel, the metaphor of the bell jar, although hidden more deeply in the poem than in the novel, stands as a symbol of that complex relationship.

Double Exposure, 1962–63

Plath wrote very few poems in the five months during which she wrote *The Bell Jar*. She seems to have worked very differently during the writing of her next novel, *Double Exposure*. There are several poems Plath wrote during this period that deal with some of the subject matter that also went into the novel. In 'The Fearful', of 16 November 1962, the second poem she wrote after the *Ariel* collection was complete, she retells in brief lyric form the central event of the plot of *Double Exposure*. The tone of the poem is one of undisguised contempt. The title of the poem reviles both the male and female characters for the fear that governs the conduct of their love affair. The man is a 'worm', wriggling behind the mask of his lies (*CP* 256). The woman, as Assia Wevill had done, 'says she is a man, not a woman', in a line phrased so that her deception over the telephone amounts to a moral failure to be a woman. Her love is selfish, and in the metaphorical progression of the poem, therefore, deathly. She 'hates' the idea of children, since a child would be a 'stealer' of her good looks, preferring to be 'dead and perfect, like Nefertit' (*CP* 256). Plath calls the woman so vain, so selfish in her love, that this moral failing amounts to the refusal of life to children. Her love is a place 'where the child can never swim' (*CP* 256). Tim Kendall has argued that 'Plath's narratives of adultery rarely allow a comfortable apportioning of blame', but in 'The Fearful', there is no trace of the empathetic understanding or the constructive humour with which Plath describes her novel, in which she also portrays the love affair of the woman who pretends to be a man on the telephone.[29] Plath allows herself to express an emotion to its fullest extent, and without any kind of moral counterbalance, in the lyric. The speaker of the poem simply gives full vent to her anger and her contempt for the characters, accusing them of the most heinous of moral crimes. Wevill told Nathaniel Tarn that there were 'only miserable sinners' in the novel, but it was presumably difficult for her to evaluate Plath's portrayal of her objectively. From Wevill's description, it also seems that the negative characters were offset by the positive portrayal of the central character. From Plath's own descriptions of the novel, she combined in it the negative emotions of 'The Fearful' with a positive, humorous style of narration.

Plath returned to her condemnation of the childless woman in her post-*Ariel* poems. Wevill was at that time childless, and Plath believed that earlier abortions had made her barren. 'Childless Woman', of 1 December 1962, curses the figure of the childless woman for her self-absorption and for her death-like quality. In that her lover achieves relationship only with her, and not with any children through her, she is 'ungodly as a child's shriek' (*CP* 259). If the woman of 'The Fearful' refuses life to children, the speaker of 'Childless Woman' is associated with their death. Connotations of abortion cluster around both this image and those of the earlier poem. In the later poem, she compares the speaker to a spider, a negative image in Plath's poetic lexicon, and one she used for the bad mother figure of 'Widow', who spins only mirrors in which to love herself. In 'Childless Woman', Plath makes some explicit anatomical references in order to denigrate the speaker, associating her infertile sexual organs with death, 'uttering nothing but blood'. Her 'forest' is her 'funeral', and her 'hill' is 'gleaming with the mouths of corpses' (*CP* 259). The contempt of 'The Fearful' becomes powerful hatred in these last stanzas of 'Childless Woman'. It would be very illuminating to be able to compare the character of the childless rival in *Double Exposure* to the childless women Plath wrote about in her poetry at the same time. If she is right that her sense of humour is constructive, then her novelistic treatment of the character based on Wevill would be more complex, offset by the humour and even the understanding expressed in other parts of the novel, than the sheer, single emotions Plath uses the lyric form to express.

The same can be said about 'Gigolo', of 29 January 1963, in which

Plath expressed both the contempt for the faithless man of 'The Fearful' and some of the hatred for the women with whom he sleeps of 'Childless Woman'. After calling his lovers 'bitches' and making a derogatory reference to the 'cellos' of their 'moans', the speaker of the poem ends on a similarly narcissistic note to the woman of 'The Fearful'. He says that he is like a beautiful fountain, above whose waters 'I tenderly / Lean and see me' (*CP* 268). The same can be said for the character of the husband as he would have appeared in *Double Exposure* as we said for the character of the rival. In the form of the lyric, Plath allows herself to express fully a single set of emotions, whereas in the novel she suggests that she counterbalanced these emotions with humour and understanding into a more complex portrayal of these characters in their full social context.

We may get a glimpse of this kind of complex portrayal of the recent events of Plath's life in the poem 'Burning the Letters', of 13 August 1962. Plath wrote several poems about events in the break-up of her marriage that probably either did or would have gone into her semi-autobiographical novel, such as 'Rabbit Catcher', 'Event' and 'Words Heard, By Accident, Over the Phone'. 'Burning the Letters' is one of these poems – it is about an event in the summer of 1962 which may well have become part of the narrative of *Double Exposure*, in which Plath built a bonfire out of her husband's letters and other papers after the telephone call in a man's voice confirmed to her that he was seeing another woman. The last eight lines of the poem are a comparison of the speaker's state of mind to the killing of a fox by a pack of hounds, Plath speaking powerfully and fluently in her *Ariel* voice. The earlier sections of the poem, however, although dealing with an obviously traumatic event, take a gentler, even conciliatory tone, finding some positive elements in the experience the speaker describes:

> At least it will be a good place now, the attic.
> At least I won't be strung just under the surface. (*CP* 204)

The 'carbon birds' of the burnt letters are 'beautiful' and even 'console' the speaker. Given Plath's descriptions of her second novel as funny and empathetic, it may be that a similar kind of balance of emotions could be found in it as she put into 'Burning the Letters' alone amongst the poems which deal with the events surrounding the end of her marriage.

Chapter 3

The Politics of Plath's Fiction

It is surprising for how long critics have been arguing, against a tendency to interpret Plath's work in personal or psychological terms, that Plath was a politically engaged thinker and writer. Stan Smith made this case in 1982.[1] Twenty years later, Tracy Brain could still argue, against 'the conventional personal readings to which [Plath's writing] is customarily subjected', that Plath's work is 'deeply, politically engaged with [the] world'.[2] Although so influential a critic as Sandra Gilbert could claim that Plath 'did not have an explicitly political imagination', more recent studies have shown that Plath was constantly thinking and writing about the political discourses and events with which she was surrounded, from the time she went to Smith College to the end of her life.[3] Al Strangeways has argued that Plath's work articulates a complex intellectual, emotional and aesthetic invest-ment in contemporary history and politics.[4] Robin Peel has demonstrated how thoroughly Plath's thought and work are saturated by contemporary political discourses, from philosophy books and lectures to magazines and radio programmes.[5] Whilst Peel has dealt in some detail with *The Bell Jar*, the tendency amongst studies of Plath's historical and political writing has been to focus on her poetry, and on her later poetry in particular. In this chapter, I discuss the political views Plath developed throughout her writing life and trace her expression of these views in her fiction.

Political Development

Pat Macpherson has studied *The Bell Jar* in the light of the dominant ideologies of the 1950s. The central concept of her study is 'paranoia', by which she describes both official anti-Communism and individual dissent from it, such as Esther's.[6] Recent studies of 1950s, however, have emphasised the greater complexity of ideological forces at work in American culture. Richard Fried writes:

It is tempting to infer that the dominant force was stability, and that the dissenters constituted a lonely group on the defensive. But that conclusion may miss the extent to which opposing trends were symbiotically connected.[7]

Martin Halliwell bases his recent study of American culture in the 1950s on the premise that 'the decade is best characterised as a struggle between conflicting forces', and his study aims to 'recover the diversity of cultural forms from the ingrained view that cold war culture is monolithic and one-dimensional'.[8] As Stephen Whitfield puts it, 'Serious social and political criticism was freely articulated in the decade, even if not as heeded as its authors wished'.[9] Joanne Meyerowitz has argued that gender discourse in particular in the 1950s is ideologically complex. She describes her 1994 collection *Not June Cleaver*, as a revisionist approach to the history of American women in the 1950s, which 'places the domestic stereotype in historical context and questions both its novelty and its pervasiveness'.[10] In her essay 'Beyond the Feminine Mystique', she argues that the women's magazines of the era articulate this complexity of ideological forces and discourses.[11] In an essay in the 2001 collection *Rethinking Cold War Culture*, she argues that women's organisations such as the National Federation of Business and Professional Women's Clubs and the American Association of University Women were actively lobbying and publishing to promote women's greater participation in the public sphere, and were even using anti-Communist rhetoric to do so. Meyerowitz also points to the nascent gay rights publications which used democratic and nationalistic rhetoric to make their claims. She calls these discourses 'faint counterpoints . . . to the more conservative clamour' of the decade.[12] Plath's politics developed in a complex ideological world, in which militant anti-Communism was politically dominant, but in which many dissenting voices, although more faint than the clamour of this discourse, were also to be heard.

Plath grew up with a very strong belief in both the rights and the responsibilities of the individual. Her father, although intended for the Lutheran ministry as a young man, had become an atheist by the time his daughter was born, and was also committed to pacifism. Aurelia had been brought up a Catholic, but broke with the Church when she was a college student because of its 'repressive and controlling ideology', and became a Methodist.[13] After her husband's death, she joined the Unitarian Church in Wellesley and taught in its Sunday School. She brought up her children to believe, as she and her husband had done, in 'directing one's life toward an idealistic goal in order to build a strong inner life' (*LH* 31). She also shared with them the pacifism in which she and her husband believed. In the context of the Unitarian Church, which allowed a range of theological views so wide as to include atheism amongst its members, Plath's own atheism was held in conjunction with a strong belief in the responsibility of the individual to create her own life for herself. She told Eddie Cohen that, although she was a Unitarian, she did not attend church regularly because she was committed to the principle that each person has to work out and create her own life for herself.[14]

An early father figure in Plath's life was Wilbury Crockett, her English teacher during her last three years of high school. He was deeply committed to the idea of liberal education, and he expected his students to be as well versed in the social and political issues of the day as with the literary texts he set them to read. His reading lists included essays on current events, such as John Hersey's *Hiroshima* (1946) and Wendell Wilkie's *One World* (1943). In an essay on Crockett, one of Plath's peers at high school, Harold Kolb, writes:

> Our class conversations . . . dealt with important events and ideas of the day, including the Korean War, the United Nations, the use of the atomic bomb, civil rights, post-World War II refugees, the Cold War, Communism, the establishment of Israel, world religions, and world peace.

'The common denominator in these discussions', he adds, 'tended to be social justice'.[15] Al Strangeways has pointed out that Plath may have had similar discussions with her history teacher, Raymond Chapman.[16] Plath's early play, 'Room in the World', written during her senior year in high school, owes much to these classes. The play is a family drama, set in the home of a laid-off factory worker who decides to picket the factory with his small children, giving them signs to wear that ask for their father to be given another job. Even his son's Popeye doll has one. This first of Plath's engagements with political ideas in fiction contains in embryonic form the most fundamental gesture of all her writing about politics: public events are portrayed in their effects on the lives of women. The worker's daughter has been embarrassed during the protest because a girl she has a crush on at school has seen her. The play ends with everyone upset and the father sadly agreeing not to take his daughter to picket for him again the next day.[17]

Crockett encouraged his students to publish their work in contemporary journals. In an article co-written with Perry Norton, 'Youth's Plea for World Peace', published in the *Christian Science Monitor* in March 1950, Plath expressed her commitment to peace in the name of 'the basic brotherhood of all human beings'.[18] The essay is an argument against the development of the hydrogen bomb. Whilst the authors supported 'democracy and the capitalistic system', in the belief that America had the best form of social government currently in existence, they argued that peace can be achieved by the 'power of attraction' rather than that of mutual deterrence. Observing that the human race has already managed to kill or maim a significant number of its members, they asserted that 'destruction, unfortunately, is always mutual'. As Langdon Hammer points out, few public statements in 1950 acknowledged America's destruction of enemy civilians during the Second World War so openly.[19] Young people in particular, Plath and Norton argue, are 'essentially idealistic', believing that world peace is possible, and looking beyond 'the present dilemma of nationalism' to the brotherhood of all human beings. They cite the United World Federalists, of which Plath was a member, and the Experiment in International Living, in which her brother would participate, as examples of the real possibility of the kind of world peace in which young people are able to believe. In a 1950 résumé, Plath listed her own membership of a United World Federalists group, which she had joined in order to contribute to the cause of peace.[20]

Also at Crockett's encouragement, Plath began to correspond with a West German student, Hans-Joachim Neupert, a practice she continued throughout her first two years at Smith. The two frequently turned to politics in their correspondence. In August 1950, Plath wrote that news of the Korean War made her physically sick. She described her summer work on Lookout Farm, the beauties of nature, the handsome men who worked alongside her on the farm and her own thought that war is simply folly when life, especially life in the natural world, is so rich. She told Hans-Joachim that her fellow-workers were continually discussing the war, and she put this experience into poetry in 'Bitter Strawberries', a poem she had originally entitled 'Swords into Plowshares'.[21] At talk of bombing the Russians into oblivion, a 'little girl with blond braids' pleads, '"Don't"', and her 'blue eyes' swim with 'vague terror' (*CP* 299–300). The poem ends with an image of the strawberry-pickers both protecting and damaging the plants they pick. At just seventeen, Plath expertly captures the sense of foreboding clouding the lives of ordinary Americans as the Korean War begins. The following month, Chicago student Eddie Cohen, with whom Plath had also begun a correspondence, testified to the same sense of foreboding among his peers, whose main topic of conversation was the latest news from their draft board.[22] Plath's letters to both Cohen and Neupert are full of references to her constant state of fear concerning the war and the atomic bomb. She could never entirely suppress this fear in the superficial entertainments of college life, she wrote, so deeply disturbed was she by the possibility of atomic war.[23] Plath added two distinctive beliefs of her own to the liberal anti-war stance she shared with peers like Neupert and Cohen.

First, she believes that killing is not natural to human beings.[24] Second, she is against war as a woman, because it destroys the love and family life which she values. As she puts it to Cohen, politicians do not consider the interests of young women like her who need a foundation of peace to build a loving family.[25] Indeed, as Plath puts it most explicitly, 'I could love a Russian boy – and live with him', because it is life together that matters most to people, not the ideological beliefs that oppose them to one another (*J* 46). Kathleen Connors sees these ideas expressed in some of the paintings Plath did at this time for her freshman course Art 13, such as 'Two Women Reading' and 'Woman with Halo'. She argues that these paintings, which picture women at leisure or in the company of friends, in a countryside depicted in beautiful bright colours, constitute feminist 'alternatives' to the 'dark visions' of 'the facile anti-Communist rhetoric of the time'.[26] Langdon Hammer has argued that 'war and the erotic came into conjunction in Plath's imagination' throughout her life and work.[27] Whilst Plath's fantasy life is indeed complex and does indeed link violence and the erotic, her association of the folly of war with the desirability of the men it destroys is in my view primarily a feminist commitment to living out in society her desires for love, marriage and a family.

Plath continued to debate political issues throughout her time at college. In July 1952, she recorded discussing Whittaker Chambers' book *Witness*, about the ex-Communist's role in the Alger Hiss trials, with her date Art Kramer, who had also given her a copy of one of Adlai Stevenson's speeches.[28] In October, she urged her mother to vote for Stevenson, praising his individual policies and criticising Eisenhower's susceptibility to conservatives in the Senate like McCarthy, Jenner and Taft.[29] Her mother replied in some detail, enclosing a newspaper article, to which Plath responded that reactionary senators would have too much power in an Eisenhower administration. On 6 November 1952, Plath wrote bitterly to her mother that she got up the day after Eisenhower's victory feeling that everything she had believed in was dead.[30] Plath also heard and commented on a variety of political figures who came to speak at Smith. In February 1951, she heard Nobel laureate Ralph Bunche, who encouraged his audience to rise above contemporary fearmongering and aggression, and to put into everyday practice the democracy in which they believed.[31] In April 1952, she heard Senator McCarthy speak (*LH* 84), but made no comment on his lecture except to compare it unfavourably with that of Patrick Murphy Malin, executive director of the American Civil Liberties Union, who she felt was an inspiring alternative of political morality and sincerity.[32] As a guest editor at *Mademoiselle* the following year, Plath suggested Malin as the subject of a future article.[33] In March 1952, she had also heard Dirk Struik, the mathematics professor from MIT recently suspended for his Communist Party membership. She was extremely interested in what he had to say, and wrote up his talk for the local press.[34]

Plath witnessed her own professors and those of her peers summoned before the House Un-American Activities Committee. In February 1952, Dick Norton sent her a newspaper article about Yale's response to charges that faculty members were indoctrinating students with Communism.[35] The following year her creative writing professor, Robert Gorham Davis, was called before HUAC to account for his Communist past.[36] McCarthyism touched Smith most closely when, in 1954, a letter was sent to college alumnae discouraging them from donating to the college whilst it employed Communists such as Davis. Plath wrote to Phil McCurdy about the meeting in which President Wright of Smith College robustly rejected the letter, scarcely able to contain her outrage at its scandalous and baseless attacks. She expressed her support for Davis, and noted with anger that this public smear had left him in need of medical treatment.[37] This letter was written by a woman from the influential Buckley family, with whom Plath had socialised briefly as a sophomore, when Maureen Buckley, who lived with her in Haven House, invited all her housemates to her coming out party. Maureen's brother, William F. Buckley, Jr., who had just published the controversial *God and Man at Yale*, spoke at Smith later that month. Cyrilly Abels, Plath's managing editor at *Mademoiselle*, expressed her delight at the rejection of the letter by Smith's President and students, calling it an inspiring response to the disturbing climate of McCarthyism.[38] In May 1953, Plath described a visit to New York City with Ray Wunderlich to see a new production of *The Crucible*. Afterwards, she wrote, they and their dinner companions at Delmonico's held an animated discussion long into the night in which they discussed philosophy and politics of all kinds.[39]

Race Stories

The first time Plath dealt with her political concerns in fiction was in 'The Perfect Setup', a story she wrote in September 1951 for her creative writing course English 220a. She sold the story for $25 to *Seventeen* magazine, which published it in October 1952. In this story, she portrays her political ideas at work in and affecting people's lives together, especially the lives of women. 'The Perfect Setup' deals with anti-Semitism amongst the social elite of Cape Cod and the dilemma this causes the young heroine, who is working as a mother's helper for a wealthy WASP family during the summer. Plath herself had worked as a mother's helper for the Mayo family in Swampscott, Massachusetts, in the summer of 1951, and Lisa, the heroine of 'The Perfect Setup', does a similar job. She befriends a Jewish girl, Ruth Jacobs, on the beach, who is working as a child-minder for a Jewish family. The two girls enjoy their work, the beach, the children they look after and their friendship. This is the 'perfect setup' of the story's title. When Lisa's employer discovers that she has befriended Ruth, however, and that her children are playing with the Jewish children Ruth minds, she awkwardly asks Lisa not to let the children play together. Plath's story deals with the emotions of the women involved in this structure of racial prejudice. She portrays Mrs Bradley's shame at asking what she nevertheless insists on. Her words are 'big and ugly and ashamed of themselves', hiding behind the kind of smile that 'you practice in front of a mirror first'.[40] Although Plath was just nineteen when she wrote the story, and although it was well tailored to *Seventeen*'s rhetorical requirements, she was nevertheless adept at exploring the effect of social structures on the emotional lives of the women who live within them. Mrs Bradley's speech is a model of contradiction:

> 'I like Janey to play with her own kind . . . Not that we're intolerant or any-thing . . . but the whole street across the way is just full of those people in the summertime.'

This speech plunges Lisa into turmoil. She wants to throw things and scream. The drama of the story lies in Lisa's emotional conflict, which is not between whether or not to do the injustice her employer asks of her, but between her certain obedience and her feelings about it. She reflects, 'I wasn't going to be the card that didn't collapse with all the rest'. Rather, Lisa thinks, she will just go on 'staying safely in the middle of the road' and doing as her employer asks.[41] She simply has to live feeling very bad about it. The story ends with Lisa telling Ruth that she and their employ-ers' children can no longer play together, narrated with all Plath's gift for portraying intense emotions under the surface of socially acceptable actions: 'When I got all through talking, she was staring hard at a stick or something in the sand'. The girls try to be nice to each other about the racist structure in which they have become enmeshed. They arrange to meet at Lisa's employer's house, but both know that Ruth will not come. She bravely gives a friendly smile and leaves to go swimming. The story ends with Lisa wanting to 'worm my way down into that sand' so deep that Ruth can no longer see her. This is the way in which Plath begins to portray political structures at work in her fiction. The social systems and policies against which she was committed in principle are portrayed at work in the ordinary lives and relationships of women. Racism, for Plath, as she portrays it in 'The Perfect Setup', is a crime against the love of others in which she wants to live and in which she believes that both she and every other individual should have the right to live.

Renée Curry has discussed the complexity of Plath's portrayal of whiteness.[42] She restricts her discussion to Plath's poetry, but we can add here that Plath's portrayal of race is as complex in her fiction as it is in her poetry. Having clearly portrayed the suffering caused by anti-Semitic prejudice in 'The Perfect Setup', Plath is less critical of Esther's attitudes in *The Bell Jar*, which lack the kind of anti-racism that characterises the narrator of the earlier story. In the episode in which Esther argues with a black hospital worker, she describes him as 'the negro', marking him only by his race. Kate Baldwin has pointed out that, although an able-bodied adult, he is portrayed as the equivalent of a feeble, elderly white man.[43] Usually a 'shrunken old white man' brings the patients their food, Esther tells us, but on this particular day it was the negro (*BJ* 173). He is subordinate to a white woman, who is giving him orders. Esther despises the black worker for his subordinate position, saying that he was 'grinning' and 'chuckling' in response to the orders in a 'silly' manner (*BJ* 173). She reduces him to a series of racial stereotypes, in which visible difference connotes moral inferiority, saying that he 'gawped' at the patients with 'big, rolling eyes'. She does something similar when she says that Doreen, as she allows herself to be reduced to nothing but her sexuality with Lenny Shepherd, looks like a 'bleached blonde negress' (*BJ* 11).

Esther and the black worker marginalise one another. Esther infers from the orderly's stares that she and her fellow-patients are his 'first crazy people' (*BJ* 174). The two of them fight verbally and physically in order to establish which of them, both subordinate in society in general, should be subordinate to the other. Esther speaks to the black orderly like a servant – '"We're not done . . . You can just wait"' (*BJ* 175). He responds with mimicry, making signs of mock respect and giving her a mock title, 'Miss Mucky-Muck' (*BJ* 175). Esther will not stand for this, however, and turns to physical violence, positioning herself out of the nurse's view and kicking the man in the leg. His response is stereotyped thrice over – he gives a 'yelp' like an animal; he 'rolled his eyes', marking his racial difference; and his speech is transcribed as non-standard. Esther savours this victory, looking right at him and saying, '"That's what *you* get"' (*BJ* 175). As one of the marginalised group of mentally ill people, Esther feels better than almost no one. She can and does, however, feel better than a black man, and she does so by means of verbal and physical violence.

Plath makes clear that Esther is not thinking rightly in this episode. Esther kicks the orderly because he brings the patients two types of beans, which she knows one should not do. She tells us that he was 'trying to see how much we would take' (*BJ* 175). This is obviously nonsense, since the orderly is only serving the meal, and has not been responsible for preparing it. Esther is genuinely paranoid at this point. She does not seem at any point in her narration of the episode to acknowledge as much, however. She writes her story when she is 'all right again', but narrates this episode in which she acts with racial prejudice without any criticism of her actions or even of her state of mind at the time which might mitigate them.

Race appears again in *The Bell Jar* in the form of a series of images of non-white women in whom Esther sees herself, most frequently in a mirror. Several times in the novel, Esther sees another woman looking back at her from a mirror, who appals her with the hidden truth about herself that she ordinarily conceals. In one case, after Esther has been crying in Jay Cee's office, it is the face of a prisoner who has been badly assaulted (*BJ* 98). In two other cases, it is a woman of another race. After her night in New York with Lenny and Doreen, Esther sees in the mirrored wall of the hotel elevator a 'big, smudgy-eyed Chinese woman' looking 'idiotically' back at her. Although she knows it is her own reflection, she is 'appalled' to see that she looks so 'wrinkled' and 'used-up' (*BJ* 17). As she leaves New York at the end of the month, with Marco's blood still streaked across her cheeks, she looks in her make-up mirror and sees a 'sick Indian' (*BJ* 108). Dorothy Wang has argued that racial doubles in Plath's work interact with her anxieties about the borders of femininity.[44] It is certainly social norms that are at work in the images of non-white women that Esther uses in her story. On both occasions when she sees a non-white woman in her mirror, this woman represents the hidden, shameful truth that Esther is not all that her society requires women to be. She is not pretty, not well-dressed or made-up, and she is not an attractive object of the male gaze. The Chinese woman is wrinkled and used-up, the Indian woman is sick. Both women, like the beaten-up prisoner Esther also sees in the mirror, fail to be 'feminine'. Something similar occurs in a deleted passage of *The Bell Jar*, in which Esther has a series of clinical psychology tests, in one of which she has to draw a picture of a woman. She feels disgusted by the contours of the female body, so she sketches a woman in a costume that covers her from head to toe, with just her eyes visible from behind her veil, like an Arabic woman.[45] When Esther is deeply disturbed by the difficulty and undesirability of living out the gender role prescribed for her, it is with the image of a non-white woman that she expresses this emotion.

Unconsciously, she equates not being fully a woman with not being fully white.

Curry argues that, in her poetry, Plath articulates the complex nature of contemporary white subjectivity.[46] This is true. In her fiction, Plath articulates the complex racial politics of her time and place. Perhaps the most characteristic expression of the contradictions in American discourse on race in the 1950s was the Supreme Court's ruling in *Brown II* that desegregation in schools be implemented 'with all deliberate speed' by the federal district courts. President Eisenhower, although considering himself a racially tolerant man, was privately critical of *Brown v. Board of Education*, the earlier Supreme Court ruling that segregation in public schools was unconstitutional, and in public did not endorse it. In the absence of direction from the executive or the judicial branch concerning desegregation, it was a decade in many Southern states before the process began. Charles Ogletree writes:

> From the White House to the city councils of the smallest towns, those in power found ways to either subtly defer or defiantly oppose desegregation. Thus the words 'with all deliberate speed' effectively lost their meaning.[47]

Plath's preferred candidate for President, Adlai Stevenson, had argued in his 1956 campaign that desegregation 'must proceed gradually, not upsetting habits or traditions that are older than the Republic'.[48] The racial politics of *The Bell Jar* proceed in a similar way, with all deliberate speed. The novel is committed to anti-racism in principle but has not eradicated in practice all traces of racism from its world. Although at the very cutting edge of the history of gender politics, *The Bell Jar* is less in the vanguard than Plath would have wanted it to be, with her conscious commitment to the rights of every individual, in the history of racial politics.

Cold War Stories

Plath first dealt with the Cold War in fiction in 'Brief Encounter', a story written for her creative writing course Eng 220b in February 1952. She rewrote it the following month, with the new title 'Though Dynasties Pass', according to her instructor's comments. The later draft cuts several long passages from the earlier story, which the instructor had presumably not liked. On the second draft, the instructor has written, 'There is no *bathos* here', which perhaps had been his criticism of the deleted passages. In my view, however, the passages Plath cut out are well written, and the earlier, longer story is the better one. It is about a female college student who meets a young, wounded Korean War veteran on a train, and it deals with his conflicted relationships to other people, including his family. The relationship that he and the girl strike up, with its erotic undertones, is portrayed as a competing and better way to live than fighting the Cold War. It is a story that prefers love and family over war, including war for America's anti-Communist ideals. 'Brief Encounter' begins with the veteran's sense of no longer belonging in the prosperous society for which he has been fighting. People see his wound (he walks on crutches) then look the other way, knowing they cannot help him. In a trope very characteristic of Plath's early fiction, the soldier looks into the night outside the train window and feels it speaking to a corresponding darkness within him. It tells him he has no place in the bustling train compartment, but only in the blank night outside. In order to stave off this inner darkness, the veteran strikes up a conversation with the girl he is sitting opposite. She is portrayed quite erotically – as she looks up at the soldier, her clothes emphasise her attractive figure and her red lipstick adds to her sensual appearance. At the same time as being portrayed sexually in this way, however, the veteran sees that she is a well-brought-up girl. She talks to him kindly and with respect, unlike his sister, who simply cries when she visits him, treating him as an object of pity, and unlike a woman on the subway earlier that day who had offered him her seat, calling into question his masculinity.[49] The girl understands how little this kind of behaviour respects the humanity of the veteran and gets very angry with these people on his behalf, in the second draft of the story even using some strong language as she imagines talking back to them.[50] The soldier appreciates her honesty, however, reflecting that this kind of plain speaking is just what he needs to feel normal again. It is not just an erotic relationship with the girl that represents the right way to live in this story, better than war and society's hypocritical relationship to its veterans; it is also family life. She is not just an erotic good in herself; she is also a well-brought-up girl, the kind of girl a young man like the soldier could marry, and she puts him right concerning his awkward relationship to his family. She insists that he go to his sister's house that night, rather than staying in a hotel first as he had planned, since he feels awkward about meeting her new husband. She tells him to go straight there, because his sister will not want to lose any of the time they could be spending together as a family. Love, marriage, home and family – these are the values the story privileges, in direct contrast to war and to the basis of America's participation in the Cold War. Thomas Hardy's poem 'In Time of "The Breaking of Nations"', from which Plath took the title of the second draft of this story, concludes with the image of two lovers 'whispering by' and the thought that love like theirs will outlast wars.[51] Plath's story genders this thought. It says that women know better than men – they value love and family, and these are the principles on which society should be based, not the principles which have led America into the Korean War.

Crazy About the Rosenbergs

Plath's next Cold War story is *The Bell Jar*. As Pat Macpherson and Marie Ashe have emphasised, Esther's story is set within the story of Julius and Ethel Rosenberg. The couple were arrested and charged in 1950 with having conspired to pass on details of the atomic bomb project at Los Alamos during the Second World War to the Soviet Union, with the help of Ethel's brother, David Greenglass, who worked as a machinist on the project. The historical record shows that any details Julius Rosenberg managed to pass on had little or no significance to the Soviets' ability to produce an atomic bomb. At the time, however, the couple were branded 'atom spies', without whom Soviet scientists would have been unable to develop an atomic bomb for years. After a sensational trial, which included Greenglass testifying against his own sister, the Rosenbergs were sentenced to death. A substantial protest movement, the National Committee to Secure Justice in the Rosenberg Case, was formed, organising rallies, printing critical newspaper articles and a 'Fact Sheet' arguing that there were serious flaws in the government's case. In January 1953, the couple were granted a stay of execution to petition the President for clemency, following which the White House was flooded with such petitions, including letters from Albert Einstein and Pope Pius XII. Protest spread across Europe – Pablo Picasso published a poster of the couple sitting hand in hand in electric chairs, and Jean-Paul Sartre wrote vitriolic criticism of the United States in the French press. After a dramatic series of stays and orders to vacate those stays in June 1953, the couple were executed in Sing Sing prison on 19 June.[52]

Plath spent June 1953 in New York as a guest editor for *Mademoiselle* magazine. A journal fragment survives from 19 June, in which she wrote about the executions scheduled for that night, and in which she expressed precisely the concerns she would later give to Esther in *The Bell Jar*. First, she cannot help but imagine the details of the experience of being electrocuted. She recalls a newspaper article about these details, which makes her 'sick at the stomach' (*J* 541). Janet Wagner, one of her fellow guest editors, recalls a kind of physical reaction Plath had to the executions, writing that, at the time when Plath thought they were taking place:

She . . . held out her arms to me and there were, raising up on her arms from her wrists to her elbows, little bumps. Soon they sort of bled together like welts from burns.[53]

Second, Plath was upset by the response of another of the guest editors, who yawned and spoke exactly the words she gives to Hilda in *The Bell Jar*, 'I'm so glad they are going to die' (*J* 541). Finally, she was appalled that this inhuman response was that of most the country. No one seemed to care, she wrote, that 'two real people' who 'took centuries and centuries to evolve' in all their complexity, were being put to death. Most Americans would simply dismiss the fact with a 'casual and complacent yawn' (*J* 542).

When Plath revisited these events in *The Bell Jar*, she gave Esther very similar reactions to her own. Esther cannot stop thinking about the Rosenbergs, and that is how she knows that 'something was wrong' with her (*BJ* 2). She says that the execution is 'all there was to read about in the papers', but this is not true – many other events of international significance were making the headlines at the same time. On 18 June, armistice talks in Korea broke down as South Korean President Syngman Rhee released some 25,000 Communist prisoners-of-war, the question of whose repatriation constituted the major obstacle in the armistice negotiations. Tens of thousands of workers rioted in East Berlin in protest at the Communist government and were put down with Soviet tanks. Alongside the story on the Rosenbergs on 18 June, the front page of the *New York Times* reported on both these stories with the headline 'Korean Anti-Red P.O.W.'s Freed By Rhee in Defiance of the U.N.; Soviet Tanks Fight Riots in Berlin' and a photograph of Soviet tanks moving through jeering crowds. Another headline reported, 'Prisoners' Flight Dims U.S. Optimism' concerning the armistice in Korea.[54] The following day, again next to news of the Rosenbergs' execution, the headlines read, 'Reds Accuse U.S., See Test of Faith; West Condemns Soviet on Berlin'. The sub-headline reads, 'Rhee Rebuffs Eisenhower', and there is even a story entitled 'Red Plot to Slay McCarthy'.[55] There is no doubt that the execution of the Rosenbergs was in the headlines, but Esther singles out this story as the sole news item in a period full of major international events on which to focus.

What is it about the Rosenbergs that fascinates Esther, not only in the sense that many people spent June 1953 deeply concerned about the executions – indeed, Phil McCurdy, one of Plath's high school and college boyfriends, was taking part in a protest march in Washington on 19 June – but to the point of neurosis? First, she is disturbed by the pain that is to be inflicted on the Rosenbergs. She cannot imagine anything worse than death by electrocution, and describes it as an especially intense form of torture focused on the most sensitive organs of the body – it is to be 'burned alive all along your nerves' (*BJ* 1). Second, she is disturbed that she lives in a society which legally imposes this kind of torture on its citizens, and which on the whole approves of it. This is made clear in Chapter 9, set on the day of the executions. The chapter begins with, and twice repeats, Hilda's comment, 'I'm so glad they are going to die' (*BJ* 95). An early draft of Chapter 9 makes clear that Plath wanted to emphasise this point. It does not begin, as the final version does, with Hilda's comment, but with the next sentence of the final version. Plath types eight lines of the text, and then, on the ninth line, just the first two words of Hilda's comment.[56] It seems that she had begun to type the line 'I'm so glad they're going to die', and then, in the act of doing so, decided that she also wanted to begin the chapter with it, in order to emphasise the inhumanity of the reaction of most Americans to the executions.

Pat Macpherson criticises Plath for 'depicting McCarthyism . . . as a problem of female bitchery' in this scene.[57] Plath's portrayal of Hilda does not slip into sexism, however. Rather, in addition to a critique of the inhumanity of her view, Plath is criticising its lack of femininity. A woman, in Plath's view, should know better. Esther had seen a play the previous night in which the heroine was possessed by a dybbuk (a Yiddish word for the spirit of a sinner). When the dybbuk spoke from inside her, its voice was such that it was impossible to know 'whether it was a man or a woman' (*BJ* 96). Hilda's voice sounds like the dybbuk's. Plath herself had seen this play, Solomon Ansky's *The Dybbuk*, in New York with Richard Sassoon in January 1955.[58] It is a love story in which the poor lover of the heroine dies when he hears that her father is going to marry her to a rich man, and on her wedding day, possesses her in the form of a dybbuk. The story ends happily – exorcised from her body, the spirit of her lover asks to enter her soul. She agrees, and this is the marriage with which the play ends.[59] The most lasting impression this play has made on Esther, however, is that when the dybbuk speaks from the heroine's mouth, it is impossible to know 'whether it was a man or a woman' (*BJ* 96). Hilda's view is so appalling to Esther that it seems to be that of a person who is not entirely a woman. Plath used the metaphor again the following year in her review of Malcolm Elwin's *Lord Byron's Wife*. She quotes Byron's sister's account of his wife after their separation, with her 'deep hollow tone of voice and a calm in her manner quite supernatural', and comments, 'How clearly one sees the killing dybbuk of self-righteousness in possession'.[60] The metaphor of the dybbuk in Plath's lexicon stands for a woman who has allowed herself to become something less than Plath believed a woman ought to be. Hilda not only expresses the view of the majority of American society of the Rosenbergs, but she also fits into that society perfectly. She is an all-American girl, well adapted to her feminine role as a consumer of fashion commodities and a beautiful object of the male gaze, and she is a successful college student who has won a competitive guest editorship at the country's top magazine for 'smart young women'. On the outside, Hilda seems to be all that an American woman ought to be. Her unthinking hatred of the Rosenbergs, however, makes her precisely the opposite. Plath begins to work out a counter-ideology of femininity here, which includes a commitment to the dignity and rights of every human being that supersedes immediate partisan or nationalistic ideologies.

Like Plath's, Esther's response to the execution of the Rosenbergs is not only political but also psychological. Esther closely identifies with the condemned couple. We see this process at work on the novel's first page, with Esther 'wondering what it was like' to be electrocuted as the Rosenbergs would be (*BJ* 1). Marie Ashe has argued that Esther's name represents the private side of Ethel Rosenberg, whose full name was Ethel Esther Greenglass Rosenberg. The fact that Plath changed her heroine's name to Esther Greenwood only at her publisher's request makes this unlikely to have been her explicit intention. Nevertheless, it is clear that Esther identifies with the Rosenbergs. Pat Macpherson argues that both are punished for their failure to conform to the oppressive norms of the 1950s.[61] Ashe put the case more precisely, that Esther's journey represents a figurative 'killing' of Ethel Rosenberg, 'a troubling model of 1950s public woman' and a 'haunting' return of her ghost.[62] I am not sure that killing and haunting is the right metaphor to describe Esther's ideological journey, but Ashe is right to argue that Esther's anxiety about her gender role is at the root of her identification with the Rosenbergs. Esther sees in the Jewish couple examples of ordinary American citizens like herself whose thoughts, feelings and desires leave them simply no place in American society. Part of the attraction of the story of the Rosenbergs to the 'goggle-eyed' newspaper readers of *The Bell Jar* was that a couple with such an apparently dreadful secret life could also appear to be an ordinary American family. As Andrew Ross writes, 'Official calculations of the enormity of their alleged crime seemed to escalate in direct proportion to the increasingly mundane revelations of their everyday middle-of-the-roadness'.[63] Esther's emotional identification with the Rosenbergs is based on her sense that she too is capable of looking like the right kind of person on the outside, of appearing to conform to middle-class norms of thought and action, but is in reality the kind of person whose identity is so terrible, so unacceptable to her society, that it would leave her simply no place in it.

The motif of electrocution suggests that, as Macpherson argues, it is Esther's ECT therapy that links her most closely to the Rosenbergs, as individuals punished for their failure to conform. In my view, however, it is Esther's suicide attempt which most closely expresses her sense of identification with the Jewish couple, in that she comes to see herself as she sees them, people whose true thoughts and feelings simply have no place in American society. Esther sees in the Rosenbergs her own fate – pretend to be someone else or die.

Ronald Radosh and Joyce Milton argue that if the Rosenbergs' two years of appeals against their death sentence had lasted into 1954, when the Korean War had ended and McCarthy had been censured by the Senate, it is likely that their appeals would have been successful.[64] In the early 1950s, however, following the news in August 1949 that the Soviet Union had exploded its first atomic bomb, no identity was more demonised in American ideology than that of the Communist spy. In a *Reader's Digest* article of May 1951, J. Edgar Hoover described 'The Case of the A-Bomb Spies' as 'The Crime of the Century'. It begins with a dramatic illustration of the global significance of the work of the atom spies, pictured as stereotypically shady characters, with the atoms whose secrets they have betrayed circling the world itself, with America at its centre. The title-page sets the tone of the article:

> The lives of these two men, now brought to justice, testify to the utter darkness of the Communist way . . . it blights the moral strength of man, leaving him only a puppet to be manipulated at will.[65]

The *Reader's Digest*, despite its apparently neutral form as a summary of current writing, was staunchly anti-Communist. It featured articles such as 'Why We Must Outlaw the Communist Party', 'Red Spy Masters in America' and 'The FBI Wants You', which begins, 'You have been asked by the President to help in the most important man hunt in our history – the rooting out of Communist spies in America'.[66] In 'The Communists Are After Our Minds', published in *The American Magazine* in October 1954, Hoover writes that 'the Red conspirators in our midst' are waging a 'relentless campaign to pervert our thinking and undermine our freedoms'.[67] In sentencing the Rosenbergs, Judge Irving Kaufman wrote that their crime was 'worse than murder'. Although no evidence had been presented to this effect, and although it would have been irrelevant to the crime with which they were charged if it had been presented, Kaufman argued that the Rosenbergs had 'caused . . . the Communist aggression in Korea, with the resultant casualties exceeding fifty thousand, and who knows but that millions more of innocent people may pay the price of your treason'.[68] As Communist spies, the

Rosenbergs represented the most terrible, the most unacceptable form of identity possible in Esther's society.

Ethel Rosenberg in particular represented for Plath a woman who failed to be all that society required a woman to be. Plath may have read newspaper and magazine reports, based on Ethel's apparent lack of emotion on the witness stand, that she was the dominant partner in the marriage and the conspiracy. This view reached as far as President Eisenhower, who wrote to his son that, whilst it went 'against the grain' to allow a woman to be executed, there were more important facts to consider. In particular, he wrote, Ethel was the 'strong and recalcitrant character' and her husband the 'weak one': 'she has obviously been the leader of everything they did in the spy ring'.[69] Since Ethel does not conform to Eisenhower's concept of what a woman ought to be, a member of the weaker sex, he allows himself to supersede his chivalrous instinct to protect her. Hoover, the driving force behind the convictions, who had idealised his own mother and held a highly conservative view of motherhood, was also reluctant to send Ethel to her death, until he convinced himself that she was a bad mother.[70] There was testimony to this effect at the trial.[71] In fact, although devoted to her children, Ethel had found it difficult to cope with them, and in 1949 had suffered a nervous breakdown and begun psychotherapy. Esther identifies with the Rosenbergs because, like them, and like Ethel in particular, she sees no place for herself in American society. She closely identifies with them because she feels that her inner life, her secret self, is as unacceptable to society as theirs.

Plath repeatedly expresses a fantasy in which the corruption beneath the surface of her skin is about to bubble out through her eyes. In 'Tongues of Stone', the first time she puts the events leading to her breakdown into fiction, she wrote that the heroine had been pretending for months to be 'clever' and 'gay', while in reality 'poisons were gathering in her body', which would soon 'break out behind the bright, false bubbles of her eyes', shouting to the world, 'Idiot! Imposter!' (*JPBD* 271). In her journal for November 1952, just eight months before her own trip to New York, Plath wrote of a similar fantasy of her own: she was afraid that 'the blank hell in back of my eyes will break through, spewing forth like a dark pestilence' (*J* 150). She expressed it a third time in 'Dialogue', written for Robert Gorham Davis's class in January 1953, just a month before Davis would testify before HUAC.[72] In an early draft of *The Bell Jar*, Esther's feelings are similar. She reflects that she would never be able to enter the medical profession, because she finds people who are ill, especially mentally ill, so revolting that she would want to crush them like vermin. The reason for this, she knows, is that she recognises herself in them, the real self she hides beneath the properly feminine appearance which she presents to society.[73] Although not expressed as such, it is a fantasy like this one that leads to Esther's obsession with the Rosenbergs. They represent the social truth of Esther's fantasy, similar to Plath's own and to that she gives to the heroines of 'Tongues of Stone' and 'Dialogue', that her real self, as opposed to the mask she wears for society, is so terrible that there will be no place for it in that society. Like the Rosenbergs, if the truth were known about her, she would have to be put to death. Like Ethel in particular, this is because she is simply not what society requires a woman to be.

'I Could Love a Russian Boy'

The Cold War also enters *The Bell Jar* in the person of Constantin, the Russian interpreter from the United Nations. In 1950, reflecting on the possibility of atomic war with the Soviet Union, Plath had written that she 'could love a Russian boy'. In the episode of *The Bell Jar* in which Esther attempts to seduce Constantin, she enacts precisely this claim. On her schedule for her month as a guest editor, Plath underlined the dates Tuesday, 16 June 1953 and Wednesday, 17 June, marking a Tuesday evening date with Kamirloff with a big star.[74] In her calendar for June 1953, Plath noted the events of her date with Kamirloff and gave it four stars.[75] In a letter of 21 June to her brother, Plath described Kamirloff as 'brilliant', 'wonderful', 'magnificent' and 'lovable' (*LH* 120). In *The Bell Jar*, she emphasised that Esther enjoys Constantin's company in the same way, across the ideological divide that separates American and Soviet citizens. In April 1956, Plath had a similar ideological experience when she travelled to London with the editor of Cambridge's *Varsity* magazine to attend a reception for the Soviet premier Nikita Khrushchev and prime minister Nikolai Bulganin. She described meeting a Russian businessman who told her 'what a good thing it was for Russians and Americans to get together personally and find out about each other'. If each side were to exchange a thousand students, he opined, 'there would be no trouble'.[76] Kate Baldwin has argued that in the episode of *The Bell Jar* in which Esther meets Constantin, Plath restaged the Russian–American encounter of Vice-President Richard Nixon and Secretary Khrushchev in the much-publicised 'kitchen debate' of July 1959. She sees in Esther's identification with a female Russian interpreter an illustration of the contemporary interdependence of American femininity and its Soviet other.[77] Something simpler occurs between Esther and Constantin, however: Esther believes in making love not war.

Plath emphasises that Constantin is a foreigner. Although outwardly like an American in many respects, his 'intuition' marks him out as different from any of the men from her own country Esther has dated (*BJ* 70). In an early draft of this chapter, she explicitly prefers the Soviet Constantin to the American men she meets on college campuses all over New England, with their uniform look and utter inability to understand her.[78]

In *The Bell Jar*, Constantin is an interpreter at the United Nations, a position that makes him an excellent candidate for espionage for the Soviet Union. In his anti-Communist primer, *Masters of Deceit*, Hoover specifically mentions 'Russians assigned to the United Nations' as potential Communist spies.[79] Esther sees Constantin neither as a potential spy nor as a potential enemy, however, but as a potential lover. She makes no attempt to discuss the progress of the war between UN and Communist forces in Korea, a subject which could be expected to arise between an American and a Soviet citizen as they toured the United Nations building and watched a debate between member states, especially at that crucial period in the armistice talks. Rather, the debate fades from Esther's consciousness as she thinks of the difficulties of her life as a young woman in a patriarchal society. Plath completely rejects the conflicting claims of capitalism and Communism, portraying them as simply irrelevant to Esther's concerns. In *The Bell Jar*, the Cold War is a war fought by men, American and Soviet, without reference to the interests of women. Plath expresses her most fundamental political belief in this episode, that society should be governed in the interests of women. In the face of the article 'In Defence of Chastity', which comes to her mind after her tour of the United Nations, Esther attempts only to break the patriarchal rule of female chastity.

Strange Love

This belief is also expressed in Plath's Cold War collage, which she made in the summer of 1960, some nine months before writing *The Bell Jar*. The political concerns of the two works dovetail so closely that the collage can be described as a visual illustration of the novel.[80] The central figure in the collage is President Eisenhower, who sits at his desk in the official White House portrait, holding a hand of cards, whilst a bomber flies over his head, its weapons pointed at the abdomen of a model reclining in a swimsuit beside the caption, cut from a lingerie advert, 'Every Man Wants His Woman on a Pedestal'. In the top right-hand corner of the collage, two grown men in suits are playing with a Scalextric set, whose track runs directly into the tail of the bomber. As Jacqueline Rose and Robin Peel have argued, the collage says that Eisenhower and Nixon (pictured by the American flag in Eisenhower's Office) govern a society founded on military technology, which is funded by large corporations (indicated by a job advert for an arms manufacturer on Eisenhower's desk).[81] We can add here that this military-industrial complex, according to the collage, is justified by a host of ideological discourses. First among these is religion. Plath sticks a caption in the top left of the collage which originally referred to the evangelist Billy Graham, but in her photomontage refers primarily to the President, which reads, 'America's most famous living preacher, whose religious revival campaigns have reached tens of thousands of people, both in the United States and abroad'. Eisenhower was much given to the use of religious rhetoric. He began his inauguration speech with a prayer and repeatedly used the Declaration of Independence's reference to the Creator as evidence that, in the American view, 'free government is founded primarily in a deeply-felt religious faith'.[82] Communists were 'the enemies of this faith', who 'know no god but force, no devotion but its use'. Plath needed to look no further than the next pages of *Life* magazine from which she cut this caption for the close relationship between religious rhetoric and Cold War militarism. On the pages immediately following the article by Graham, which is entitled 'Men Must Be Changed Before a Nation Can', there is a two-page spread on Rear-Admiral William Raborn, the naval officer in charge of the Polaris nuclear missile programme, which 'will be ready this summer – three years ahead of schedule'.[83] It features a photograph of the Polaris missile next to one of the rear-admiral at home with his wife, niece and dog, juxtaposing without any difficulty a picture of the ideal American family with the technology that threatens to destroy it.[84] Graham had called Douglas Macarthur 'one of the greatest Americans of all time' and claimed that Christianity had suffered a blow when President Truman dismissed him in 1951.[85] Plath found a similar complex of patriarchy and militarism at work in her experience of the Anglican Church in North Tawton. She felt that the doctrine of the Trinity preached there, unfamiliar to her as a Unitarian, was a male construct, putting the Holy Spirit in the place of the mother between the Father and the Son.[86] Three months later, she stopped attending after the rector identified the possibility of a nuclear holocaust with the second coming of Christ, an idea Plath described simply as 'insanity' (*LH* 449). According to the collage, the religious language which suffuses American society from the President down is no more than a hollow ideology, contradicting the reality of the lives of American women. The Scalextric set and the golf ball (a reference to Eisenhower's favourite pastime, at which he was frequently photographed) indicate that the military-industrial complex is a kind of macho game for overgrown boys. As Plath said of the Korean War ten years earlier, men make wars as if they were little boys playing with toy guns.[87]

Above all, in Plath's collage, war is against the interests of women and children. She expresses a similar complex of ideas to those of Stanley Kubrick's film *Dr. Strangelove*, made three years later. The 'strange love' satirised in the film is precisely the link between militant anti-Communism and patriarchy criticised in Plath's collage. Both texts make full use of the phallic symbolism of bombers and bombs, and both explicitly link these to misogynistic male fantasies. In *Dr. Strangelove*, General Jack D. Ripper, named after a killer of women, sends B52s to bomb the Soviet Union. He believes that he came to understand the nature of Communism 'during the physical act of love'. Women are to men, in Ripper's view, as Communists are to Americans: both 'sap and impurify our precious bodily fluids'; both cause 'loss of essence'. 'I don't avoid women', he says, 'but I do deny them my essence'.[88] The difference between the two works is perhaps more significant than their similarities, however. In *Dr. Strangelove*, Ripper is explicitly identified as mad. His ravings about bodily fluids are contrasted with the moderate, albeit weak, voice of the President, played by Peter Sellers to resemble Plath's preferred candidate in 1952 and 1956, Adlai Stevenson. In her 1960 collage, by contrast, there is no such moderate voice to be heard. In the world in which Eisenhower rather than Stevenson became President, the strange love of Jack D. Ripper is not that of an individual rogue general, but is shared by everyone, from the President down. All men, Plath's collage says, at least all those in power in the United States, share Ripper's love of war and hatred of women. In the society they govern, women must conform to the desire of the male gaze, like the model in the swimsuit, but in reality become the kind of worn-out drudge pictured in the bottom right-hand corner of the collage next to the caption, 'Fatigue-build-up . . . America's growing health hazard'. Plath's critique takes a positive form in the caption in red capitals on Eisenhower's desk: 'CHANGE YOUR THINKING'.

Growing Up in the Second World War

Plath had a strong sense of her German and Austrian heritage, to which little critical attention has been paid. As Langdon Hammer writes, 'Even when she seems most American, Plath is a German-American, as she was fully aware'.[89] Plath's father, Otto, was born in the Polish Corridor, or West Prussia as it was then known, a part of the German Empire, in 1885. He emigrated to America in 1900, where he learned English and became a citizen (*LH* 8). Plath's mother was the daughter of Austrian immigrants, who continued to speak German at home until Aurelia entered school. When she was five, her father taught both her and his wife English. Both of Plath's grandparents always spoke English with a German accent. Anti-German hysteria ran unchecked during the First World War, and Aurelia Schober, with her German name and 'early mispronunciations' (*LH* 4), became a target for abuse in the Italian and Irish community in which her family lived. She was 'ostracised' by the other children in the neighbourhood, who called her 'spy-face', and when she was pushed off the steps of the school bus, the driver simply ignored the fact and the bus left without her (*LH* 4). It was the study of German language and literature that brought Plath's parents together, Aurelia being Otto's student of Middle High German at Boston University. In the photograph of Otto standing at the blackboard, which Plath puts into her poem 'Daddy', he is teaching a German language lesson. Indeed, as Hammer puts it, his German textbook is 'next to his heart'.[90] In 1950, Plath wrote to her German penpal that she was always conscious of her German heritage, feeling a kind of ethnic identification with a writer like Thomas Mann.[91] Her 1953 calendar is printed in German, with a picture of a different Austrian beauty-spot for each month.[92] In May 1956, she told her mother that she has been reading Rilke's poetry and Grimms' fairy tales to Ted Hughes, first in the original German, and then translating them (*LH* 256). Aurelia had given Sylvia her 'dear' copy of *Märchen der Brüder Grimm*, inscribing it, '*für ein gutes Kind von ihrer liebenden Mutter*' ('for a good child from her loving mother').[93] In July 1958, Plath was carefully working through the text of this edition, telling her mother that she was 'extremely moved' as she thought of her Austrian and German heritage (*LH* 346). This followed an experience with the Ouija board in which the spirit Pan had told Plath to write a poem on the Germanic myth of Lorelei, one of the Rhine maidens, because these maidens are her 'own kin' (*LH* 346). In the summer of 1958, she set her children's story 'The It-Doesn't-Matter Suit' in the fictional German town of Winkelburg. The hero, Max Nix, has six brothers, two of whose German names are Plath's father's, Otto and Emil (*CCS* 17–37). In London, Plath told her mother several times how much she enjoyed the company of Daniel Huws' German wife Helga, who spoke to their baby in her native language, cooked German dishes and embodied German culture in general to Plath.[94] In the summer of 1960, Plath enjoyed meeting Helga's mother, who spoke only German, and wrote to Aurelia hoping that the two would be able to meet the following summer.[95] In late 1962 and early 1963, as her calendar shows, she was learning German over the radio.[96] In October 1962, she told Peter Orr in a radio interview, when he suggested that 'Daddy' could not have been written by a 'real American', that she was not a 'general American':

> My background is . . . German and Austrian. On one side I am a first generation American, on one side I'm second generation American.[97]

It was her German and Austrian heritage, she explained, that led to the imagery of 'concentration camps and so on' in her poetry. It was also because she was 'rather a political person', she added, explicitly linking her political concerns to her ethnic background.

Plath dealt with this background in two short stories, 'Superman and Paula Brown's New Snowsuit' and 'The Shadow'. The first was written for Alfred Kazin's class in the Fall semester of 1954, and was published in the *Smith Review* the following spring. The second was written in Boston in December 1958 and January 1959 for submission to literary periodicals like the *New Yorker* and the *London Magazine*. In both stories, an injustice done to the narrator by another child, and by the neighbourhood to her family, is set in the contexts of the international horrors of the Second World War – both narrators see a propaganda film of Japanese guards torturing Allied prisoners-of-war – and of the injustices done to the German community in the United States. In 'Superman and Paula Brown's New Snowsuit', the narrator recalls the family anxiously listening to the radio each night after America's entry into the war. Uncle Frank believes that German citizens in the United States will be imprisoned while the war lasts, and the narrator's mother can only repeat, 'I'm only glad Otto didn't live to see this' (*JPBD* 155). The Smith Act of 1940 required all aliens resident in the United States to register for an internal passport, have their fingerprints taken and submit to questions about their political beliefs and activities. Once war was declared, all German residents were declared 'alien enemies', required to carry certificates of identification and forbidden to travel by air or to possess firearms or radios. Although less well known than the forced relocation of over 100,000 Japanese-Americans from the West Coast during the war, the FBI arrested over 6,000 German aliens during the war, and detained them in some fifty internment camps across the United States.[98] Plath knew about these camps from Gordon Lameyer, whom she dated between 1953 and 1955. Lameyer's father was a German citizen and had been interned in one of these detention camps. In notes for his unpublished memoir, *Dear Sylvia*, Lameyer writes that

neither his nor Plath's father had been Nazi sympathisers, but that both had been proud of their German heritage, an unpopular position to take in America in the late 1930s. Although Lameyer's father had lived in the United States since 1928 and had returned to Germany only once to visit his mother, he was interned for three and a half years. Lameyer adds that, in his view, Plath saw his German father as a surrogate for her own.[99] When Plath told herself in her journal to read about the 'German concentration, I mean American detention camps' (*J* 475) which she puts into both 'Superman and Paula Brown's New Snowsuit' and 'The Shadow', it was to Lameyer's reminiscences that she was referring.

Commenting on Plath's high school projects, Langdon Hammer writes, 'Memories of World War II colour Plath's sense of the post-war world'.[100] 'Superman and Paula Brown's New Snowsuit' and 'The Shadow' make it clear that prominent among these memories are Plath's recollections of the injustices done to German Americans during the war. These injustices, as well as those of the war itself, are an essential part of the loss of the childhood sense of justice Plath describes in these two stories. The first is based on an autobiographical event. When Plath wrote to her mother about reading the story to her creative writing class, she reported that it was based on the real episode of 'Paula Brown's snowsuit' (*LH* 148). In both stories, the narrator loses the belief she had as a young child in the inevitable triumph of good over evil she read about and listened to each week in stories of heroes like Superman and the Shadow. At the beginning of 'Superman and Paula Brown's New Snowsuit', not only does the narrator dream about the superhero and act out his exploits in games, but he also seems to have a real presence in the world in the person of Uncle Frank, who bears an 'extraordinary resemblance' to him (*JPBD* 155). When war is declared, however, not even this heroic figure can prevent the internment of innocent German-Americans; he simply says that they may be detained while the war lasts. In both stories, Plath portrays the evil the narrator learns about in her experience of the Second World War destroying the sense of justice she has learned from her superhero comics. In 'Superman and Paula Brown's New Snowsuit', she sees a war film about Japanese soldiers sadistically tormenting their prisoners-of-war. Although she had previously dreamed every night about Superman, this film gives her a sense of evil so real that it expels the fictional superhero from her dreams. The atrocities committed in the war, as well as the injustices done to German-Americans, shatter the narrator's sense, which she identifies as a child's sense, of justice. With the war, she grows up, coming to disbelieve in imaginary heroes and in the justice they embody. The childish injustice of the episode of Paula Brown's new snowsuit takes place in the wider context of the evils of the war in which it occurs, and the two events are not distinct in the story of the end of the narrator's childhood. The heroic Uncle Frank, unlike Superman, can right neither wrong – he cannot prevent America entering the war nor its internment of innocent German aliens; nor can he see justice done in the neighbourhood over the snowsuit – he agrees to buy Paula a new snowsuit, even though the narrator was not responsible for spoiling the last one. As war is declared, she is left with the sense that not only is Superman a childish fiction, but so is the justice that he never fails to execute. Her dreams of both vanish into oblivion in the darkness of her bedroom at the end of the story. She concludes simply, 'That was the year the war began, and the real world, and the difference' (*JPBD* 160).

In 'Superman and Paula Brown's New Snowsuit', local and the international events are fused only in the narrator's consciousness. There is no explicit connection made between the German-American internment camps of which Uncle Frank speaks and the neighbourhood's belief that it is the narrator, rather than Paula Brown, who is lying. In 'The Shadow', the connection is made explicit. After an incident similar to that in 'Superman and Paula Brown's New Snowsuit', in which the narrator, Sadie Shafer, is accused unfairly of biting another child, the neighbourhood adults again believe the other children's version of the story over hers and ostracise her family as a result. Again, this incident occurs during America's entry into the war. This time, however, the two events are linked. Not only do the neighbours cut their ties with Sadie's family, they do so because they are a German family. On the way to school, Sadie is told as much by the angelic Maureen Kelly. 'It's not your fault for biting Leroy', Maureen tells her, 'My mother says it's because your father is German' (*JPBD* 341). With America's declaration of war against Germany, and the institutional declaration of German citizens like Sadie's father as alien enemies, a childish squabble quickly descends into racism among the parents. Suddenly, everything different about the object of this racism adds to his evil in the eyes of the community. When Sadie protests that her father is from the Polish Corridor, Maureen insists, 'He's German . . . Besides, he doesn't go to church' (*JPBD* 341). This prejudice against German-Americans occurs at the local level because it is sanctioned institutionally. Sadie's father has been required to leave his family and go to an internment camp for German-Americans. When she returns home from school, expecting her mother to explain why Maureen Kelly was wrong to slander him, Sadie is surprised that she cannot. 'In one way', her mother says, 'he is' German, exactly as Maureen had charged (*JPBD* 342).

Unlike the narrator of 'Superman and Paula Brown's New Snowsuit',

Sadie has generalised the lesson she had learned each week from the Shadow's radio programme, that 'crime does *not* pay', into a view of American society. She has come to think of the 'powers of good', arrayed in 'circle after concentric circle' around her: 'the FBI, the President, the American Armed Forces' and even the superheroes of her childhood culture. All ultimately circled by 'God himself' (*JPBD* 341). With America's entry into the war, however, Sadie's sense that society constitutes these concentric circles of justice is shattered. She had felt that there was something missing from this view of the world when she had seen the propaganda film about the Japanese guards. When she realises that the kind of irremediable injustice of which the film first made her aware occurs in America too, to her and her family, she realises what was missing. The concentric circles of justice are a childish fiction, just as the Shadow is. Although as pleasant a story as those of the Shadow's perpetual defeat of evil, in the reality of war, they simply do not hold. Plath ends the story with a sense of a completely empty world, without any of the institutional guarantees of justice in which children alone believe. She tells her mother she does not believe that 'there is any God' if 'such things can happen'. Her mother responds simply, '"Some people think that"' (*JPBD* 344).

Chapter 4

Gender and Society in *The Bell Jar*

'We're stargazers this season, bewitched by an atmosphere of evening blue'.[1] Thus begins the text Plath wrote for '*Mademoiselle*'s Last Word on College', the summary of the work she and her fellow guest editors had done on *Mademoiselle*'s 1953 College Edition. The text goes on, in the characteristic extended metaphor of the fashion blurb, to speak about what the editors see in the 'fashion constellation', the 'astronomic versatility' of sweaters, and to praise *Mademoiselle* as the 'star of the campus'. It appears beneath a photograph of the twenty guest editors dressed in the fashions to which the text refers, standing in the shape of a star, with Plath herself at the top. The page embodies Plath's complex relationship to the gender discourses in which she grew up, showing that she could write fluently, indeed appear with her entire person, in precisely the kind of discourse against which her work is also a protest. The College Board Contest, the competition Plath won in order to become a guest editor, was advertised the year she entered as 'a step ahead on a career', 'a trail blazer for the future' and 'real brain work'.[2] The twenty guest editors, in the issue on which Plath worked, were said to be 'the best, the very best' of college students from across the country.[3] Nonetheless, the crowning achievement of this elite contest is the kind of vacuous fashion blurb, 'silver and full of nothing', as Plath put it in *The Bell Jar* (*BJ* 95), that she wrote for the 'Last Word on College'. An advert in the same issue is headed 'S^n', which the copy explains: 'Separates raised to the highest power, that's what this symbol says'.[4] The mathematical symbol is posited as an example of the kind of intellectual discourse with which a college student can be expected to be familiar, but is instantly emptied out, for female students, into the discourse of fashion and beauty. The advert goes on, 'To quote the girls at Sarah Lawrence, who are modelling, "Separates save our lives"'.[5] In the next two chapters, I examine Plath's fiction in the cultural context of the gender discourses within which she lived, thought and wrote. In this

chapter, I focus on *The Bell Jar*, and in the next on her short stories. In both cases, I argue that her fiction is as complex a body of work as these discourses themselves.

Sex

Plath grew up, dated, had relationships with men and married in a time in which expert opinion on marriage, sexuality and family life was almost universally regarded as a discourse possessing all the authority of science. This was the period of the 'expert' in marriage and family life, which began with the marriage education movement on college campuses in the 1930s and flourished until second-wave feminism rejected its claims to objectivity in the mid-1960s. As Beth Bailey writes, in her history of courtship in twentieth-century America:

> The new arbiters of convention were academics – social scientists in the main – who sought to bring youth's experience in courtship and marriage under the authority of educators and experts . . . Hundreds of thousand of students passed through their classrooms and read their textbooks, popularised versions of their scientific expertise reached the general population through mass-circulation magazines.[6]

The consensus of expert opinion was overwhelmingly against premarital sex as damaging, both to the individual and to society as a whole.[7] One of the most popular marriage textbooks during the 1950s was Judson and Mary Landis's *Building a Successful Marriage*, which went through seven editions between 1948 and 1977. In the 1953 edition, the authors argue against premarital sex on several grounds. It leads to 'mental and emotional conflict' in girls; it is a mistake to believe that sexual experimentation prepares a couple for marriage, in fact, the opposite is true: 'there is a strong possibility that their ability to achieve psychic union as well as physical after marriage will be limited'; overemphasis on sex before marriage can lead to a misguided choice of partner with whom you have nothing but sex in common; and you will acquire habits of self-gratification that you may not be able to unlearn after marriage.[8] Many sections of the chapter on premarital sex are not based on research data but are ethical views, given the appearance of scientific fact by the citation of such data elsewhere in the book. In *Making the Most of Marriage*, another social science textbook, Paul Landis presents a similar argument, concluding, 'Evidence available to date suggests that marriages of the chaste are most successful under the culture pattern of the United States'.[9] The message is the same in the advice manuals for a more popular audience. In *Woman's Guide to Better Living*, from 1957, Dr John Schindler compares premarital sex to opium-smoking and an 'uncontrolled automobile' in its capacity for harm. He writes:

> The reasons for social regulations and tabus in this field of sex are intrinsically sound and they cannot be thrown out without destroying human society.[10]

Plath herself encountered this discourse in many forms. In her first semester at college, she attended a talk on 'Sex Before Marriage' by Dr Peter Bertocci from Boston University, a philosopher of religion who had published a book on sexual ethics for college students the previous year, entitled *The Human Venture in Love, Sex and Marriage*. In this book, Bertocci argues that sexual experience, in order to contribute to the good life as a whole, must be reserved for the loving and responsible context of marriage and the home, which are 'among the supreme values of human existence'. Premarital sex is, 'in the light of all the demands that life is to make upon one', an obstacle to the experience of 'mutuality', 'the desire to express physically the unity that [two people] feel spiritually', that sexual relations express within marriage. It erodes the confidence of each partner in the other to control themselves in the name of an ethical principle, even that of the other's good; it can prevent sex from expressing a mutual desire for unity with a future spouse; it can cause the break-up of otherwise constructive relationships; it can lead to pregnancy; and this last fact is a constant emotional burden, especially to the woman. Bertocci concludes:

> When [two people's] love for each other can *include their biological without excluding their social interests*, their self-respect, their mutual exploration of values, their ambitions and responsibilities, then, indeed, it can be a continued blessing.[11]

When Plath heard Bertocci's talk at Smith the following year, she wrote to her mother that she admired his not 'dodging the issue' and that she was quickly 'lost in the sound maze of his contentions' (*LH* 58). Getting lost in a maze is an odd metaphor with which to describe following a logically persuasive argument, and it seems to connote a simultaneous rejection of the argument along with the socially required acceptance of it. Bertocci's book uses specific examples with which to illustrate his ethical arguments, and Plath told her mother that he used the same device in his paper at Smith, inviting students to conclude for themselves, on the basis of real-life examples, that premarital sex was harmful. She accepted his 'cold, clear logic', she wrote, in part because 'Emile' was not there to 'make my emotions fight reason' (*LH* 58). The Emile to whom Plath referred was the college junior whom she had seen four times the previous summer. She recorded their first date in her journal as a deep experience of the effects of the double standard of sexual morality on women. She was very attracted to him, and when he tried to seduce her late in the evening, she wanted to respond to his advances, but knew that the social consequences of doing so made it impossible. At one point, Emile asked her if she was feeling all right, to which she recorded her unspeakable thoughts in her journal, 'Oh yes. Yes, thank you' (*J* 15). In reality, though, she could not act on these thoughts – she broke away from his embrace, and he took her home. The long, erotic account of the date in her journal can in no way be reduced to the duality between emotions and reason in whose terms she later referred to the experience, in the light of Dr Bertocci's talk at Smith, to her mother. There is no sense in the journal that it would be irrational, wrong or unpleasant to have slept with Emile. It is the fear of the social consequences of pregnancy that kept Plath from doing as she desired, and she expresses no sense that these consequences, and the ethical standards from which they follow, are rational or justified. Two years later, as she wrote to Ann Davidow about Dick Norton's revelation that he had slept with several women, she drew the same conclusion. It is not the fact that Norton had had several sexual partners that infuriated her, but the fact that contemporary social standards did not allow women to do the same.[12] Her response to the double standard is a structural protest – 'the whole thing sickens me' (*J* 10). It is the entire system of institutions and discourses by which the double standard was maintained that Plath found irrational, and not at all the female sexuality which was inscribed within them.

Aurelia Plath wrote that the Emile to whom Plath referred in her letter home was the date on whom her story 'Den of Lions' was based (*LH* 58–9). In this story, Plath transforms the sexual conflict she recorded in her journal into an entirely social conflict, in which the heroine has to hold her own socially against the cruel and mocking attitudes of Emile's older, more sophisticated friends. At one point Plath uses the same words she used in her journal to describe the erotic encounter to refer to the social encounter in the story – 'I had gone under twice; I was drowning'.[13] In the journal, this phrase referred to her overwhelming attraction to Emile as she danced with him; but in the story, the dance is only very slightly erotic – indeed, as they dance, 'Marcia felt the fragments of her composure come back again' after the intense verbal conflict with his friends – and the words refer to her feelings during precisely that conflict. The end of the story is based on Plath and Emile's final encounter, later in the summer of 1950, in which they parted. In the story, in response to Emile's words, 'I like you, but not too much. I don't want to like anybody too much', Marcia replies, 'I'm not going to see you any more'.[14] In reality, however, when Emile spoke these words, Plath herself 'blurted' – in comparison to Marcia, who could either 'bid or pass' – 'I like people too much or not at all' (*J* 18). In response, Emile told her that she would never know him, and she commented simply, 'So that was it; the end' (*J* 18). All the emotions are displaced from the erotic encounter in the journal to the social encounter in the story. Some passages in the story seem to have a coded sexual significance as a result, such as Marcia's reflection that 'no matter how much she liked Emile . . . she would never pay the price', which would mean having to 'compromise things that were intangible, yet terribly important'.[15] The differences between the journal entry and the story which is based closely on it indicate two things concerning Plath's sense of her situation within the ideology of sexual ethics at this early stage of her writing life. First, female sexuality seems unspeakable to her, just as contemporary ideology told her that it was. If she is to publish a story about the conflict she feels towards Emile, it cannot directly deal with the conflict between desire and the double standard that she recorded in the privacy of her journal, but must be transposed into the less transgressive register of social relationships. Second, the story represents a place in which Plath can portray a young woman in control of her relationships to men, since these relationships are not sexual. In reality, at least as she recorded it in her journal, Plath felt only just in control of the conflict between desire and the double standard. It is only in her maturer fiction, such as *The Bell Jar*, that she felt able to portray this conflict as such. In 1951, the conflict between the reality and the ideology of female sexuality was such that it remained entirely unspeakable in the kind of fiction that Plath could imagine publishing.

Despite her rejection of the entire culture in which the double standard was allowed to flourish, it is the experts' advice that comes to Plath's mind during an experience she recorded in December 1950, in which an older date, a war veteran from Amherst in his twenties, attempted to force himself on her. As Plath described this incident in her journal, she recalled that although the man was attractive, she knew, '"Once a woman has intercourse, she isn't satisfied." "You need time and security for full pleasure"' (*J* 42). Plath frequently heard the advice that pre-marital sex can lead a woman to become over-attached to her lover. She wrote to Ann Davidow, in a way that assumes that Ann would feel the same way, that she did not want to let her desires control her relationship with Dick Norton to such an extent that she would either be forced to marry him or never to see him and his family again.[16] In an early draft of *The Bell Jar*, Esther's mother warns her that a woman becomes a kind

of emotional slave to the first man she sleeps with.[17] It is thoughts like these that came to Plath's mind in the experience that she described in her journal. Plath initially cursed the man for to trying to take advantage of her because he was 'never worried about having babies' (*J* 42). Real as this fear was to Plath, her words sounded superficial to her, as if she were 'playing a part' (*J* 42). So she began 'explaining weakly how it is', telling him that, whilst attracted to him, the social consequences of sex for her made it impossible. The conflict Plath felt over the situation is physically evident in her journal as she recorded and re-recorded it. Having initially written, 'You will go out with him again if he asks' at the end of this account, she changed the word 'will' to 'won't'. Her final sentences had been 'But you will see him if he asks again. You are a girl'. Here she changed 'But you will' to 'And you won't', and deleted the final sentence, which she had originally underlined, altogether (*J* 43, 678).[18] Despite seeming to have resolved this conflict verbally, in fact Plath did see the man again (*J* 678). Plath's experience of sexuality under the double standard was a highly conflicted one – one about which she could not adequately speak or write, not to her mother, and ultimately not even to herself.

In her notes for the talk she gave at the Wellesley College Club, Aurelia Plath recorded that she and her daughter read widely together on the subject of sexual ethics, including books by Havelock Ellis, Bertrand Russell and Langdon Davies' *Short History of Women*. They discussed the work of Margaret Sanger, 'the unfairness of the double standard and the forces that lay behind it', and the cultural variation of sexual ethics. Aurelia taught her children that sex was 'a serious commitment with another's life', which should only be entered into once they had allowed themselves to 'develop a degree of maturity', which meant at least completing their college educations. She added finally, 'The decision had to be theirs'.[19] In *The Bell Jar*, Esther's mother sends her an article from the *Reader's Digest* called 'In Defence of Chastity' (*BJ* 76). This is a fictional transformation of an event in Plath's own life, in which Aurelia gave her a book called *The Case for Chastity* by the novelist Margaret Culkin Banning, which was also published in a shorter form in the *Reader's Digest* (*J* 432).[20]

Banning's book is a brisk, no-nonsense essay, based on the author's sense of contemporary research in psychology and sociology, on the many individual and social dangers of premarital sex. In addition to the risks of venereal disease, unwanted pregnancy, the infection and death that can follow an abortion, Banning claims that 'petting' (that is, forms of sexual contact other than sexual intercourse) creates habits of satisfaction that make it impossible to adjust to 'normal marriage relations'. For girls who pet, 'the chances of satisfaction and compatibility in marriage are very poor' – indeed, 'many of such cases are in danger of becoming perverts'. She discusses the 'serious' 'effect of unchastity on the nervous system' caused by the stealth, hurry, unpleasant surroundings, fear of discovery and guilt associated with premarital sex. Girls who break their own and society's codes in this way can become hardened into liars, obsessed with guilt, lonely, socially outcast, and although 'many of them would have made fine wives or mothers', they are usually deserted by a man who ultimately 'preferred a virgin for a wife'. Such women may become promiscuous, feel inferior and be unable to enjoy sex even if they do later marry. In short, premarital sex 'will almost surely have a perma-nent effect on the life of any girl involved and . . . in most cases alters her psychology as well as her physiology'.[21] Although *The Case for Chastity* strongly advocates chastity for both sexes, Banning's book is aimed primarily at female readers, and she acknowledges a kind of historical inevitability to the double standard. 'Any law which approaches a single standard of morality for men and for women, is almost impossible to enact'.[22] Indeed, Banning claims that there is an 'ancient instinct' which 'makes a man prefer a virgin for a wife'.

There is one major difference between the real and the fictional article. In *The Bell Jar*, Esther says that the 'main point' of the article her mother gives her is that 'a man's world is different from a woman's world', as are a man's 'emotions' from a woman's, and that it is only by marrying that men and women can live together happily (*BJ* 76). This is not the main point of Banning's book. In just one paragraph – the only paragraph in which she makes a feminist point, namely that men make the laws about sex, although they don't keep them themselves – Banning speaks about a difference in the reasons men and women have for for-mulating sexual ethics:

> Women think of their own personal protection and that of their individual children in influencing and upholding marriage codes. Men think of the safety of the race.[23]

This is as close as Banning gets to saying that a man's world is differ-ent from a woman's, or that the same is true of man's emotions and a woman's, and this is the sum total of her thoughts on the subject. Perry Norton told Plath in spring 1951 of his mother's view that women want 'infinite security', men a 'mate', and that 'both look for different things' (*J* 54), a statement Plath took and used in *The Bell Jar*. Wherever she heard the view that a man's world is different from a woman's as an argument against premarital sex, Plath used it in the novel as an example of the kind of discourse used by women who have bought into patriarchy against the interests of women like Esther who want to criticise and change it.

Plath received her mother's advice on the double standard, along with her gift of Banning's book, as a life-denying experience. In her therapy notes, she listed her mother's giving her the book and her advice on virginity as two of the reasons for which she hated her. Tim Kendall has argued that *The Bell Jar* 'might . . . be described as a misogynistic text, were it not that the male characters are no more attractive'.[24] As an account of the novel as a whole, I disagree with this claim, but it is never more true than when Esther describes the women in her society who compromise and collude with the double standard. Before providing the financial assistance which buys Esther the kind of care with which she can recover from her breakdown, Mrs Guinea sends a telegram asking, 'Is there a boy in the case?' (*BJ* 178). She 'couldn't, of course, have anything to do with it', Esther observes drily, if this was the case (*BJ* 178). In the correspondence between Aurelia Plath and Olive Higgins Prouty, on whom the character of Mrs Guinea is based, there is no communication to this effect, neither in the telegram Prouty sent to Aurelia when she first heard that Plath had been found, nor in the longer letter she sent that day. She says, 'If I am to help in any way, I must know all the facts', but this refers to the medical treatment Plath was receiving.[25] In her reply, Aurelia gave Prouty all the medical details she asked for, but made no attempt to deny that a relationship with a man had contributed to Plath's breakdown. In fact, the words were Aurelia's own. The *Boston Herald*'s report on Plath's disappearance, of which Aurelia kept two copies, reads, 'Chief MacBey quoted Mrs Plath as saying "There is no question of a boy in the case"'.[26] Plath made a deliberate aesthetic choice in *The Bell Jar* to emphasise how widely the double standard of sexual ethics is accepted and enforced by women in Esther's society. With the exception of the period following her split from Dick Norton, Plath seems to have admired his mother, on whom the character of Mrs Willard is based. In 1959, after visiting her, she told Aurelia how much she liked Mrs Norton's brisk, outgoing character.[27] In the novel, Mrs Willard puts the beautiful rug she has made out of her husband's discarded woollen clothes on the kitchen floor, where it is trampled on by an unappreciative family. In reality, Mrs Norton's rugs were admired and treasured even after her death by her family.[28] The portrayal of anti-feminist characters like Mrs Willard and Mrs Guinea in *The Bell Jar* derives much less from the actual women on whom they are based than from a conscious aesthetic choice by Plath to emphasise how deeply women in Esther's society buy into the double standard, and so how difficult it is for a young woman like Esther to articulate a protest against it.

Medicine

One of the major factors in Esther's recovery is her prescription for contraception, an event which was also part of Plath's therapy.[29] It was illegal to use, prescribe or give out information about contraception in Massachusetts in 1954 – it only became legal in 1967 for married women and in 1972 for single women like Esther. Contraception is an experience of 'freedom', for Esther, in which she becomes her 'own woman' (*BJ* 213), but in order to take possession of her own body in this way, she has to break the law. Plath's critique of the patriarchal laws and discourses that criminalise contraception is part of the wider critique she articulates in the novel of the institutions of science, medicine and psychiatry, which form a kind of continuum in and through which a society run by men defines and controls women. It is in particular the politics of medical science to which Plath draws attention in *The Bell Jar*, pre-empting the more explicit and theoretical feminist critiques of the health care institutions that were developed in the 1960s and 1970s. As John Ehrenreich argues, these feminist critiques were part of a series of discourses – including the work of black and socialist critics – on the institutional practices of medicine in the US during this period. He identifies these discourses as a 'cultural critique' of modern medicine, which argues not so much for a more equitable distribution of existing resources in health care as for fundamental changes in the way that health care is practised. He sums this critique up as follows:

> Modern medical care . . . does not consist of the administration by doctors of a group of morally neutral, essentially benign and effective techniques . . . The 'scientific' knowledge of the doctors is sometimes not knowledge at all, but rather social messages . . . wrapped up in technical language.[30]

In Irving Zola's words, modern medicine has become an 'institution of social control', replacing and to an extent incorporating the traditional institutions of religion and the law:

> [Medicine] is becoming the new repository of truth, the place where absolute and often final judgements are made by supposedly morally neutral and objective experts . . . in the name of health.[31]

In a technological and bureaucratic society, Zola argues, which 'has led us down the path of the reluctant reliance on the expert', the medical profession has become an unquestioned source of expertise and authority over an increasingly wide area of human existence.

Feminists have paid particular attention to the power exercised over women by the institution of obstetrics and gynaecology. In a study of gynaecology textbooks from 1943 to 1972, Diana Scully and Pauline Bart argue that 'gynaecology is just another of the forces committed to the maintenance of traditional sex-role stereotypes, in the interest of men and from a male perspective'.[32] Scully sums up their findings as follows:

> Women were portrayed as most appropriately fitting into traditional sex roles: anatomically destined for motherhood, they were fulfilled as people only by reproducing, mothering, and attending to their husbands.[33]

Scully and Bart found a tendency, from the 1940s through to the 1970s, for gynaecology textbooks to define pregnancy as a 'step towards maturity', and to castigate in psychiatric terms women who refused this traditional role as expressing 'unconscious anxiety, conflict or inadequacy'. Before Kinsey's 1953 study, they found women described as much less sexually responsive than men and as finding sexual pleasure above all in reproduction and mothering. Even after Kinsey, his findings were used selectively, so that 'the textbooks often state that the male sets the sexual pace in marital coitus . . . but nowhere is it mentioned that women are multiorgasmic – a Kinsey finding which raises questions concerning the stronger male sex drive'.[34] Even after Masters and Johnson's work in the 1960s, there are textbooks which define the female sex drive and personality as passive and submissive. Scully and Bart cite a text from 1968 which states, 'An important feature of sex desire in the man is the urge to dominate the woman and subjugate her to his will; in the woman acquiescence to the masterful takes a high place'.[35] As Gena Corea puts it, in her study of the sexual politics of the American medical institution in the 1970s:

> Gynaecologists . . . could control women through medical theories that were assumed to be scientific discoveries but which were, in fact, permeated with stereotypes about women's nature and role.[36]

In *The Bell Jar*, Plath expresses this feminist critique of the medical institutions with which her characters interact. She is most critical of obstetrics and gynaecology as a patriarchal institution, in which men alienate women from themselves by assuming control, under the beneficent guise of care, of women's bodies. Her critique is at its most explicit during the scenes in which Buddy takes Esther to watch a woman give birth in a teaching hospital. Plath herself had been to the Boston Lying-In Hospital with Dick Norton during the Christmas vacation of 1951–52. She later wrote that she had been afraid of giving birth herself ever since this episode, 'having seen a ghastly delivery in a charity ward in Boston at a very impressionable age'.[37] In *The Bell Jar*, Esther describes the delivery table as an instrument of torture: the very sight of its 'stirrups', 'instruments', 'wires' and 'tubes', making it look like a 'torture table', strikes her dumb (*BJ* 61). In an early draft of this section, Esther notices that the woman being lifted on to the table looked very badly disfigured. She was making a noise that reminded Esther of a bull she had once seen slaughtered in an especially cruel bullfight in Spain.[38] Plath did not have available the work of feminists who argued in the 1970s that the lithotomy position in which Esther sees this woman (lying on her back, with her knees drawn up and spread wide apart by 'stirrups'), according to contemporary research, was used only because it was more convenient for the obstetrician, and that it 'tends to alter the normal foetal environment and obstruct the normal process of childbearing, making spontaneous birth more difficult or impossible'.[39] She can see clearly, however, that the woman has become a passive, inert object of the institution of obstetrics, and that the obstetrician has become the subject of the process of birth. As Adrienne Rich recalls her own experience of childbirth in the 1950s, 'We were, above all, in the hands of male medical technology'.[40]

Plath emphasises the wresting of control of the process of birth from the woman Esther sees with her dehumanisation. She is first described as 'a trolley with a big white lump on it'. Even as Esther gets to see her more closely, she is just an 'enormous spider-fat stomach' with 'two little ugly spindly legs', making an 'unhuman whooing noise' (*BJ* 61). In the second draft, Plath tried ten synonyms to describe this noise, one of them twice.[41] Even her final choice, 'unhuman', retains in its awkward solecism Plath's sense of how little the woman's experience can be understood and expressed in her society's discourse. As the Boston Women's Health Book Collective wrote ten years later, 'In medicine there is scarcely any woman's viewpoint, and very little – if any – language for that viewpoint'.[42] The woman needs an episiotomy, because 'the baby's head stuck for some reason' (*BJ* 62), possibly because of the lithotomy position in which she had been placed. As Doris Haire points out, one of the disadvantages of this position for the mother is to 'increase the need for episiotomy because of the increased tension on the pelvic floor and the stretching of the perineal tissue'.[43] By the time she has been cut and stitched, the mother in Plath's account remains, as she began, a semiconscious, inert object in the birth of her own child, control of which has been entirely assumed by male medical technology. When one of the attendants finally tells her the sex of the baby, she does not even 'raise her head' (*BJ* 63).

Plath's critique of this technology is most explicit as she portrays Esther's reaction to Buddy's account of the effects of the Twilight Sleep medication given to the woman during the delivery. On this medication, a mixture of the analgesic morphine and the amnesiac scopolamine, women screamed and thrashed in pain during delivery, but woke with no memory of the experience.[44] When it first became known in the United States in 1914, following an article in *McClure's* magazine, women's rights activists quickly organised a national campaign to promote its use.[45] In her 1915 book on Twilight Sleep, journalist Hanna Rion urged, 'Take up the battle for painless childbirth where I have left off . . . Fight not only for yourselves but fight for your sister-mothers, your sex, the cradle of the human race'.[46] Women of Plath's generation, however, took a different view. Grantly Dick-Read's book *Childbirth Without Fear*, published in 1945, had popularised the idea of 'natural child-birth' and the elimination of unnecessary medical interference. Plath's copy indicates that she was not impressed with Dick-Read's patriarchal views.[47] Indeed, she was 'disgusted' with his claim that childbirth is not fundamentally physical and his tendency to '[go] ga-ga over the Spiritual Nobility etc. of it all'.[48] Nevertheless, she took his specific prescriptions, such as those on diet, seriously and methodically. Although she had had some initial concerns, partly because her Wellesley doctor had warned her against it, Plath was extremely happy with her experience of home birth.[49] There was none of the 'impressive flashing' of medical technol-ogy and personnel that occurred in the United States, she told Lynne Lawner, but just a 'primitive homeliness', which did her a great deal of good.[50] In *The Bell Jar*, written between the births of her two children, she took a critical view of Twilight Sleep, calling it 'the sort of drug a man would invent' (*BJ* 62). In an early draft of the novel, Esther had added that it deceived women into repeated experiences of agony, and that it preyed on her mind afterwards.[51] In 'Sweetie Pie and the Gutter Men', which she called her 'obstetrician story' (*J* 499), the heroine is similarly critical of Twilight Sleep, describing it as a 'fraud' invented by men to keep women producing children for them. She reflects that women should 'refuse childbearing altogether' in the face of such treat-ment (*JPBD* 354). By 1961, Plath had come to see obstetrics, even at the very point which had seemed to be a positive development to an earlier generation of feminists, as an institution of patriarchal control. As Gena Corea would write fifteen years later, 'the doctor's motive in treatment was something other than the woman's well-being, something connected to his view of woman's function in his world'.[52]

Esther also has a gynaecological examination after her first sexual encounter leaves her haemorrhaging. Plath portrays this examination as a similarly structured power relationship to those involved in the birth scene. The doctor makes no attempt to hide his surprise as he treats Esther, saying, '"It's one in million it happens to like this"'. When she asks if he can stop the bleeding, he is amused, and replies, '"Oh I can fix it, all right' (*BJ* 223). The doctor's amusement, his use of the neuter pronoun and his unwillingness to address Esther as a responsible adult are all depersonalising experiences. He establishes no caring or supportive relationship with her, a fact that Diana Scully noticed was still built into the training of obstetrician-gynaecologists in the 1970s. In a three-year study of residents in obstetrics and gynaecology in two large US teaching hospitals, she observed, 'Residents were not encouraged to treat women in a positive or supporting way. No attempt was made to understand the problems and stresses of concern to women'.[53] She argues that the lack of care structured into the training programme of obstetrician-gynaecologists tends to foster this attitude once residents graduate into professional practice:

> When training takes place in an atmosphere of uncaring, where patients are treated like objects to be exploited for their training value, the attitudes acquired become a permanent part of the physician's pattern of relating to people.[54]

This is precisely the kind of depersonalising gynaecological care that Esther receives twenty years earlier. Nancy Hunter Steiner, in her recollection of the event on which the fictional episode is based, writes that the doctor who treated Plath for the same kind of haemorrhage that Esther experiences attempted to put her at ease – 'The doctor kept up an easy banter, encouraging us to relax . . . He flashed us a conspiratorial smile'.[55] Indeed, Steiner recalls that his words conveyed precisely the opposite of those Plath puts in the mouth of the gynaecologist in *The Bell Jar*, and that he said, 'Don't start thinking you're exceptional. I've seen a number of cases just like yours'.[56] The problems of biography in reading Plath's work are well documented, and it would be wrong to assume that Steiner's recollection, nineteen years after the event, is simply true. Whatever the nature of the experiences on which Plath drew as she wrote this episode, however, she wanted to convey in her novel her sense of the gender politics at work in the institution of obstetrics and gynaecology.

Psychiatry

Plath reserved her strongest critique of the gender politics of health care in *The Bell Jar* for the institution of psychiatry. Maria Farland has argued that the novel shares the concerns of the anti-psychiatry movement of the 1960s.[57] In my view, this is true only to the extent that feminists in the 1970s used the work of anti-psychiatrists to develop a specifically gendered critique of the institution of psychiatry. These critics argued that psychiatry is a patriarchal practice, which, in Phyllis Chesler's words, posits 'certain misogynistic views of women and of sex-role stereotypes as "scientific" or "curative"'.[58] Chesler's *Women and Madness* was the first major feminist critique of psychiatry. She makes several points there which resonate closely with Plath's concerns in *The Bell Jar*. First, the statistics concerning gender in the psychiatric profession during the period of Plath's encounters with it are significant. In 1960, 91 per cent of the American Psychiatric Association were men, as were some 85 per cent of clinical psychologists.[59] Women, on the other hand, 'constituted the majority of private psychotherapy patients, as well as the majority of patients in general psychiatric wards, private hospitals, public outpatient clinics, and community mental health centers'.[60] Hence, Chesler writes, 'A predominantly female psychiatric population has been diagnosed, psychoanalysed, researched, and hospitalized by a predominantly male professional population'.[61] Second, she argues that these statistics reflect the way in which psychiatrists diagnose and treat women. Drawing on her own experience of psychiatric training in the 1960s, Chesler argues that professional training encourages psychiatrists to think and act professionally in ways that, under the guise of scientific objectivity, reinforce patriarchal and misogynistic beliefs and practices. She describes this as 'clinical ideology', the 'major biases' of which are clearly evident in Plath's portrayal of psychiatry. The first of these biases is that 'everyone is sick'. Citing a 1968 study which shows a predisposition in psychiatrists to diagnose mental illness where it did not in fact exist, Chesler writes, 'Most clinician-theorists are trained to find "pathology" everywhere: in women, in children, in men, in nations, in entire historical epochs'.[62] This is the case in *The Bell Jar*. When Esther scatters the torn-up pieces of her badly written letter to Doreen on Dr Gordon's desk, there is no question in the latter's mind that she may be responding in a normal way to an extremely difficult situation. Although Esther explains her anger as a response to the fact that Dr Gordon was 'slow to understand' (*BJ* 129), and makes no attempt to establish any kind of caring relationship to her, it takes just this one incident for him to conclude that she is mentally ill and needs the physical intervention of ECT.

The second bias which comprises what Chesler calls clinical ideology is that 'only men can be mentally healthy'.[63] This claim was demonstrated in a 1970 study by Inge Broverman at Worcester State Hospital, Massachusetts. Her team set out to test the hypothesis that 'clinical judgments about the traits characterizing healthy, mature individuals will differ as a function of the sex of the person judged'.[64] Broverman gave a questionnaire to a group of 79 psychiatrists, psychologists and social workers, both men and women, ranging across all ranks of all three professions, and aged between 23 and 55. This age range, as well as the institutional location of all five members of Broverman's team in Massachusetts, makes her study especially relevant to Plath's experience – the psychiatrists and other health professionals by whom Plath was treated could themselves have been members of the sample studied. These clinicians were given thirty-eight bipolar pairs of character traits, one pole of which a previous study had confirmed was regarded as stereotypically either masculine or feminine, such as 'Very aggressive / Not all aggressive', or 'Doesn't hide emotions at all / Always hides emotions'. One group was asked to say which pole of these characteristics defined a mature, healthy man; another group was asked which pole defined a mature, healthy woman; and a third group was asked which defined a mature, healthy adult (sex unspecified). The questionnaires yielded these results:

> The clinicians' concepts of a healthy, mature man do not differ significantly from their concepts of a healthy adult. However, the clinicians' concepts of a mature, healthy woman do differ significantly from their adult concepts.[65]

As Broverman puts it, 'A double standard of health exists for men and women'. Furthermore, there was a strong correlation between the qualities regarded as healthy in both adults and men with the stereotypes that an earlier study had shown were regarded as socially desirable. Put simply, in the midst of a population that thought it was good to be a man, the physicians added that it was also mentally healthy to be a man, and for the same reasons. They responded that healthy women differed from healthy men in being more submissive, less independent, less adventurous, more easily influenced, less aggressive, less competitive, more excitable in minor crises, having their feelings more easily hurt, more conceited about their appearance, less objective and disliking maths and science. As Broverman comments, 'This constellation seems a most unusual way of describing any mature, healthy adult'.[66] To be a woman and to be mentally ill, Broverman's study confirms, or at least to be constantly on the verge of mental illness, are closely related concepts in patriarchal ideology.

Over and over again in the writings and records of hospitalised women, throughout the nineteenth and twentieth centuries, one sees the equation in the ideas and practices of the clinicians responsible for their care of mental health in women with cultural norms and stereotypes of femininity. Although to be a woman, in Plath's culture, was to be on the verge of mental illness, to be mentally healthy was to be 'feminine', to act as a woman should. This is made clear in the Bay Area data, analysed historically by Carol Warren in her book *Madwives: Schizophrenic Women in the 1950s*. These data are the case histories and interviews, conducted between 1957 and 1961, of seventeen women who were diagnosed as schizophrenic, institutionalised in the Napa State Hospital in California and subsequently released. As Warren writes, 'The mental hospital of the fifties quite explicitly used the marital relationship and the housewife role as criteria for mental health assessments'.[67] After failing her discharge conference twice, and confiding in the interviewer that she had finally learned 'what to say' at these conferences, the woman known as Kate White was successfully discharged once she said that her marriage had improved and that hospitalisation had helped her:

> Dr B then asked 'Do you think your hospitalization has helped you any?' Mrs White: 'It sure has.' 'How do you and your husband get along now?' 'Wonderful.' 'Better.' 'We sure do.' (indefinite leave, 4 January 1959).[68]

During the period following their return from hospital, the women's husbands overwhelmingly judged their mental health by their ability to perform housework efficiently.[69] A 1961 study of female former mental patients showed that women who refused to function domestically, in terms of cleaning, cooking, childcare and shopping, were those who were recommitted to mental hospital.[70] As Phyllis Chesler writes, of the criteria used in admitting women to and releasing them from mental hospitals, 'Adjustment to the "feminine" role was the measure of female mental health and psychiatric progress'.[71] In order to be considered mentally healthy in the 1950s, a woman needed wholeheartedly to embrace – or to least to tell her doctors that she did – the 'feminine' role of housewife and mother.

The roles of wife and mother were not the only aspects of femininity that were taken to be signs of mental health for women by clinicians during the period of Plath's encounter with the psychiatric institution. Women were expected to be docile, submissive and obedient if they were to be regarded as mentally healthy. Lenore McCall, hospitalised in the 1930s, learned this lesson:

> Because I could control the dreadful paroxysms of weeping which, incidentally had done much to spend me physically, and could conduct myself with more of an outward semblance of conventionality, it was assumed I was improving.[72]

In Janet Frame's novel *Faces in the Water*, Istina Mavet describes the goal of ECT as 'an improvement which was judged largely by your submission and prompt obedience to orders', and she calls ECT the 'new and fashionable means of quieting people and of making them realise that orders are to be obeyed and floors are to be polished without anyone protesting and . . . weeping is a crime'.[73] R. D. Laing's patient Ruth Gold was considered mentally ill by her parents, as well as by other psychiatrists, when she was abusive and resentful towards her parents, dressed like a beatnik and tried to be a writer. In response to Laing's question, 'Do you feel you have to agree with what most of the people round you believe?' she replied, 'Well if I don't, I usually land up in hospital'.[74]

It was not just the submissive and docile elements of the feminine role in the 1950s that were used as criteria for mental health in women. Beauty, grooming and dress were all taken by physicians as signs of a recovery from mental illness. One of the women Chesler interviewed went to see a psychiatrist because a sexual predator had broken into her apartment and the police had thought, because of her hippie appearance, that she had encouraged him. The psychiatrist's advice: 'He kept saying I should wear my hair long instead of pulled back because it was more feminine'. Another woman was advised, 'Why don't you fix yourself up? . . . You look like a hobo – I'd almost think you were afraid of men'.[75] As Elaine Showalter puts it of British women in the twentieth century, 'Female sanity is measured against a detailed standard of grooming and dress'.[76] Sexual desire for men other than their husbands was also taken as a sign of mental illness in women. Joyce Noon, one of the Bay Area wives, was recommitted to hospital against her will by her husband when he found her in a bar late at night talking to a man, having left their son at home. Another of the wives was recommitted by her husband when he discovered that she was having an affair with a fellow-patient.[77] When Esther meets Dr Gordon, then, he acts in a culturally typical manner in sending her for ECT treatment and hospitalisation. Her intelligence and ambition, as shown by her frustration at not getting into the prestigious writing class at Harvard summer school and at her inability to write a thesis on *Finnegans Wake*, would have been characteristic signs to a young, self-confident male psychiatrist of a young woman pathogenically rejecting her feminine role. The fact that she had not changed her clothes or washed her hair for three weeks when he first interviewed her would confirm this. Plath ironises his unquestioning acceptance of the dominant images of femininity, as he praises, in increasingly inappropriate situations, a previous generation of students at Esther's college as a 'pretty bunch of girls' (*BJ* 126). When Esther, looking far from pretty, rudely scatters torn-up pieces of a letter on his desk, his response is very typical of that which many other hospitalised women experienced. Esther was judged mentally ill because she was failing to conform to cultural norms of femininity.

Warren argues that much of the trouble experienced by the Bay Area housewives, although pathologised as mental illness, can be traced to social structures of oppression. Although conformity to the role of housewife was seen as a sign of improved mental health, in fact it was precisely the stresses of this role that caused much of the women's distress in the first place. What is presented as the cure for distress is in fact one of its causes. As Charlotte Perkins Gilman wrote, 'I went home and obeyed [my doctor's] directions for some three months, and came so near the border of utter mental ruin that I could see over'.[78] Many of the Californian wives, Warren writes, 'traced their troubles to the demands of the housewife role'.[79] One of the women expressed her sense of injustice as being diagnosed and treated for mental illness when her distress derived from her relationship with her husband: 'Shock treatment is a helluva way to treat marital problems – the problems involved both of us'. The structural cause of the trouble of the Bay Area wives, Warren argues, can be seen from the extent to which hospitalisation 'cured' this trouble, namely not at all. Many of them formed optimistic plans in hospital for renegotiating the terms of their marriage, but in every case this proved impossible in long-term practice, against the grain of the dominant ideologies and practices of marriage and the family. 'Only those women who had been forcibly removed from the traditional family, with its obdurate structures, escaped an ultimate reabsorption' into them and into the distress they had initially caused. This is the lesson that second-wave feminism learned from the anti-psychiatrists of the 1960s, for whom madness was a name given to behaviour which breaks social rules, and its diagnosis and cure ways in which to marginalise and disempower individuals who commit such behaviour. As Jane Ussher writes, 'The earlier dissenters may have been correct in pointing out that psychiatric labels serve society: what they omitted from their analysis was that it is a *patriarchal* society'.[80]

This is very much the view Plath expresses in *The Bell Jar*. In a chapter outline for the novel, she notes that the chief psychiatrist of Esther's private hospital is treated with excessive reverence.[81] She is clearly and passionately angry at the marginalisation of Esther by Dr Gordon, whom society pays well and respects highly for what it believes to be his ability to treat her, but who in reality only increases the distress he is supposed to be alleviating. Esther imagines that her psychiatrist will be the kind of person who can help her, 'kind', 'ugly' and 'intuitive', someone who will understand her and be able to guide her back to health (*BJ* 123). She needs only kindness and intuition to get better, but instead she gets arrogance, expertise and the physical intervention that follows from the contemporary psychiatric belief in the biological determination of mental illness. In Plath's own experience, the psychiatrist she first consulted reminded her of Dick Norton, who had come to represent for her precisely the ways in which the discourses of science and medicine reinforce the patriarchal values and institutions of contemporary society (*LH* 124). In the third draft of the novel, Plath had included an episode in which a psychoanalyst visits Esther in hospital, who initially seems to be the opposite of Dr Gordon. He is an old man, a European, and his book-lined study makes Esther think he may be the only doctor she has met so far who might understand her. But whilst he seems to represent all that Dr Gordon lacks, in fact he turns out to be no more help to Esther than Dr Gordon. Although he gives her a plausible psychoanalytic account of the derivation of her feelings from her relationship to her father, before she is able to ask what advice he can give her on the basis of this insight, their session is over. The next day, because he is at the top of his profession, he goes away on a long vacation.[82] Even the doctor who appears to be the kind, ugly intuitive man Esther is looking for fails not only to help her, but even to listen to her.

When Esther sees the photograph of Dr Gordon's family on his desk, placed so as to be clearly visible to his patients as well as to him, she says, 'For some reason the photograph made me furious' (*BJ* 124). So furious indeed, does it, and by metonymy Dr Gordon's entire approach as a psychiatrist, make her that she is still violently angry about him at the time of narration, when she is 'all right again' (*BJ* 3). She enacts a kind of narratorial violence towards the picture, breaking it up, dismembering it, as she would like to do to Dr Gordon, as she represents it. Although the woman in the family picture is obviously his wife, when Esther first describes it she says that she 'could have been Doctor Gordon's sister' (*BJ* 124). Why would Esther suggest something that she knows is so unlikely to be true? She is insulting Dr Gordon, working in an aggressive impulse under a socially acceptable form of words, accusing him of incest, and effacing the existence of his wife, murdering her in words as she would like to do in fantasy to her husband. Something like this occurs again when she seems to remember a dog in the picture, but then adds that perhaps it was just the 'pattern in the woman's skirt' (*BJ* 124). Again, under a perfectly acceptable form of words, Esther is expressing her aggression towards Dr Gordon, through the characters in the picture in which he has represented himself. In the fashion magazines of the early 1950s, skirts are usually plain, or if they are patterned, these are either simple spots, stripes or checks, or they are floral patterns. In *Harper's Bazaar*, for example, from January 1953 until August, when

Plath was hospitalised, there are just two pictures of skirts with animal patterns (fish and butterflies), and one of these is an advert for fabrics inspired by artists.[83] Esther is insulting Dr Gordon's wife here, calling her skirt ugly, as a disguised expression of the much worse insults she would like to level at her husband. Even at the time of narration, Esther's anger towards the man who claimed to be able to treat her, but in fact distressed her even more, remains intense and violent.

One of the reasons why the photograph makes Esther so furious is that it seems impossible that a man like Dr Gordon, with his perfect family 'haloing him like . . . angels', could understand her in any way (*BJ* 124). Her anger at the photograph is a metonymy for her anger at her entire treatment by Dr Gordon – that instead of helping her back into well-being and social functioning, his treatment functions from beginning to end, under the respected forms of science and medicine, as a way of marginalising and disempowering a woman already in distress. There is a circle, well symbolised by Plath's metaphor of the halo, described between the family in the photograph and the doctor on one side of the desk, from which the patient on the other side is firmly excluded, a circle of social acceptability, of membership and power in society. Esther is positioned by her psychiatrist outside the discourses of health, knowledge and power, and Plath is deeply critical of the injustice of this experience. His very first question, in which he asks her what she thinks is the problem, confirms her fears, with its implication that there is in reality no problem. From the very beginning of her treatment, Esther is constituted by her psychiatrist as outside the circle of knowledge, health and power. This is well symbolised in her second meeting with Dr Gordon, in which, after she scatters her torn-up letter on his desk, he simply ceases to talk to her, to acknowledge her existence as a subject. His last words to Esther are, 'I would like to speak to your mother' (*BJ* 130).[84]

Most women who have written about ECT describe it as a frightening, coercive and damaging experience. Two-thirds of those treated in the 1950s, as today, were women, and it was used most commonly for depression, as well as for schizophrenia.[85] Since its adoption in the United States in the 1940s, ECT has been highly controversial. It almost always causes memory loss, both retrograde (in which past memories are lost) and anterograde (in which new memories are not retained), which is often extensive and permanent.[86] Plath never wrote about this symptom, which was extremely distressing to writers, since many of the memories on which they need to draw for material were lost, although Linda Wagner-Martin records that she occasionally spoke about it to college friends. 'She said it was like being in a dream; she never knew whether she was awake or asleep and dreaming. It was as if she had lost events, people, years from her life'.[87] In the 1960s, the treatment was modified with the use of a muscle relaxant to reduce the risk of damage to the bones and muscles during the convulsions induced by the shock, along with an anaesthetic to prevent the sensation of suffocation caused by the effect of the muscle relaxant on the respiratory system.[88] Plath's description of the excruciating pain Esther goes through during ECT indicates that the treatment was administered to her incompetently. When the treatment is given correctly, the electric shock instantly induces unconsciousness.[89] The experience which Plath describes in *The Bell Jar* is one in which, like her own, the electric current passed through the patient's brain is not strong enough to produce immediate unconsciousness. Olive Higgins Prouty, who assumed the cost and control of Plath's treatment, wrote scathingly to Dr Peter Thornton, the psychiatrist who first administered ECT to her, about this mistake:

> She was not properly protected against the results of the treatments, which were so poorly given that the patient remembers the details with horror.[90]

Thornton responded to Prouty with a letter in which he called her 'poorly misinformed' and 'psychiatrically ignorant', and described Plath's response to the treatment as 'favourable'. Like Dr Gordon in *The Bell Jar*, Dr Thornton ends by simply refusing to speak to a woman who presumes to criticise his practice as a psychiatrist, asking Prouty not to 'burden' his office with 'any further communications'.[91]

In an essay entitled 'The Electroshock Quotationary', Leonard Frank has assembled quotations from over 100 different accounts of ECT. In no other account but Plath's does the patient remain conscious and in agony during the treatment.[92] What Plath's account shares with those of other patients, however, is that Esther interprets the experience as a punishment for transgressing her feminine role. As Elaine Showalter writes of British women's narratives of hospitalisation in the mid-twentieth century, 'They transform the experiences of shock, psychosurgery and chemotherapy into symbolic episodes of punishment for intellectual ambition, domestic defiance and sexual autonomy'.[93] In *The Bell Jar*, Esther says, 'I wondered what terrible thing . . . I had done' (*BJ* 138). Virginia Cunningham, who receives shock treatment in *The Snake Pit*, wonders exactly the same thing:

> What had you done? You wouldn't have killed anyone and what other crime is there which exacts so severe a penalty? . . . Dare they kill me without a trial?[94]

Gordon Lameyer, whom Plath was dating during the summer of her breakdown, recalls that the electric shock machine with which Plath was treated reminded her of a collection of torture instruments. As the nurses connected her up to it, she told Lameyer, it was as if she had been sentenced to death in the electric chair.[95] Plath's therapist at McLean, Ruth Beuscher, when asked forty years later about her treatment, confirmed that, in her view, even the properly administered shock treatments she had given Plath had been successful only as a deterrent: 'She just didn't want to have any more shock treatments, so she reorganised herself inside so she wouldn't have any more'.[96] Feminist critic Ollie Mae Bozarth, herself a survivor of shock treatment, explicitly links the violence of ECT with domestic violence:

> Many husbands beat up their wives . . . Other husbands just sign consent for the 'medical treatment' called shock, and let the experts do it for them.[97]

This critique continues up to the present day. In a 2006 article, which thoroughly reviews the literature on the subject, Bonnie Burstow argues:

> Although the medicalisation camouflages the assault, overwhelmingly electroshock constitutes an assault on women's memory, brains, integral being. And this being the case, electroshock may be meaningfully theorised as a form of violence against women.[98]

For Plath in *The Bell Jar*, Esther's incompetently administered ECT treatment is the nadir of her experience of the institution of psychiatry as one in which women are controlled by and forced to conform to the norms of patriarchal society.

Beauty

In *Life* magazine's special issue on 'The American Woman' in 1956, the first article is a ten-page series of photographs of beautiful young women from all over the United States entitled, 'The American Girl at Her Beautiful Best'. The first of these, a full-page photograph, is of a 23-year old Californian woman on a beach, wearing only a towel. The ideological message of such a feature, and of its position as the leading article in the magazine, is clear – to be a woman is first of all to be an attractive object of the male gaze. This issue of *Life* also features, in its second section, 'Women's Problems', an article on the American beauty industry entitled, 'Billions of Dollars for Prettiness'. The article points out that 'big industry thrives on woman's struggle to stay young'. Amongst photographs of women in beauty salons, health spas and exercise regimes, it says:

> [The American woman] . . . is shaken on tables, beaten by machines, starved, steamed, packed in mud and needled with cold water. In earnest conference she picks her hair shades and face powders.

It points out that the 'defense budget' of American women – that is, the amount they spend each year on beauty products – adds up to more than twice the defence budget of Italy.[99] In the 1955 college issue of *Mademoiselle*, staff health and beauty columnist Bernice Peck writes that personal appearance is of such importance to young women that it ought to be taught for credit in college. 'It seems purely practical', she writes, 'to study, along with political science and principles of economics, that lively lighter science – personal appearance'. She praises Stephens College, Missouri, for its course Personal Appearance 1, 'with a five-teacher department instructing in all phases of good looks', taken by 400 women a semester. 'Some sweet day', Peck argues, all colleges will offer such courses, since they are 'a soundly sensible way to help graduates introduce their gifts of higher learning to a competitive post-college world'.[100]

In a man's world, the advice books tell young women of Plath's generation, you must be attractive to men, whether you are trying to get a husband, a job or both. It is also important in keeping these things once you have got them. In his advice book *Woman's Guide to Better Living*, Dr John Schindler makes this point. The tone of his book is on the whole sympathetic. Schindler is aware how difficult and demanding the roles of housewife and mother are. He points out that they involve two or three times as much work, without any of the rewards, as the average paid job, and his book advises women how to cope with the difficulties of these roles. Nevertheless, when it comes to personal appearance, his tone suddenly shifts to one of prescription. The essence of his advice, he writes, can be summed up in a remark made by a 'wonderful elderly housewife' of his acquaintance to her daughter, who turned out as a result to be a 'fabulous housekeeper': 'Be sure and comb your hair before breakfast'. Before her husband and older children get home, that is, and difficult as this may be, Schindler's reader must, like a salesman, 'put up a front' – dress nicely, fix her hair and put on a smile. He tells his readers that, whatever they wear around the house, they can look either 'neatly feminine' or 'like a rag and a bone and a hank of hair by wearing sloppy slippers, dowdy slacks, grimy shirt tails and a mat of hair anchored to a sullen face by a forest of pin curls'. He warns:

> A wife who is habitually slovenly and dowdy is neither a happy thought for a husband nor a pleasant sight to meet. The desire to come home to it, the courage to face it, gradually and slowly weakens.[101]

Although sympathetic to almost every other difficulty faced by the housewife and mother, Schindler has no patience for a woman who does not look her best. If her husband leaves her because he cannot stand such an unattractive sight evening after evening, he says plainly, she has only herself to blame.

It is not surprising, therefore, that, throughout *The Bell Jar*, Esther is fascinated by the commodities of the beauty and fashion industries. Indeed, she is obsessed by them, in the dual sense that she loves what does her harm. She describes her fascination with the fashion industry early in the novel, as she reflects on Doreen's 'fashion-conscious' college, where the students match every outfit with every accessory with a devotion that Esther says 'attracted me like a magnet' (*BJ* 5). Clothes, hair, make-up, accessories, grooming, manners, style – these aspects of personal appearance are all integral to Esther's world in *The Bell Jar*. There are few characters whom she does not describe with a detailed account of their appearance. Indeed, she describes herself in this way, right from the novel's opening pages, 'tripping about in . . . patent leather shoes I'd bought in Bloomingdale's . . . with a black patent leather belt and black patent leather pocket-book to match' (*BJ* 2). In the very same paragraph, she describes the outfit she wore to a cocktail party one evening in New York. Esther has fully interiorised the ideological message of the beauty and fashion industries, that a woman is to be judged by her appearance. She also holds others to the same rigorous standards, despising Lenny Shepherd's friend Frankie in part because he dresses badly. As Esther says, 'If there's anything I look down on, it's a man in a blue outfit' (*BJ* 11). Not only does this indicate the extent to which Esther has accepted the ideological message of the value of one's appearance, but the present tense in which she expresses it indicates that she still feels this way at the time of writing. That a woman's appearance is an integral part of who she is an ideological message that, for all its contribution to her breakdown, Esther never learns to reject. Although the pressure to conform to society's standards of femininity, and the lack of satisfaction she finds in working on a fashion magazine, which is supposed to be a pinnacle of achievement for an intelligent woman, are contributing factors to her breakdown, Esther is never able directly to criticise the ideologies of beauty and of fashion. Naomi Wolf's argument, thirty years later, that the ideology of beauty was the only element of the feminine mystique of the 1950s with the strength to survive the critiques of second-wave feminism, is borne out by Plath's novel.[102] Esther directly criticises the institutions of medicine, psychiatry and marriage, as well as contemporary sexual ethics and laws, but not once does she rise to a similar level of protest against the values promoted by the beauty and fashion industries. Her only protest is the silent one of her breakdown, during which, among other symptoms, she ceases to change her outfit or wash her hair. Throughout her recovery, however, and right up to the end of the novel, Esther continues to attach great importance to her appearance. As she ends her narrative, on the threshold of recovery and return from hospital, she tells us in detail what she is wearing. Calling into question the complete nature of her recovery, Esther ends the novel as she began, with her sense of identity deeply bound up in her appearance. She even calls her red outfit 'flamboyant as my plans' (*BJ* 233), a description of her personal appearance as an expression of her inner self which positions her squarely back within the discourses of the fashion industry in which she began and which contributed to her breakdown in the first place.

Marriage

During the 1940s, with young men away at war, a sense that there was a shortage of available men to date and marry became increasingly acute amongst college women and did not subside after 1945. On the contrary, popular books and magazines focused on the 'man shortage'. An often quoted, although misleading, statistic in these years was that one in seven women who wanted to marry would not be able to for lack of a partner.[103] A four-part *Ladies' Home Journal* article entitled 'How to be Marriageable', which ran from March to June 1954, began with an interview with Dr Paul Popenoe, director of the American Institute of Family Relations, who tells its readers:

> By their 30th birthday 82 per cent of all American women are married. The woman of 30 who is unmarried has only about one chance in five of finding a mate.[104]

As Beth Bailey puts it, the 'early-marriage ideal was changing the face of college life'.[105] In 1958, *Mademoiselle* published a dating map for college girls, with a detailed key to all the men's, women's and co-educational colleges on the east coast, from Maine to South Carolina.[106] As the article which accompanies the map says, 'It's trying to get an education and a man at the same time that's the number one problem and strain on any college girl, co-ed or women's college student'.[107] Plath had met the author of this article, Jobs and Futures editor Polly Weaver, during her month at *Mademoiselle* five years earlier. She was a Smith graduate and had held the Press Board job there that Plath herself was doing in 1953, writing news releases about the college for the local papers. It is someone with precisely Plath's cultural background, a realistic model of the kind of work she can expect to do after graduation, who is drawing the dating maps for college girls.

It is not only college women who are trying to find a husband in Plath's America. In an article entitled '129 Ways to Get a Husband', *McCall's* tells its readers:

> In the United States today, there are sixteen million women over the age of seventeen who are not married. Presumably the vast majority of them would like to be.[108]

Some women are going to miss out on marriage, the article warns, and those who do not are going to have to take responsibility for achieving their goal. *Woman's Home Companion* agreed: in an article on true and false popular beliefs about marriage, Judith Chase Churchill confirms that 'a girl's chances of marriage drop sharply after thirty-five'.[109] The most frequent theme in *McCall's* 129 ways to get a husband is to pretend to be helpless, incapable or in some way inferior to him. They include:

> 19. Get lost at football games.
> 31. Stumble when you walk into a room that he's in.
> 34. Wear a Band-Aid. People always ask what happened.
> 40. Stand in a corner and cry softly. Chances are good he'll come over to find out what's wrong.
> 47. 'Accidentally' have your purse fly open, scattering its contents all over the street.[110]

A frequently given piece of advice to women trying to attract a man was not to appear more intelligent than him. According to Aurelia Plath, Sylvia had used this advice in dating since she was a teenager.[111] In a series of biographical notes about her daughter, she wrote that they agreed that it would be best for Plath to attend a women's college, at which 'one could work as diligently as one pleased without the punishment of rejection by boys who would refuse to date a girl with a reputation for being a "grind"'.[112] As *McCall's* puts it, 'Hide your Phi Beta Kappa key if you have one – later on junior can play with it'.[113] In *The Bell Jar*, Esther takes very similar advice to this, letting her baby play with one of the free gifts she received as an editor at *Ladies' Day*. In her *Mademoiselle* article on college dating, Polly Weaver takes this behaviour for granted, as she writes that one of the difficulties of co-ed classes is, 'in a class where you're brighter than he is, not daring to speak up'.[114]

In the January 1952 issue of *Mademoiselle*, there are two articles on the extent to which young women of Plath's generation have absorbed this ideology and made it their own. In an article entitled 'Have College Women Let Us Down?', Howard Mumford Jones complains that the present generation of college women lack the intellectual curiosity, political commitment and professional ambition of earlier generations. Their goal during their college years, Jones writes with disapproval, is primarily to meet a husband who will provide a secure home for them in which to bring up children. If they think about work at all, it is in terms of a 'job' rather than a 'career' – something which can be fitted around marriage and family commitments.[115] The most revealing thing about Jones' article is the lack of controversy it generated. *Mademoiselle* invites readers' responses at the end of the article, but despite Jones' hostile and even misogynistic tone, only 20 per cent of *Mademoiselle*'s readers disagreed with him; 66 per cent agreed with him, and the remaining 14 per cent agreed with some of what he said. Of the 20 per cent of readers who objected to Jones' characterisations, *Mademoiselle* prints a reply by one, a Radcliffe student named Loretta Valtz. Even in this rebuttal, however, Valtz tacitly agrees with Jones that most contemporary young women are as concerned about marriage and family as women of Jones' generation were about politics. She simply denies that this is a bad thing:

> Our dedication is not to sweeping and evanescent theories about the salvation of the world . . . Our dedication is to marriage and to the family – the roots from which are nurtured stable individuals and a stable society.

In fact, this is all that Valtz's piece is about – that college women of Plath's generation are committed primarily to marriage and family, and that this constitutes their political responsibility and commitment. She also accepts Jones' complaint that college women are looking for 'jobs' rather than 'careers', but again denies that this is a bad thing:

> We declare ourselves . . . for real marriages and children sound in mind and heart as well as in body, for 'jobs' that give us valuable contact with the world rather than 'careers' that suck all our creativity and energy.[116]

This article was published during the period in which Plath was expressing most intensely in her journals her struggle to imagine a marriage that did not drain her creativity but rather expressed it. She found little help in this struggle from the popular discourses by which she was surrounded. If she had read an article published two months earlier on the history of working women in the US, she would have had a similar experience. Entitled 'The White-Collar Girl . . . And How She Grew', the article traces the history of working conditions for American women since the mid-nineteenth century and ends with a reflection on modern young women's attitudes to work. The author, Helen Beal Woodward, writes that the dilemma of 'Marriage v. Career', which exercised American feminists in the 1920s, now concerns the majority of educated young women much less. 'The educated girl, model 1952', she writes, is indeed looking for a good job, partly for 'self-support', partly for 'the chance to use her abilities', but mostly because it 'puts her in a bargaining position, the better to look around for what she *really* wants, a good husband.[117] In an article on dating and marriage in *Mademoiselle*'s college issue of 1954, Jane Whitbread and Vivian Cadden describe the 'increasing seriousness about marriage' amongst American college students, and their 'conscious effort . . . to learn to develop mature emotional attachments'.[118] The following month art historian Russell Lynes, who had bought some of Plath's poems in his capacity as managing editor of *Harper's* magazine the previous year, nostalgic for the more radical views of his own generation, wrote gloomily about the life goals expressed in questionnaires sent out by *Mademoiselle*'s Jobs and Futures department to college girls all over the country. 'The family is, of course', he observed, 'the ultimate measure of success' as far as these respondents are concerned, 'its solidarity, its community of interest, the well-being of the children'.[119]

Lynes points out that it is extremely difficult to imagine how unusual people like artists, scientists and philosophers will manage to flourish in a culture which so massively privileges the normal, the ordinary and the 'well-rounded'.[120] In his graduation address to Plath's class of 1955 at Smith, Adlai Stevenson made the same point: 'One looks back with dismay at the possibility of a Shakespeare perfectly adjusted to bourgeois life in Stratford'.[121] Plath enjoyed Stevenson's speech, with its 'hypothesis that every woman's highest vocation is creative marriage', calling it 'witty' and 'magnificent'.[122] Nancy Hunter Steiner felt more ambivalent:

> We loved it even if it seemed to hurl us back to the satellite role we had escaped for four years – second-class citizens in a man's world where our only possible achievement was a vicarious one.[123]

Stevenson seems to have offered Plath more questions than answers. He was critical of contemporary society in a way that resonates with Plath's own concerns, as a culture governed by male, scientistic discourses and practices, a culture in which the Henry Mintons of the world dominate the Elizabeths:

> You will live, most of you, in an environment in which 'facts', the data of the senses, are glorified, and values – judgments – are assigned inferior status, as mere 'matters of opinion'.

In this environment, art is considered no more than an 'adornment of civilisation' rather than a 'vital element' of it. Stevenson was even aware that American housewives were unhappy with the sexual division of labour:

> Once they read Baudelaire. Now it is the Consumer Guide . . . There is often a sense of contraction, of closing horizons and lost opportunities.

Despite sharing these critiques of contemporary society with Plath, Stevenson had no more to offer as a solution than a variation on the theme of the gender ideology which is Plath's concern in the first place. Women like the Smith class of 1955 had the important role of civilising their husbands and children, he concluded: 'What you have learned and can learn will fit you for the primary task of making homes and whole human beings'.[124] Stevenson's speech is an example of what Barbara Ehrenreich and Deirdre English call 'sexual romanticism', the ideology that ascribes to the private sphere of the home, and to the woman who governs this sphere, all the human values driven from the public sphere of the market. This kind of thinking, Ehrenreich and English write, chooses 'not to remake the world, but to demand that women *make up* for the world'.[125]

During her years at Smith, Plath found the dominant ideology of marriage intolerable, and articulated a constant struggle against it in the pages of her journal (*J* 88, 97–102, 103–8). She told Ann Davidow that she did not want to give herself up to supporting the progress of her husband's job, but to progress in all kinds of interesting jobs herself.[126] This is precisely the view she gives Esther in *The Bell Jar*, who does not want to be 'the place an arrow shoots off from' but to 'shoot off in all directions' herself (*BJ* 79). In just the same way, Plath had told her mother in February 1955, shortly before graduation, that she has no intention of acquiring secretarial skills because she did not want to be someone else's secretary.[127] She did not want to be subordinate to the creative work of others, but to do her own creative work, precisely the view she attributes to Esther in *The Bell Jar*, who does not want to 'transcribe letter after thrilling letter' but to write her 'own thrilling letters' (*BJ* 72). Plath rejected the idea of marrying Gordon Lameyer for the same reason – she wanted to live her own life to the full.[128] It was during the years she was dating Dick Norton in particular that Plath struggled most intensely with the ideology of marriage, for Norton, she felt, articulated this ideology especially clearly. Plath writes that his idea of a wife is that of a 'physical possession . . . like "a new car"', increasing his status in society (*J* 101). This comparison of women to cars was a common trope in 1950s gender discourse. In 'The *Esquire* Girl, 1951 Model', *Esquire* magazine ran a thirteen-page feature, in which twelve full-page pictures of scantily–clad models, one for each month of the year, were compared to twelve cars turned out by the magazine's 'production line':

> You now have the 1951 model of the Esquire maid before you; available in
> 12 body types, all with substantially the same superb chassis, the finest com-
> bination of everything that biology and industry can devise.[129]

This sense of a woman as a prize possession was one which contemporary ideology encouraged in young men, as Plath acknowledged when
she wrote that her boyfriend's comparison of a wife to a new car was
'only normal' (*J* 101).

Plath did not agonise over marriage again to the extent that she had
done during her first years at Smith. Throughout the first six years of
her marriage to Hughes, however, she consistently thought of their successful marriage as a kind of miracle, and of Hughes as the one man she
had ever known with whom she could have both a fulfilling family life
and also pursue a career as a writer (*J* 271, 274, 287, 336, 341, 361,
376, 395, 421, 434, 500, 517, 519).[130] In *The Bell Jar*, she portrays her
conflicted feelings during the years of dating Dick Norton. Although
she repeatedly fantasises about marriage and children, Esther says that
she 'never wanted to get married', as it would mean a life of domestic
drudgery for a man who was himself leading a fulfilling life at work
(*BJ* 79). Esther can see that this has been Mrs Willard's life, who is evi-
dently intelligent and educated, and even had a teaching career of her
own before marriage. If anyone could be expected to continue to live a
creative, intellectual life as a married woman it would be her, but all she
does is 'cook and clean and wash' all day (*BJ* 80). In *Woman's Guide to
Better Living*, Dr Schindler confirms Esther's view. His wife, whom he
credits with arriving at the conclusions he synthesises in his book along
with him in family discussions, had been a college professor, but for
all her input into the book she is not named once in the text, except as
'the mother'.[131] Dr Spock provides another example. Plath consulted his
bestselling book *Baby and Child Care* so assiduously that she thought
it would disintegrate before her baby was a year old.[132] In an article
in the *Ladies' Home Journal*, of September 1957, Spock tells the story
of writing this book. He would dictate it to his wife. It was slow and
painful work, he writes, and he often suffered from writer's block.
Nevertheless his wife would patiently sit at the typewriter waiting for
him to formulate his thoughts:

> What was most remarkable of all was that, though she had perfectly good
> opinions of her own about child care, she never made suggestions about how
> to say it until I asked for help.[133]

Mrs Spock does, and is highly praised for, precisely the kind of work
Esther does not want to do in *The Bell Jar* – secretarial work for a man.
In precisely the way that Esther fears, the identities of Mrs Schindler and

Mrs Spock – their creative work, and in the former's case even her name – are altogether subordinated to those of their husbands.

In *Life* magazine's special issue on the American Woman, the article on marriage – which significantly is placed in the section on 'women's problems' – consists of a synthesis of the views of five psychiatrists on 'our disturbing divorce rate'. They conclude unanimously that, in the words of the article's sub-title, the problem is 'wives who are not feminine enough and husbands who are not truly male'. There is even a technical term for the problem – 'they are suffering from what the psychiatrists call sexual ambiguity'. The article begins with some sexual metaphysics, on what men and women are 'by nature'. It also speaks of the 'God-given' characteristics of the genders. In the view of *Life*'s psychiatric panel, 'Men are designed by nature to sire children and women to bear them, and from these elementary facts . . . come their differences in emotional needs'. The 'primary feminine qualities' are 'receptivity, passivity and the desire to nurture', the male qualities are 'dominance', 'exploitiveness' and 'responsibility'. What disturbs *Life*'s psychiatrists is that these 'natural' roles are no longer those to which American men and women are gravitating – 'The emerging American woman tends to be assertive and exploitive' and her male counterpart 'passive and irresponsible'. They think of feminism as one of the major expressions of this problem, the root cause of which is women wanting to be like men. Although *Life*'s psychiatrists feel able, in 1956, to dismiss feminism as 'moribund' since the winning of the vote, it has produced a contemporary expression of sexual ambiguity, the 'career woman'. Dr John Cotton, a member of the panel who practises in New York City, even coins a technical term for the complex of symptoms displayed by such women – the 'New York career woman syndrome' – arguing that the reason there are so many psychiatrists in New York is that there are so many career women there who need their help.[134]

As Esther records Buddy Willard's repetition of his mother's articulations of this ideology of femininity – a man is 'an arrow into the future' and a woman is 'the place the arrow shoots off from' – she says that Buddy would tell her these things till they 'made me tired' (*BJ* 67). The tiredness she speaks about here is that of her constant struggle to define and defend her desires against the weight of ideology which tells her that they are misplaced or deviant. The *Saturday Evening Post* articulated Mrs Willard's ideological view precisely, publishing a short piece entitled 'How to Help Your Husband Get Ahead', which reminded its readers, 'A wife is a crossbow that catapults a man into the business day, his eye clear upon the target'.[135] Esther is tired, and ultimately breaks down, because of the impossibility of publicly being who she is, an ambitious woman who wants to be a writer as well as a wife and mother. In 1955, *Time* magazine interviewed 183 male college seniors from the graduating class of 1955, Plath's own class, about their expectations of what their lives would be like in fifteen years' time. David Riesman, who analysed these interviews, pointed to 'the resentment which appears again and again in [them] toward the . . . career girl'.[136] One Princeton senior described his future wife as 'the Grace Kelly type, camel's-hair coat type':

> Although an Ivy League type, she will also be centered in the home, a housewife. Perhaps at forty-five, with the children grown up, she will go in for hospital work and so on.

Grace Kelly, in giving up her successful career as a Hollywood film star once she married, a story repeatedly told in interviews and articles, became a public symbol of contemporary gender expectations, 'the ultimate fifties woman who had sacrificed a career for the joys of marriage and family'.[137] A Harvard senior interviewed by *Time* recognised that the desire, frequently expressed by the men of the class of 1955, for a wife who is college-educated but becomes a housewife and mother once she marries, is contradictory:

> I want someone who would stay home and take care of the children, but on the other hand I want someone who can stimulate me intellectually, and I don't know if those things are compatible . . . If a woman goes to Radcliffe and takes up economics, she isn't learning how to bring up children.[138]

For all that this student recognises the incompatibility in his standards for the kind of woman he wants to marry, he continues to hold these standards.

It is precisely this ideological contradiction in which Esther is caught. Plath's poem 'Ariel', written a year after *The Bell Jar*, indicates the intensity of this contradiction. In *The Bell Jar*, Esther rejects the idea of being the 'place an arrow shoots off from', but wants to 'shoot off in all directions herself' (*BJ* 79). In 'Ariel', the poem's speaker fulfils Esther's wish, and herself becomes 'the arrow, / The dew that flies / Suicidal' into the 'cauldron of morning' (*CP* 239–40). Many critics see these lines as positive. For Linda Wagner-Martin, the speaker of 'Ariel' has 'finally overcome Mrs Willard's curse'.[139] For Susan Van Dyne, she has erased 'the dichotomy between male ambition and envious female desire'.[140] According to Judith Kroll, she is 'dissolved and transformed'.[141] In my view, such readings are too sanguine. Rather, Sandra Gilbert is right to argue that the speaker of the poem is looking for a way out of her gender role that she cannot find without destroying herself.[142] As

Christina Britzolakis puts it, the poem ends 'ambiguously suspended between celebration and mourning'.[143] 'Ariel' expresses the experience of the cultural contradiction in which Esther is caught in *The Bell Jar*. The effort it takes to define herself against the massive pressure of the dominant gender ideologies is so great that it drives her to breakdown and attempted suicide. To become the arrow of Mrs Willard's proverb, as Esther wants to do, is to cease to exist as a woman in the way that the concept of woman is publicly defined. The weight of the gender ideology against which Esther struggles to be herself seems to leave her no option but to leave the world altogether.

'Femininity'

Despite her feminist critique of the patriarchal institution of marriage, Plath had also absorbed the ideology of marriage to a considerable extent. In December 1955, after her first term Newnham College, she told Olive Higgins Prouty, 'I love cooking and "homemaking" a great deal'. She added that she was 'neither destined to be a scholar . . . nor a career girl' (*LH* 201). The following month, she reassured her mother that she would not devote herself to a career: 'I am . . . *meant* to be married and have children and a home' (*LH* 208) She made frequent and detailed references in her letters to her mother to the meals she cooked, repeatedly asking Aurelia to post her copy of *The Joy of Cooking* to Cambridge, which she finds it hard to do without (*LH* 242).[144] On one of the occasions when she made this request, she wrote that she felt destined to cooking, which was one of her greatest pleasures.[145] She made repeated references to how much she was looking forward to making meals for Ted, making a beautiful home for him and even making the sandwiches he took to work during his time as a teacher in Cambridge.[146] In 1961, when her mother sent her two copies of the *Ladies' Home Journal*, Plath wrote of her 'joy' in receiving them, and anticipated with pleasure 'trying the luscious recipes' (*LH* 438). Several months later she referred again to wanting to 'try the exotic recipes' she read in her 'beloved' magazine (*LH* 455). She wrote in Britain of her longing for a modern kitchen with modern appliances, of the kind she was used to in America, and enthused in detail to her mother about the new oven and refrigerator she bought for their first home in London in February 1960.[147] She told Aurelia that she could not stop cleaning them, because she loved to make them shine.[148] Two years later, she was equally enthusiastic about their new Bendix washing machine.[149]

One of the ways in which Plath began to feel better after the breakdown of her marriage was with new clothes and a new hairstyle. She wrote about these to her mother, 'My morale is so much improved . . . Men stare at me in the street' (*LH* 479). In her next letter, she went into great detail about the outfits and accessories she had bought, which made her feel like 'a new woman' (*LH* 480). A month later she spent a gift from Olive Higgins Prouty on fashionable clothes from a London department store, which made her 'feel and look like a million' (*LH* 491). It was 'amazing', she wrote to her mother, how much better they made her feel (*LH* 492). She drew deeply on the ideology of fashion when she wrote to Prouty that her new wardrobe and hairstyle would be the beginning of her transformation into a new woman.[150] You become a new woman, this ideology says, by looking like one, by buying new fashion and beauty products. Indeed, despite Plath's observation to her mother on the good value of her hairstyle, it had to be redone at the local hairdresser's every week (*LH* 480).

For all her critique of patriarchal marriage, Plath was even more critical of unmarried women. She repeatedly disparaged the female dons by whom she was taught at Newnham, her most frequent term for them being 'grotesque'. She calls her supervisors 'bluestocking grotesques, who know about life secondhand', relics of the 'Victorian age of emancipation' (*LH* 219). Plath's own model of emancipation for women was explicitly differentiated from that of the suffragists of an earlier generation. 'God forbid that I become a Crusader', she reflected in her journal, as she thought of earlier women's rights activists like Lucretia Mott, reflecting that they sought the sense of identity and purpose in feminism that they had lost in marriage (*J* 100). Plath has absorbed the feminine mystique to a sufficient extent for the concept of 'career woman' to deviate in her mind from the concept of 'woman'. She had learned this ideological lesson early, writing to her mother in her freshman year at Smith about her thoughts on a future career, and then interjecting, 'Ugh – I hate the word' (*LH* 68). She found in Dorothea Krook the single exception to the rule she saw among her Cambridge lecturers that a woman cannot be both a professional academic and fully a woman at the same time.[151] In her article in Oxford University's *Isis* magazine, she called for a new culture at Cambridge in which a female student 'keeps her female status while being accepted as a human being', dismissing as a counter-example of this well-rounded femininity 'those blue-stockinged . . . women who brood in the University Library until closing time'.[152]

This critical attitude towards feminists of an earlier generation emerges in *The Bell Jar*, in Plath's account of the female poet who teaches at Esther's university. She lives with a 'stumpy' female classicist, who wears her hair in a 'cropped Dutch cut' (*BJ* 210). When Esther had mentioned her plans for marriage and a family to the poet, she had been appalled, exclaiming, '"But what about your *career*?"' (*BJ* 211). This well-known poet is a fictional transformation of the well-known novelist and scholar Mary Ellen Chase, whose partner was classicist Eleanor Shipley Duckett. Plath told Chase, who strongly disbelieved that marriage and a writing career could coexist, about her forthcoming marriage whilst the latter was visiting Cambridge in 1956. She wrote to her mother that her reaction was one of 'shock' (*LH* 292), and later described her 'disapproval' (*J* 435). Choosing a career in preference to marriage is a denial or repression of one's femininity, for Esther, as for Plath herself. Esther is genuinely concerned when Buddy Willard raises the question of how she will be able to get married after having been in a mental hospital. Both of them know it is a cruel question, an attack on her sense of identity as a woman. Although Esther does not articulate this desire as explicitly as Plath, she too wants both marriage and a fulfilling working life outside her home. There is no sense in the novel of how the two are to be done at the same time. They remain simply conflicting desires, whose conflict contributes significantly to Esther's breakdown and remains unresolved at the end of the novel. Whilst she asserts that she does not want to marry, Esther continually fantasises about marriage throughout the novel. In her fantasy life as Elly Higginbottom, she dreams that she will marry a 'virile, but tender, garage mechanic', with whom she will have a 'big cowy family' (*BJ* 127). When she meets a prison guard at Deer Island, where she used to live, she reflects that if she had never left home, she could have become his wife. She would have 'piles of little kids', a few farm animals, and would spend her days happily around the house with her 'fat arms' and 'pots of coffee' (*BJ* 144). In these passages, a fulfilling marriage for Esther remains entirely within the realm of fantasy. In both daydreams she marries a working-class man, unthinkable in reality. She cannot even imagine what a fulfilling marriage would be like for the middle-class, college-educated woman she is. Furthermore, in both fantasies, she has abandoned her desire to pursue a public career, picturing herself in a kitchen, with her family as her single achievement. The reason she gives for not wanting to get married is that she wants 'change', 'excitement' and to 'shoot off in all directions' (*BJ* 79). Even at the level of fantasy, however, it is simply impossible for her to reconcile this desire with the idea of marriage. In an early draft of the novel, Esther had begun her comments about shooting off in all directions with the reflection that her personality was more masculine than feminine.[153] She ends as she began, with no idea as to how, as a woman, she can both marry and have a career. Although we can infer from the fact of Esther's baby at the time of narration that she has married, Plath gives us no sense as to how this came about. The gap in the novel between Esther's narrating, when she is 'all right' (*BJ* 3), and the end of her narration, about to enter her discharge conference in hospital, is absolute. If she has managed to move from one state to the other, it is, like Plath's own sense of her happiness in marriage at the time of writing, a miracle.

Chapter 5

Gender and Society in Plath's Short Stories

In a series of notes for a story she planed to call 'Coincidentally Yours', which would later become 'The Smoky Blue Piano', Plath wrote that it would be told from the perspective of a young woman who is essentially her. She listed a series of characteristics that this heroine and narrator would have – cheerful, fun-loving, popular, pretty but not convention-ally so – and noted that it was herself on whom this character is based.[1] These notes were written in the Fall semester or Christmas vacation of 1954. As Plath's fiction developed, she created narrators and protago-nists who are not recognisably versions of herself, as in 'The Invisible Man' and her later women's magazine fiction. Nevertheless, the major-ity of Plath's stories are based on experiences and events in her own life. Fiction is, for Plath, above all a medium in which women's lives can be portrayed. In this chapter, I discuss the range of ways in which she does so.

Plath's Women's Magazine Fiction

Plath was an avid reader of women's magazines throughout her life. From Britain, she asked her mother to send her a feature from the *Ladies' Home Journal* about small children.[2] When Plath was ill with a cold, Aurelia sent her a *Ladies' Home Journal*, and Plath replied that she had loved the entire magazine (*LH* 370). In 1961, she described herself as 'homesick' for the journal (*LH* 433). There are numerous references to it in Plath's letters – in 1961, Aurelia responded to her request for a subscription as a Christmas gift, which Plath was repeatedly enthusiastic to receive, and Aurelia renewed the subscription the following year.[3] Not only did the *Ladies' Home Journal* in particular remind Plath of American life, but she also enjoyed making use of the practical articles and features published in women's magazines (*LH* 433). Aurelia sent her a copy of *Good Housekeeping* with an article about savings under-lined for Plath's attention, to which Plath responded in detail.[4] She was delighted with a design for a baby's crib in one of the copies of *Woman's Day* her Aunt Marion sent her one Christmas, and she referred repeat-edly to her mother to trying the recipes she found in the *Ladies' Home Journal*.[5]

Plath was always both willing and able to write for a wide variety of different markets, from literary periodicals like the *New Yorker* to women's magazines like the *Ladies' Home Journal*. After her Christmas vacation with Richard Sassoon in Europe in 1955, in which they visited the Matisse chapel, Plath planned out a story about this experience, writing to her mother that she planned to write it up in several styles, first that of the *New Yorker*, then that of the *Ladies' Home Journal* and finally as a non-fictional account (*LH* 208). In 1957, she wrote in her journal of 'at least five' stories that she was attempting to write at the same time. These are 'The Day of the Twenty Four Cakes', which she described as 'McCalls or SatEvePost naturalism and introspection'; a story she calls the 'Eye-Beam story', which she described as 'Atlantic Monthly: weird, very Kafka symbolic'; *Falcon Yard*, for which she thought of learning from Hemingway; 'Operation Valentine' and 'The Laundromat Affair'; and finally a feature for *Harper's* magazine (*J* 292). Not only is Plath able to write a single story, like 'The Matisse Chapel', in different styles, but she constantly juggles writing different pieces in numerous styles. She worked on fiction in the styles of literary authors like Kafka and Hemingway at the same time as she worked on stories about cakes and laundry for women's magazines. Indeed, in a passage like this one, Plath made no marked distinction in value between liter-ary and non-literary writing. The stories she mentioned in the passage above are not divided into these two groups, but come to Plath's mind together, as a single group. Indeed, she described herself as 'hung between the equal . . . pulls' of these stories (*J* 292).

Christina Britzolakis argues that Plath's ambition to write in several genres, both 'popular' and 'literary', represents a split in her self-consciousness that she tries and fails to unify.[6] Plath did not see writing fiction for women's magazines as a problem to be solved, however. She recognised the distinction between literary and non-literary writing which her English degrees at Smith and Cambridge had drummed into her, reflecting that she could work on women's magazine stories 'while keeping my art intact' (*J* 366). This kind of distinction between art and other kinds of writing is rarely found in Plath's reflections on her work, however. Marsha Bryant has argued that, in *Ariel*, Plath writes in a 'surreal' style which incorporates both high literary and everyday popular discourses, contrasting this style to Plath's fiction, which 'may tend to pit art and domesticity against one another'.[7] There is no such opposition, however, in Plath's fiction. When she sketched out the plot for 'The Day of the Twenty-Four Cakes', she wrote that the style would be 'either Kafka lit-mag serious or SATEVEPOST', and that she would work in each of these styles until she was satisfied with the result (*J* 288). This lack of distinction between the relative value of the two genres is the most characteristic feature of Plath's reflections on her fiction. On the very same day that she distinguished in her journal between art and working on women's magazine stories, she remembered the spring of 1956, when she ended her relationships with Gordon Lameyer and Richard Sassoon during her European holiday and returned to Cambridge for a new relationship with Ted Hughes, and reflected that she was going to work these experiences into fiction for *McCall's* and the *New Yorker* (*J* 366). In all her notes on her plans for publishing stories, she made no distinction in value between the literary fiction published by the *New Yorker* or the *Atlantic Monthly*, and the women's fiction published by *McCall's* or the *Ladies' Home Journal*. They are simply different genres in which Plath aspired to write well. When the *Saturday Evening Post* rejected 'The Trouble-Making Mother', Plath wrote that it was a 'slick story, but one I consider good' (*J* 295). Linda Wagner-Martin has emphasised the dominance of male authors, critics and teachers in Plath's literary education.[8] Despite her formidable education in English Literature, however, Plath never entirely learned to privilege 'literary' over 'popular' forms of writing. The women's magazine story is not a genre she dismisses as merely popular, because she places a lower value on the concept of the literary than her teachers had done. It is rather one of many genres, each with their own criteria, which Plath enjoys and in which she aims to write well herself.

We have a good example of Plath's ability to write the same story in two styles in her rewriting of 'In the Mountains' as 'The Christmas Heart'. The stories are based on Plath's experience visiting Dick Norton at the Ray Brook sanatorium in upstate New York, where he was being treated for tuberculosis, during the 1952–53 Christmas vacation. 'In the Mountains' was written for Plath's creative writing course during her senior year at Smith, and published in the Fall 1954 issue of the *Smith Review*. In January 1955, she wrote that she had intended it to be 'understated and cryptic as Hemingway', and that she has decided to rework it into a story for *Seventeen*, for which it would need a much greater focus on the heroine's 'inner struggle' (*LH* 155).[9] In March 1956, she asked her mother to submit 'The Christmas Heart' to five different American women's magazines, having already submitted it herself to the *Ladies' Home Journal*.[10] 'In the Mountains' is, as Plath said to her mother, terse and understated, the kind of piece a creative writing student could be expected to produce in imitation of Hemingway. 'The Christmas Heart', however, which consists of the bulk of the original story more or less verbatim, contains numerous short additions and one long addition, which nearly double its length and which alter the genre of the story to the kind of romance Plath hoped would be accepted by the women's magazines to which she submitted the story.

There are two small stylistic features of 'The Christmas Heart' that immediately strike the reader of both versions of the story. First, Plath has toned down the sexual content of the earlier version. In 'In the Mountains', the heroine, sitting next to the hero on the bus, can feel 'the hard length of his thigh' next to her (*JPBD* 162). In 'The Christmas Heart', he is simply warm next to her. A book in which a woman is 'made pregnant' by the hero (*JPBD* 168) becomes one which she is simply the woman he loves.[11] Second, Plath irons out all the minor blasphemies in her characters' speech, replacing exclamations like 'God!' and 'Good lord!' with innocuous substitutes (*JPBD* 167, 168). The most substantial changes, however, are the additions of a new emotional story, about the heroine's developing feelings about her relationship to the hero. These additions are very frequent, and Plath adds a new episode, in which the hero teaches the heroine how to ski, and in which her changing feelings for him are the driving events of the narrative.

In the midst of a terse, descriptive account of the opening scene of 'In the Mountains', in which the hero and heroine take the bus to the sanatorium, Plath inserts the first sentences of the story of the heroine's emotional journey. On the first page of 'In the Mountains', we read:

> Austin put his arm around her shoulder. The old man . . . was looking at them, and his eyes were kind. (*JPBD* 161)

In 'The Christmas Heart', in between these two sentences, Plath inserts two long sentences about the heroine's feelings for Austin (or Michael, as he is called in the later story) as he puts his arm around her shoulder. She feels a world away from him now, having learned in his absence that she does not constantly have to be meeting his standards. The story Plath inserts into 'In the Mountains' in this way cannot be reduced to a single genre, nor can a single position be isolated as the one the narrator adopts toward her narration. The story is at once formulaic romance fiction – an exercise in writing for a market – and the statement of certain feminist values to which Plath was deeply committed. Hughes describes Plath's women's magazine stories as 'efforts at pastiche' (*JPBD* vii). The value of a mutually creative relationship, however, as opposed to the domination of the girl's intuitive nature by the boy's scientific outlook, privileged by the story, is one towards which Plath herself works in her journal meditations over the relationship she fictionalises here. Plath did not see romance fiction as a minor or inferior genre, but rather as a form of writing that, although often formulaic, superficial and wish-fulfilling, is at the same time potentially full of meaning for women, quite as full of meaning as the works traditionally canonised as literary have been for men. She can take a genre that is 'only' for women and express in it values to which she is as deeply committed as those great male writers she was reading at college at the time were committed to theirs. Plath wrote a scene that she would later put into *The Bell Jar*, in which the heroine has to ski down to the hero, although she does not know how to steer or stop. In 'The Christmas Heart', Sheila melodramatically compares her journey down the slope to her relationship with Michael. Both will succeed only if she is strong and courageous, his partner and not his inferior. Although this is formulaic romance fiction, Plath uses it to express a value – a creative relationship between two partners – to which she could not be more committed. This is the kind of women's magazine fiction that Plath writes. She could not help but put more into the stories she wrote for women's magazines than the magazines wanted from their authors. Plath cannot make a truly minor genre out of women's magazine fiction, but always – at least when she sets out to write it herself – finds that, as well as being dismissed as an inferior mode of writing, it is also full of potential for a woman to express herself in.

Having focused on Plath's American women's magazine fiction in Chapter 1, I focus here on the stories she wrote for the British women's magazine market in 1960 and 1961. In November 1960, Plath told her mother that she had turned again to writing for women's magazines. She had completed one, begun a second, and she and Ted were working on plots for several more (*LH* 401, 403). By Christmas Eve, she had completed the only story she ever sold to a women's magazine, 'The Lucky Stone', published as 'The Perfect Place' in *My Weekly*. Plath saw these stories as a useful source of income that could be written whilst she minded her baby, since they demanded only 'perspiration, not inspiration' (*LH* 403). The best-known of these stories, 'Day of Success', was based on an incident that occurred during the first week of February 1961. Hughes had been invited to discuss a series of children's programmes he had proposed for BBC radio with a producer named Moira Doolan. According to Anne Stevenson, Plath had taken Doolan's phone call and had formed the impression that Doolan was younger than she actually was. When Hughes was late home from the lunch meeting, which had gone well, Plath burned Hughes' notes, the drafts of the poems and the play he was working on, and his edition of Shakespeare.[12] The thought of husbands leaving their wives for younger, more attractive women had been on Plath's mind that week as Dido Merwin, the wife of Hughes' friend W. S. Merwin, had had a facelift, about which Plath wrote critically to her mother, commenting that people would still gossip, but that now they would say that Dido was afraid of her husband leaving her.[13]

There are two models in 'Day of Success' of the 'bad', failed or lacking woman, a woman who is not all that a woman ought to be. These are opposed to the heroine, a housewife and mother, a 'good' woman, with whom readers can identify, and whose goodness is rewarded with the love of her husband, precisely what is denied the others. The first failed woman is the divorcée Nancy Regan, who has substituted wealth for a home. Her husband left her when he became a successful playwright and she has become a wealthy but bitter society gossip. She is all that Ellen, the main character, does not want to become. When Ellen hears that her husband's play will soon be published for a substantial sum, she thinks about doing what Nancy would do, going out on a spending spree, but she reflects decisively, '*I'm not Nancy*' (*JPBD* 187). The story's structure is complex, however. In its system of values, according to which Nancy is judged as a negative character, her negative characteristics *follow* her punishment – her husband leaving her – and are caused by it. The distribution of rewards and punishments (one's husband staying or leaving) is, therefore, despite the apparent value-system which differentiates good from bad women, arbitrary and unrelated to it. When Ellen's husband returns home after his lunch, unattracted to the attractive producer, he has a 'mysterious glow' that has nothing to do with 'martinis or redheads' (*JPBD* 192). In the story's system of values, this glow is indeed mysterious – no account is given, or could be given according to its terms, of why Jacob stays with Ellen but Keith leaves Nancy. Ellen says to herself '*Jacob's not like Keith, Jacob's not like Keith*' (*JPBD* 191), but there is no possible explanation for this difference in the terms of the story – hence its anxious repetition. Although it seems that one woman is lovingly committed to the home, whereas the other is hard and materialistic, this is not the difference between their husbands' behaviour. The women are subject to the unaccountable whims of their husbands, who bless some and damn others without discernible reason, and with an absolute sovereignty against which there is no appeal.

The other stereotype to which Ellen is opposed is Denise Kay, the young attractive producer. Whereas Nancy is all that Ellen does not want to become, Denise is all that Ellen fears. She does not value marriage – she is having an affair with a married man and has had other such affairs in the past; indeed she is a 'professional [homewrecker]', who looks for married men in particular (*JPBD* 191). This phrase sums up Denise's negativity in the women's magazine story perfectly. Not only is she a threat to the home but she is even a professional threat – the worst kind of career woman, who makes a career of seducing the husbands of housewives and mothers. This negativity to the second power is emphasised again as Nancy warns Ellen that Denise is a 'real career girl', who always makes sure the men she picks never leave her with domestic work to do (*JPBD* 191). This is the final straw in the characterisation of Denise as a bad woman – not only is she is neither a housewife nor a mother, but she does not even want to be.

Plath thought of women's magazine stories as sites of wish-fulfilment for their readers. She described her husband as the kind of heroic character that 'unsatisfied ladies scan the stories in the *Ladies' Home Journal*' to find (*J* 376). Magazine fiction, is, in Plath's view, a fantasy space for women readers, in which they can vicariously experience the kind of relationship they do not have in reality. 'Day of Success' is a good example of such wish-fulfilment. When Ellen's husband returns late from lunch with the attractive Denise, he turns out not to have been attracted to her at all. He does not like the fact that she is 'highpowered' nor that she drinks a lot (*JPBD* 194). Rather than being seduced by the scent of French perfume, of the kind a career woman like Denise can afford, the scent he likes is that of home – Ellen's 'marvellous homemade blend of Farex and cod liver oil' (*JPBD* 193). So unequivocally committed to the home is he that the story ends with his raising their home life to a new level by putting a deposit on a little house in Cornwall with the career woman's cheque. Plath was able to write the kind of fantasy she believed the readers of women's magazines were looking for. When Ellen realises her husband prefers her to the glamorous Denise, she speaks 'dreamily' and does not walk but rather 'floated' away from her husband and child to pick up the telephone (*JPBD* 194). These words accurately indicate that the story, like a dream, is a fantasy, an exercise in wish-fulfilment. Anne Stevenson argues, 'Even in 1961 its catch-your-man-and-be-happy philosophy would have sounded naïve', but this is not true.[14] Finding love, and therefore happiness and fulfilment, is the most common subject of women's magazine stories in 1961. Tracy Brain adds, 'Even at the beginning of the twenty-first century, women's magazines are littered with short stories that purvey the "catch-your-man-and-be-happy philosophy"'.[15]

In January 1962, the fiction editor of *My Weekly* rejected Plath's stories 'A Winter's Tale' and 'Shadow Girl'. She liked their 'sense of "quality"' and 'sincerity', which she had also liked in the 'The Lucky Stone', but she felt that the wealthy publishing background of the characters was too glamorous for her readers to identify with. 'We don't want . . . anything of the kitchen-sink variety', she wrote, but simply 'nice, ordinary recognisable homeliness'.[16] With its violent emotions just beneath the surface of ordinary social interactions, 'Day of Success' would not meet this criterion. The other three stories come much closer. Peter Steinberg has argued that 'The Perfect Place' anticipates themes and motifs from *The Bell Jar*.[17] In my view, the four stories Plath wrote for the British women's magazine market in late 1960 and 1961 are more closely related in themes and styles to one another. One of the most striking features in them is the extent to which their structure privileges the country over the city. Tracy Brain has pointed to the toxic world of 'Johnny Panic and the Bible of Dreams' and the National Park setting of 'The Fifty Ninth Bear' as places in which Plath expressed her ecological vision in fiction.[18] We can add here that Plath's love of the natural world was repeatedly emphasised in her British women's magazine stories. In 'The Perfect Place' and 'A Winter's Tale', the heroine's journey leads not just emotionally to the right man but physically to the countryside in which he lives. In both stories, the anti-hero, the bad male character who wants the heroine but not for the right reasons, is from London. In both stories, he journeys from the city to the Yorkshire countryside, intending to take the heroine back as his wife. She refuses, however, in order to stay in the country with the hero with whom she has fallen in love. In 'The Perfect Place', Kenneth is from a wealthy society family. He is a successful lawyer and devoted to his work. In their Yorkshire boarding house, however, Joanna meets Simon, who loves the coastal landscape and wildlife, just as Joanna had done as a child. In three scenes in the story, they fall in love in the context of the natural world. In the first scene, Joanna and Kenneth go exploring on the rocks by the beach, but Kenneth does not like the difficult terrain. When he lets her go on alone, Joanna meets Simon, who shows her a starfish and the kind of 'lucky stone' she used to collect by the sea as a child. They sit together over a rockpool, watching a 'red-speckled crab stalk across the brilliant pebbles'.[19] When Kenneth interrupts this scene, he loses his footing on the wet rocks, dirtying his suit and getting angry at the 'grit and tar streaking the expensive material'.[20] In the second scene, Simon and Joanna are driving along the coast in the rain. Joanna tells Simon that she enjoys the rain. She used to go out in it as a child, she says, 'listening to the fog horns off the coast hooting like lost owls'.[21] This memory of her seaside childhood moves her to tears, but Simon regards this as 'natural'. He compares the two of them, with their shared love of each other and the coast, to fish in the sea. They are the kind of people, he says, for whom 'the sea's a native habitat – they take to it like fish'.[22]

A very similar journey occurs in 'A Winter's Tale', written the following year. There the bereaved heroine, Kate, lives alone on the Yorkshire moors. Her friend Irene, who works in publishing, travels up from London to persuade Kate to return there with her. She even invites Wilfred, the anti-hero of the story, who works in the same publishing house, to come up and propose marriage to Kate. His unattractive qualities are explicitly associated with city life. He stares myopically at Kate whilst he tells her about the latest financial news. When the trio get stranded in a snowstorm on the moors, Wilfred is too weak physically and too indecisive morally to get the two women to safety. He ends up only at a farmhouse where he is taken care of while the women freeze. It is Justin Blake, the hero of the story, who lives on and knows the moors, who saves them. It even seems to Kate, when she sees Wilfred again at the farmhouse, that he looks fatter after the generous meal he has been given. The story ends in precisely the same way as 'The Perfect Place', with the anti-hero wanting the heroine to return to the city with him to marry her, and with her refusing in order to stay in the country with the man she has fallen in love with. In 'A Winter's Tale', the story ends with an explicit connection between the love of the hero and heroine and the countryside which they also love. Justin brings flowers to Kate's house and, as she opens the door, she seems to fall in love both with him and with the winter landscape from which he comes.[23] In 'Day of Success', this journey to the country is about to occur as the story ends, as Ellen's husband has made enough money from his play to buy the little house on the coast of which they have always dreamed, away from the 'petrol fumes' and 'smoky railroad yards' of the city, with a 'garden', a 'hill' and a 'cove' for the baby to grow up in (*JPBD* 182). Ellen's reward for being a good wife is not only a faithful husband but also a life in the country with him.

A second feature of Plath's British women's magazine stories is that the hero is always an artist of some kind. In 'The Perfect Place', Simon is a painter. Kenneth, on the other hand, 'suspected . . . artists of self-indulgence and irresponsibility', because a man, in his view, should work at a paying job to support his family.[24] Simon is painting a seascape when he and Joanna meet on the beach, and he asks her to stay with him at the end of the story while she admires his paintings. In 'Day of Success', the hero is a poet and a playwright, and in 'Shadow Girl' he is a filmmaker and a scriptwriter. Perhaps the most significant thing about the value of art in these stories, however, is that it is never successfully maintained. It seems that the hero is an artist, symbolising his emotional understanding of the heroine, as opposed to the materialistic anti-hero who is interested only in his career and social status. In every story, however, this structure collapses. In 'Day of Success', the bad husband, Keith, is also an artist. Although he is associated with the negative values of wealth and social status, there is no suggestion that he is a bad artist, a merely commercial entertainer as opposed to the true art of Ellen's husband Jacob. On the contrary, both men seek financial success for their plays, and both achieve it. It is precisely the money which caused Keith to leave his wife (the negative value of the story) which allows Jacob and Ellen to live together in the country (the positive value). In 'The Perfect Place', it seems that Kenneth cares only about wealth and status in comparison to Simon's love of nature and art. Kenneth, however, also has considerable taste in such things as wallpaper, furniture and clothes. If he is stereotyped as an artificial man, with his greater concern for his expensive suit than the beauty of nature, it is difficult completely to contrast him to Simon, who is stereotyped as an artist, since the difference between art and artifice is so small. The wedding dress by the 'London designer', which stands for the materialism of Kenneth's family, is also the same kind of work of art which stands for the very opposite quality in Simon. Furthermore Simon, like Kenneth, is financially successful: 'My first one-man show bought our house'.[25] The negative value of wealth is associated not only with the anti-hero, who looks down on artists as too poor to support a family, but also with the hero. Precisely the same lack of opposition occurs in 'Shadow Girl'. Both the anti-hero, who feigns interest in the heroine only to get his book published by her powerful father, and the hero, who loves her for herself, are commercially successful artists. In 'A Winter's Tale', the anti-hero, Wilfred, enjoys the tasteless products for tourists in the Brontë country in which the story is set. On the other hand, he is also genuinely interested in the Brontë sisters' life and work.[26] Although he is merely a businessman, someone who cares about art only insofar as he can sell it, he also slips into being the kind of true lover of art that is the hero's quality in these stories.

Beneath the surface of the stories lies a similar confusion concerning gender roles. In 'The Perfect Place' in particular, Kenneth's masculine concern with the world of work and money makes him an emotionally inadequate character to understand and love Joanna. When she tells him she needs him to teach her, he is 'pleased' to take on this paternal role. On the other hand, Kenneth behaves in a number of feminine ways. It is he rather than Joanna who is concerned with the details of furnishing and decorating their home. While Joanna is thinking about the beauty of the northern landscape, Kenneth wants to discuss the sitting-room wallpaper, complaining that he is 'really not satisfied with the fleur-de-lis paper' they have chosen for it.[27] In a similar way, it is he rather than Joanna who is concerned with his clothes. Joanna, by contrast, is happy in a 'fisherman's' jersey. Although not sufficiently in tune with Joanna's feminine nature to be her lover and the hero of the story, Kenneth is at the same time even more feminine than she is. In 'Shadow Girl', it is the heroine who takes flowers to the hero, a motif that runs throughout the entire story. When she hears the hero speaking about breaking up with someone clingy and emotional on the telephone, she assumes he is referring to her. It turns out at the end of the story, though, that the needy partner Angus is going to get rid of is a man, a writer who has been pestering him with scripts to produce. Not only is Angus breaking up with a man, but the man who occupies this feminine position is another artist, which as we have seen is the most heroic quality of all in the male heroes of the stories.

Why do these stories deal successfully in the stereotypes of women's magazine fiction on one hand, yet fail on the other to maintain the structure of these stereotypes? In my view, it is because Plath is using ideological materials, products of collective fantasy, whose incoherent and contradictory nature become apparent as she puts them to work in her stories. As we saw with 'Day of Success', each of Plath's British women's stories has a recognisable relationship of fantasy to her own life. In 'The Perfect Place', the heroine had a childhood by the sea, just as Plath did. Indeed, Plath uses the motif of the lucky stone, which she had used for the title of that story, again the following year in 'Ocean 1212-W', as a symbol of her continued fantasy of childhood (*JPBD* 109). Both Joanna in 'The Perfect Place' and Kate in 'A Winter's Tale' are bereaved, as Plath was, and both stories portray a love that heals that bereavement. In 'Shadow Girl', as the title indicates, the heroine lives in the shadow of her father, as Plath did, and the story portrays a love that leads her out of that shadow. Furthermore, the experience of falling in love in these stories is associated with childhood, with the heroine allowing herself to become a girl again. In 'Shadow Girl', the heroine feels as carefree as a little girl on her first date with the hero.[28] In 'The Perfect Place', Joanna and Simon fall in love while exploring the beach, just as Joanna had done when she was a child. She tells him, 'I still behave like a child when I'm back by the sea'.[29] Plath believes that women's magazine stories are fantasies for their readers. It is because she is able to deal so accurately in the logic of these fantasies that her stories show them up as such, as inconsistent and contradictory in relation to reality.

Home Is Where the Heart Is

Although the women's magazine market demands that the home be the dominant value in its fiction, it is a dominant value in so much of

Plath's fiction that it is clear that it is a concept to which she was also personally committed. Although Plath protested vigorously against the contemporary attitudes to women which demanded that they become wives and mothers rather than pursuing creative work of their own, she nevertheless valued marriage, family and the home. She wrote many short stories, from her high school days to mature adulthood, which privilege the home as a value for women. These stories began early. In a piece written in 1948 for her high school English class, entitled 'The Visitor', Plath was already writing about the marriage vs. career dilemma. The story draws fully on the feminine mystique, privileging as the moral of the story marriage and family over a career as the most fulfilling choice for a woman. The visitor of the story's title is a college friend of the narrator's mother, who has chosen a career rather than marriage. They had both studied art at university and had intended to run their own clothing companies. Esther, the visitor, had achieved this goal, while the narrator's mother had married instead. During the visit, Esther repeatedly insinuates that she has achieved more than her friend. She learns by the end of the story, however, during which she becomes a part of the family, that this superiority is an illusion. She had not understood how much she lacked in her own life until she saw the ways in which her friend's family worked together as a whole. Indeed, the narrator's mother is the most fulfilled person she has ever met. Like a chorus, the narrator's father agrees with this conclusion – as the family wave Esther off on the train at the end of the story, looking tired beneath her glamorous appearance, he comments to his wife that it is not easy to live as Esther does. [30]

In 'Home is Where the Heart Is', written for a contest run by the Christophers in 1955, Plath again organised a story around the value of the home for a woman. Betty Arnold, the heroine, exemplifies Betty Friedan's 'happy housewife heroine'.[31] Like the narrator's mother in Plath's early story, Betty has given up a promising career in order to bring up her family, and she is beginning to lose her sense of identity. She had been one of the top students at university and had run the university newspaper, but now she spends her day doing domestic chores that anyone could do. She dreams of winning a holiday to Paris in a radio competition, and has just begun to compose her entry for this competition when, at the turning point of the story, her husband phones to tell her he is bringing an important client home for dinner. As in 'Day of Success', this turning point, in which the home changes from a negative to a positive value for the heroine, is effected by an event entirely out of her control. Her husband has simply changed his mind. In the first half of the story, he had not wanted to bring the important client home, which upset Mrs Arnold, although she did not show it. When he changes his mind – and as in 'Day of Success', we have no access to the reasons for his actions – all the negatives of the first half of the story turn one by one into positives. Mrs Arnold realises that she has been happy at home all along and that she has no need to go to Paris for excitement or adventure, as indeed a male character had moralistically reminded her in the first half of the story. Although the success of the dinner she puts on for her husband's client means that they will have enough money to travel, she comes to realise that what she really wants is the home and family she already has, and she throws away her entry for the holiday. The story ends with the ideological moral that the heroine belongs in her home. She realises that it was a mistake to think differently, even to the extent of wanting a holiday. She does not need to go to Paris to see beautiful buildings, she reflects, since the most beautiful building of all is her own home.[32]

It is difficult precisely to characterise Plath's own position with respect to these stories which privilege the home as the highest value for women. On the one hand, the motif occurs repeatedly throughout her fiction – in addition to 'The Visitor' (1948), 'Home is Where the Heart Is' (1955) and 'Day of Success' (1961), there are 'I Lied for Love' (1953), two outlines in Plath's 1957 journal for a variation on this theme, 'The Day of the Twenty-Four Cakes' (*J* 288, 292–3), and her children's story 'Mrs Cherry's Kitchen' (1958). Every one of these stories, however, was written with a pre-given audience in mind, to whose expectations Plath consciously fitted her work. 'The Visitor' was a high school English essay, in which Plath wrote material of which she could expect her English teacher would approve. 'Home is Where the Heart Is' was written for a student literary contest run by the Christophers, a Christian organisation which, as Aurelia Plath explained, promoted 'personal responsibility' and 'individual initiative' in public life (*LH* 153). 'Day of Success', like her projected story 'The Day of the Twenty-Four Cakes', was written for the women's magazine market. 'I Lied for Love' was written for a contest in *True Story*, a mass-circulation magazine aimed at working-class women. In a journal fragment of 1953, Plath wrote that she was writing the story for 'filthy lucer [*sic*]', aiming to 'capture the style' of the magazine (*J* 539).

In her study of *True Story*, Kathy Newman describes the stories it runs in the 1950s as 'economic fictions', 'stories centred on conflicts over money, class, and work . . . Their moral was simple: Do not desire beyond your means. If you follow this code, you will be rewarded. If you do not, you will be punished'.[33] This is precisely the kind of story Plath wrote. The heroine introduces herself as a girl who grew up on a farm, but who was seduced for a time by the lure of a wealthy and luxurious lifestyle, forgetting her family and the place she came from. Jenny dates a rich boy in school, whose parents try to keep them apart; he goes to fight in Korea and is killed, leaving Jenny pregnant, but the honest farm-worker Ivan marries her and raises her child as well as the children they have together. Since Ivan was close to Jenny's father and inherited his farm, she ends up by making her home on the family farm, as her father always wanted. At the end of the story, Jenny has learned the moral that home is what matters most in life, and in the final scene she and Ivan watch their children play in the beautiful landscape that surrounds their home.[34] Plath wrote a story for money in which a woman learns that home and family are more valuable than money, because this is precisely the kind of fiction she knows that *True Story* will buy.

Although Plath's children's story 'Mrs Cherry's Kitchen' does not set up a system of opposing values in which home and family are the positives, against negatives like a career or money or travel, it simply assumes that the place of the woman in the story – 'Mrs' Cherry – is in the home. The story concerns her kitchen appliances, which try unsuc-cessfully to swap functions, but the adult woman in the background can be assumed to be a wife, mother and housewife: 'Mrs Cherry spent the whole Monday morning scouring and scurrying around the kitchen', cleaning, cooking and doing the laundry (CCS 47). Marsha Bryant sees in Plath's poetry the influence of magazine adverts that feature magical characters in the kitchen, like the Minute Minder Man or the Jolly Green Giant, and this may also be the case with 'Mrs Cherry's Kitchen'.[35] The story was written with a magazine market in mind, the children's magazine *Jack & Jill* (J 304, 320). For all Plath's ability in catering to the popular values of her time, however, the sheer repetition through-out her career of stories which privilege the home cannot be explained simply as a skilful use of cultural codes. Nephie Christodoulides sees a psychoanalytic complexity at work in 'Mrs Cherry's Kitchen', in that Mrs Cherry imposes a maternal law on her husband, who is 'depend-ent upon her for nourishment and cleanliness', although 'ostensibly served by her' in the name of the father.[36] There is also something like a repetition-compulsion at work in these stories about the home and family as the place for Plath's heroines. Although they are consciously designed to meet the expectations of the market, these stories about home and family are too frequent a feature of her fiction to be explained merely as a series of exercises in pastiche. This is a function of Plath's conflicted relationship to the gender ideology of her time. She rejected the feminine mystique which would keep educated women at home instead of creatively pursuing the kind of work to which she was committed as a writer, but at the same time continued to value the home and the family privileged by the feminine mystique. She was well aware of the gender ideologies of the 1950s and early 1960s, and could draw on them with skill in writing for the market, especially the women's magazine market. But she never quite lost a commitment of her own to values that she also recognised were ideological. It is this irreducibly complex love-hate position towards contemporary attitudes to women that Plath's group of stories about the home ultimately articulate.

Feminine Identities

Many of Plath's women are postmodern characters, whose identity end-lessly recedes in layer after layer of image and identification, without a clearly distinguishable original over which these images are laid. 'Platinum Summer' exemplifies this well. Plath's own platinum summer began in the spring of 1954, when she dyed her hair blonde following her return to Smith after her breakdown and recovery. Plath initially told her mother that she was trying to draw focus away from the scar by her eye, but Aurelia understood her to be '"trying out"' a different 'personality' (*LH* 138). Reflecting on the first year of Sylvia's recovery, Aurelia described it as a time in which Plath was playing different char-acters in a search for a sense of who she really was.[37] Plath herself spoke of her 'brown-haired personality' when she dyed her hair back to its natural colour in the autumn, contrasting this character to her blonde-haired one (*LH* 141). In 1955, Plath put her experience of being blonde for a spring and a summer into a short story. After reading a feature in a fashion magazine, the heroine – studious, brown-haired Lynn – dyes her hair platinum blonde, which has the desired effect of drawing the atten-tion of numerous male admirers, all but the quiet and studious Eric in whom she is interested. Although she finally succeeds in bringing herself to his attention, Eric prefers her natural hair colour, and the story ends with her dyeing it back to this colour, much to his approval, and to the disappointment of the wealthy playboy Ira, who finally abandons his attempts to seduce her.[38]

The first thing that the story makes clear is that the complex network of identities through which Lynn travels is initiated by the discourse of fashion magazines. She dyes her hair because she reads a feature telling her to in a magazine. This article exhorts the reader to make herself over, and to do so by focusing on one particular aspect of her appear-ance. Lynn flicks through pages on make-up and diet until a picture of a model with bleached hair catches her eye. Lynn is interpellated by the picture in the magazine, encouraged to identify with the image and to transform herself into it. As Plath knows, this is just how the features and adverts of contemporary women's magazines work. The *Ladies' Home Journal* ran a 'Beauty Workshop' in September 1952, which featured nine 'Beauty Commandments', the fifth of which, about hairstyle, reads:

> Experiment with a new length, a new rinse or a new permanent. Change the arrangement often enough to keep you feeling and looking like an up-to-date beauty![39]

This commandment is illustrated with two photographs of women in a salon following just this advice. Plath had absorbed the discourse of fashion magazines thoroughly enough to reproduce precisely the kind of rhetorical devices at work in their adverts. She knew how they played on the anxiety and insecurity of their readers. As Lynn reads through the feature that persuades her to dye her hair, she sees a blurb that asks the reader whether her hairstyle is sufficiently glamorous.[40] There are countless questions of this kind in the adverts in women's magazines of the 1950s. Drene Shampoo demands, 'Does your hair look dull, slightly mousy?'[41] *Good Housekeeping*'s 'Beauty Clinic' column asks questions like, 'Do your curls sag on damp days or suffer from five o'clock droop?', and simply 'What's the matter with your hair?'[42] Skin care products highlight the numerous complexion flaws that need to be remedied if the reader is to look attractive – Pond's cold cream warns of six different areas of the face, each accompanied by an illustration, in which 'After 25 – drying skin begins to *show*!': 'criss-cross lines under the eyes', 'flabby, dry-lined throat', 'little creases . . . by the earlobe', 'flaky, dry skin patches', 'tiny dry lines . . . between your eyes', and 'dry skin down-lines by nose and mouth'.[43] An advert for Fresh soap features pictures of sixteen romantic moments enjoyed by a glamorous young couple in evening wear, any one of which could be spoiled by the woman perspiring in her sleeveless dress. The caption demands severely, 'Are you *always* Lovely to Love?'[44] Endless adverts for deodorants, mouthwashes, girdles, sanitary towels and other health and beauty products instil the same worries in the consumer that, without them, she will be insufficiently attractive.

Plath clearly portrayed the effect of these heavily researched, heavily funded questions: the interpellation is instantly effective. No sooner has Lynn read the blurb suggesting that her hairstyle is not glamorous enough than she examines her hair and agrees that indeed it is not. The advert then presents its suggested product in the form of a resolution to the anxiety it has stimulated. Plath also reproduces a favourite trope of beauty product adverts, that of the revelation of the already beautiful nature within. Lynn's solution, the feature tells her, is to buy and use a kind of hair dye that will emphasise the blonde tints she already has. Numerous adverts of the period promise exactly this outer emphasis of already existing beauty. Pond's, for example, ran a series of full-page spreads with headlines like, 'Within *you* – is a delightful second self' and 'That fascinating stranger – your *inner* self'.[45] In the first of these examples, a large photograph of a glamorous member of the Roosevelt family is accompanied by the caption, 'Her face speaks out to you of her enchanting Inner Self'.[46] The *Ladies' Home Journal* asserts that 'woman's desire for beauty emanates from her inner being' and that this desire can be fulfilled 'through recognition of your own inner possibilities'. In a feature on hairstyles explicitly described as a 'personality brush-up', Dawn Crowell Norman, the *Journal*'s beauty editor, comments:

> Hairdo's have lots of possibilities – and personalities! Take time to experiment with some tricks of the topknot – and you can be a new woman several times a week![47]

This is precisely the kind of article that Plath describes in her story. As Dawn Crowell Norman puts it in a later article, the 'premise' on which such features are based, which Plath had accurately represented in 'Platinum Summer', is that 'a fresh body makes a fresh spirit'.[48]

The adverts do not offer Lynn an illusory hope, moreover. In fact, the product does all that it promises. The advert makes the specious claim to bring out what was hidden within its reader all along, and yet, for all its speciousness, this is exactly what occurs. As Lynn turns platinum blonde on the outside, so she begins to turn platinum blonde on the inside, too. She starts to feel glamorous, and this shows in her demeanour. Before she knows it, she has a string of admirers competing for her attention. The hair dye seeps into her soul, or rather her soul exists on the surface of her body – in her hair, in her image. Self and image are not radically distinct in Lynn's experience, just as the discourse of the advert has suggested. She has read so many fashion features that she lives them – it takes an external product to reveal an internal quality. She has, as she reflects later on the difference between her experience as a brunette and as a blonde, a blonde identity. Christina Britzolakis argues that Plath's later works 'put into question the very possibility of a "pure" or uncontaminated knowledge of self', and this is precisely what occurs in 'Platinum Summer'.[49]

Plath turns the screw of this relationship once more, as Eric, the man in whom Lynn is interested, prefers her natural hair colour and asks her to change it back. Here a divergence in gender experience is set up. Eric wants Lynn to wear her hair in its natural colour precisely because it is natural – he agrees that she has a blonde personality, but tells her that she can be herself without external products like hair dye. For the male character in the story, Lynn is simply who she is, whatever the colour of her hair. For the female character, however, things are not nearly so simple. Now that Eric has noticed her, she reflects, he wants her to be who she really is, but it took the detour of an artificial colour for him to notice her in the first place. The very idea of who she really is is just one more image in the endlessly ramifying series of images of which Lynn's identity is constituted. She goes on to reflect that, however irrational men might say women are, women know how to manage men. What Lynn knows as a woman of the 1950s is the endless complexity of the play of images by which her identity is constituted, and about which Eric's male way of thinking is simply deluded. Hence the political nature of this reflection – although Eric might think her irrational, Lynn knows how to manage him, how to get what she wants, because of her greater understanding of the play of images which constitutes the experience of identity. The story ends with Lynn dyeing her hair back to its natural colour. She has attracted Eric by giving him what he wanted – an idea of the natural – in a story in which Plath shows clearly that, in feminine experience, nature is just one more 'look', the product not at all of the absence of beauty products like hair dye, but of a stylist even more skilful with them than the heroine herself.

Violence and Patriarchy

Several of Plath's women characters have a violent complex of sup-pressed emotions just beneath the surface of their outward femininity, which she portrays as a direct effect of their experiences in patriarchal society. 'Sunday at the Mintons' is an example of this. The story was written in April 1952 for Plath's creative writing course Eng 220b, and submitted to *Mademoiselle* for the 1952 College Fiction prize, which it won. When Plath knew the story was going to be published she wrote to her mother that she was 'scared' and 'curious' about what Dick Norton's response would be, since 'Henry started out by being him and Elizabeth me' (*LH* 87). The pair turned into elderly siblings as the story developed. Norton began a letter to Plath after he read the story by writing as Henry Minton to Elizabeth.[50] His intention does not seem to have been explicitly ironic, but the letter suggests that at some level he recognised himself in Henry Minton. Plath felt strongly during the years she dated Norton that he used the scientific, medical training he was acquiring at Yale to disparage her more aesthetic, relational way of looking at the world.[51] She told Ann Davidow in January 1952 that her ideal man would be someone just like Norton, but a little more sensitive. Their personalities were completely different, she told Ann – he lived according to reason, she to her feelings.[52]

Plath puts this opposition into the story of Henry and Elizabeth Minton. The sheer duality of the pair is the first point she wants to convey, as her character notes, written on the back of the first page of the first draft, indicate.[53] She wrote two columns, listing some twenty-five qualities for each character, all of which indicate that Henry is rational and practical whereas Elizabeth is emotional and a dreamer. Although the brother and sister live together again in the story as older adults, Elizabeth has endured a lifetime of having her temperament and characteristics judged wanting by Henry's standards. Her brother's sense of knowing and governing the world around him is gender-specific. He expects his sister to be a domestic worker, and is constantly upbraiding her for being a poor or inattentive housekeeper. Henry is sure of his right to expect that Elizabeth perform these tasks, however. God is on his side – he is the one who has access to the divinity as he prays before their meal, in a voice which sounds like a 'Biblical chant' (*JPBD* 142). Society also backs him up, as he feels able to 'moralise' to Elizabeth when she fails to perform her household tasks adequately and to give her a 'reproachful oration' on serving dinner correctly (*JPBD* 142). In his position as elder brother, who learned to give Elizabeth orders under the direction of their mother, Henry also has the family on his side. Furthermore, although this is not explicitly part of the story, his scientific and technical mindset is one that commands a powerful position in post-war American society.

The story, however, is nothing but a sustained feminist protest against this right and against all its sanctions. It is the extent of the violence into which this protest explodes that constitutes its powerful aesthetic effect. Elizabeth has long been wanting to respond to Henry's judgements, but she has no language in which to do so. There was once an occasion on which she managed to do this. She had tried to 'say something spontaneous and fanciful' about how she would like to see the thoughts inside a person's brain, but Henry had responded with a condescending joke, which left her 'deflated' and with nothing else to say (*JPBD* 147). She suffers in demure silence, choosing two responses. The first is imaginary protest. She is able to shut out Henry's criticisms by entering the 'private world' of her imagination, thinking about whatever she pleases as he talks (*JPBD* 143). She enjoys taking off her spectacles and blurring his image until he is 'thoroughly obscured' (*JPBD* 141). Plath also enacts this kind of imaginative protest on the surface of her own typescript. At the point at which Elizabeth's murderous fantasy begins, when her brooch drops onto the rocks, she exclaims, 'Whatever shall I do?' (*JPBD* 149). On the final word in this sentence, on the typescript, Plath has doodled a grinning face. The 'd' in 'do?' makes up the left ear; the question mark makes up the right ear; the 'o' makes up the left eye; and a blacked out 'o', typed in error before the question mark, makes up the right eye.[54] Sally Bayley has analysed the sketches of glamorous women Plath made on some of her high school and college assignments, describing them as a 'feminisation of the "facts"', done by a 'doodling, dreaming young Plath whose attention was often far from the narrated (and predominantly male) events of her . . . lesson'.[55] The same thing occurs on a smaller scale as Plath wrote 'Sunday at the Mintons'. She articulated on her own typescript, at the very point at which Elizabeth's rebellion against Henry's authority begins in earnest, precisely the kind of imaginative protest against discursive authority that constitutes Elizabeth's deepest desire in the story.

Plath described 'Sunday at the Mintons' as a story of the imagination.[56] Elizabeth's other response to her powerlessness as a woman is a series of imaginary fulfilments of murderous wishes, which spill out of her consciousness and permeate that of the entire text. As they walk out on the pier, Elizabeth's brooch drops onto the rocks below and she asks Henry to retrieve it. The wind and the sea have the answers to Henry's self-satisfaction that Elizabeth does not, as his words are 'flung back at him' in the 'derisive wind' (*JPBD* 150). When a wave comes to engulf Henry as he teeters on the rocks below the pier, Elizabeth's love-hate relationship to him is clear. '"Henry", she whispered in an ecstasy of horror' (*JPBD* 150). Elizabeth is horrified, and tries to warn Henry of the mortal danger he is in, but her unconscious desires are stronger – they keep her voice to a whisper, which he cannot hear. Elizabeth's horror at the prospect of Henry's death is itself drowned out by her ecstasy at it. Death is the only way she can imagine answering Henry, the only thing that silences him. After struggling and straining to stay afloat, she sees that his body is 'quieted' before it disappears (*JPBD* 151).

Elizabeth's murderous fantasy is of course no more than a fantasy. Plath makes this clear with Elizabeth's own end in the story. This ending is pure pleasure for Elizabeth, as the slightly erotic portrayal of the wind blowing up her dress, so that she is unable to 'smooth down her petticoats', already suggests. Elizabeth sails away on her wind-filled skirt with a 'triumphant, feminine giggle' (*JPBD* 152). This image of triumphant femininity consists in two things. First, Elizabeth fantasises the murder of the man, and the entire patriarchal system which he represents as her older brother, by whom she is dominated. Second, her fantasy is not only murderous but also erotic. Elizabeth remains sympathetic to Henry even after she has imagined killing him. She feels 'pity' for him and is concerned about who will take care of him at the bottom of the sea (*JPBD* 152). Plath's feminism in this story is a criticism of patriarchy on the basis of an ideal, non-exploitative sexual relationship. Henry doesn't simply die in Elizabeth's fantasy but enters into a kind of harmony with her, as her 'high-pitched . . . giggle' blends with his 'deep, gurgling chuckle' as they drift out to sea together, she above and he beneath the waves (*JPBD* 152). The image is a utopian one for Plath, one in which male and female voices speak – indeed laugh, indicating the utopian quality of the fantasy – in unison or harmony, as opposed to the domination of Elizabeth's voice by Henry's that has aroused the fantasy in her in the first place. This scene in the story articulates what Margaret Mead called a 'two-sex world', which is how she describes the way in which American society ought to reorganise its gender roles in a more constructive way for both men and women, so that both can use their distinctive abilities for everyone's benefit. 'We can build a whole society', she writes, 'only by using both the gifts special to each sex and those shared by both sexes – by using the gifts of the whole of humanity'.[57] Plath read and annotated Mead's *Male and Female* at Smith, and it is with its 'two-sex' vision of the world that she ended the first draft of 'Sunday at the Mintons'.

Plath changed her mind about this ending, however. On the typescript, after she had typed this end to the story, she hand-wrote two versions of another paragraph, the second of which becomes the final paragraph of the final version. Back in the real world, Elizabeth is roused from her reverie by Henry telling her it is time to leave. The last sentences read:

> Elizabeth gave a sigh of submission. 'I'm coming,' she said. (*JPBD* 152)

Dick Norton wrote that it was Plath's brother's idea that she should add this ending to the story.[58] She has clearly decided to end the story on a more pessimistic note than in her first draft. From having emphasised, with its position at the end of the story, Elizabeth's feminist fantasy, in which the patriarchal male dies in order to be reborn under the sea as a genuine sexual partner, she chooses to emphasise the real patriarchal conditions of the society which leaves women nothing but fantasies of such relationship. In real relations, as in real speech, Elizabeth is left with nothing to say. In her words and in her actions, she remains submissive to Henry's imperative, having discovered no possibility of changing that situation except in the violence of fantasy.

Fantasies of violence also fill Plath's story 'The Fifty-Ninth Bear', written in September 1959 at Yaddo, and inspired by an incident that had occurred two months earlier in Yellowstone National Park, when a bear raided Plath and Hughes' car whilst they listened from their tent. Tracy Brain has shown that no record exists of a bear killing anyone in Yellowstone Park during or close to 1959, despite Plath's biographers' assumption that her story of such a death in her letter to her mother is true.[59] Hughes' letter to his parents at the time, however, confirms Plath's account that a woman she met at their camp told her that a woman at the camp she had just left had been killed by a bear. The dead woman, Hughes wrote, 'shone her flashlamp' at the bear to drive it away from her cooking pots, and it 'came straight at her and killed her on the spot', making clear that Plath believed, on the basis of what she took to be an eyewitness account, that a bear had killed a woman in a nearby campsite.[60] There are many other details of Plath's own experience in the story. She and Hughes counted bears on the road to their campsite in Yellowstone, and continued to do so throughout their stay there.[61] The petrol gauge in their car was on zero for a worryingly long time before they reached the campsite. At their previous stop, in Stinson Beach State Park, the place they had expected to camp had been turned into a car park. Plath told her mother that she was on the verge of crying in frustration over this, but that Hughes had comforted her.[62]

Lucas Myers felt that 'The Fifty-Ninth Bear' was an improper story for a married woman to have published. He calls it 'unsettling'. Although based on a real experience and although 'the thought was a natural enough product of the subconscious', he writes, 'I was surprised she made a story of the killing of a husband for her husband and their friends to see'.[63] In fact, it may have been Hughes himself who suggested the idea. A list of ideas he gave Plath for poem topics suggests that this incident was one of them.[64] Plath's experience of sexual politics during her relationship with Dick Norton makes its way back into this later story in her choice of the name, Norton, for the husband. Three months before writing the story, Plath had hit upon the name Sadie Peregrine for the heroine of her novel: 'SP, my initials . . . Then Peregrine Falcon . . . And Sadie: sadistic . . . Wanderer' (*J* 498-9). The kind of fantasies that had been restricted to the consciousness of Elizabeth in 'Sunday at the Mintons' spill out of the consciousness of the female character in 'The Fifty-Ninth Bear' and permeate the entire story. The force of Sadie's fantasies turns the entire world of the story into one of sadism, one whose pleasure consists in violence and death, so that violence fills the minds of both characters, and the narrator, and at its climax the death of the male character occurs in reality, rather than in fantasy alone. It is as if the anger that has been brewing in Elizabeth Minton in the seven years since her story was written has exploded into reality in this later story.

The story is set in motion by an unnamed problem in Sadie and Norton's marriage. In visiting Yellowstone Park, they are performing a 'ritual of penance and forgiveness' (*JPBD* 84). The logic of the story's structure, in which Sadie's bear kills her husband, suggests that the marital wrong has been done by the husband – his is the penance, hers the forgiveness – for which he receives not forgiveness but justice, or at least that kind of emotional justice that characterises Sadie's fantasy life. Indeed, in the first draft of the story, Plath included a passage in which Sadie is explicitly associated with the childish tendency to displace aggressive emotions from their original objects onto others.[65] Norton takes a patriarchal relationship to Sadie – he thinks of her as a helpless child, a role Sadie has indeed adopted, pouting and crying when she does not get what she wants. With her 'sensuousness', 'enthusiasms' and tendency to live in her feelings alone, he thinks, she is so 'flimsy' that she could not cope with the real world without him (*JPBD* 88). Plath deleted a long passage from the first draft of the story, in which Norton reflects that Sadie holds on to him like a little girl, looking for shelter from the reality of the outside world. Norton even thinks that she may be a little unbalanced, unable to cope mentally with ordinary, adult life.

Whereas Elizabeth Minton has only her imagination to compensate for her domination by her elder brother and the patriarchal society he represents, Sadie, although in every sense a 'little woman', a wife-child, is also, precisely through her adoption of this ideological role, in control of her husband. As if in a kind of reverse chivalry, by allowing him to seem to dominate her, it is in fact she who dominates him. The relationship is complex – she has become a childish character within her marriage, but like a child that controls its parents, she controls her socially stronger husband. Norton does not 'care to see' that Sadie's passivity 'moved and drew him' and that 'she led . . . and he followed' her through the boiling geysers of the National Park (*JPBD* 90). Initially, Plath had gone on in this paragraph to show that this relationship also holds at the most intimate level of their marriage, with Norton snuggling up against Sadie in bed as if he were her baby rather than her husband. Sadie has led Norton throughout the Yellowstone landscape, whose heat and terrain disagree with him both physically and mentally. So demanding is this penance, indeed, that he has begun to fantasise about the death of his wife, imagining himself as the bereaved hero of his own romantic story. The narrator, too, is aware that Sadie is enacting a fantasy of violence towards her husband, telling us that Norton woke up feeling as if his eyes had been 'scoured . . . with sand' as he slept (*JPBD* 85).

The climax of the story is no more than the working out at the level of the plot, the making explicit, of the revenge Sadie is taking for whatever marital wrong resulted in their trip. She plays the game of how many bears they will see on their trip in the childlike way in which she tacitly dominates her husband – Norton secretly wants her to be right, so that she will not get upset. She bets on seeing fifty-nine bears, because that number is her 'symbol of plenitude' (*JPBD* 86). When the bear which kills Norton first appears in their campsite at night, Sadie imagines that she has willed it out of the forest, murmuring, '"My bear"' (*JPBD* 94). Sadie's will becomes so strong at the end of the story that she leads not only Norton, but controls the plot, the reality of the story itself, in a kind of wish-fulfilment. She makes Norton leave the tent and chase off the bear. When it stands its ground, Plath writes, 'There was another will working', more powerful than Norton's (*JPBD* 95). This is the bear's will only insofar as it is Sadie's – the distinction between fantasy and reality breaks down at the end of the story, which ends in pure, murderous wish-fulfilment. As the bear attacks, Norton hears a 'shrill cry', he does not know whether of 'terror' or 'triumph'. Plath writes, 'It was . . . her bear, the fifty-ninth' (*JPBD* 96). The bear is Sadie's – her symbol of plenitude is also the symbol of her murderous desires towards her husband.

In the first draft of the story, Plath emphasised with the imagery she used to describe the couple that Norton's death was a kind of revenge enacted by Sadie. Early in the first draft, Norton thinks of himself as a bear in his relationship to Sadie, rough and clumsy as he undresses her in the bedroom. He thinks that Sadie gives herself to him like an orchid opening its petals. These images are then picked up in Plath's initial account of Norton's death. In the story's penultimate paragraph, in which Norton is killed by the bear, Plath had written that he felt as if he were trapped in the throat of an orchid. The images of Norton's death were the same images used to describe his marriage. What he had taken from Sadie in marriage, they made clear, she was giving back to him with the bear's attack. Whereas Elizabeth Minton's fantasy was a kind of utopian reworking of patriarchal gender relations, Sadie's idea of plenitude, her idea of fullness, of satisfaction, includes no such utopia. She wants only the death of her husband, and her violent fantasies of this death are so strong that they permeate into the reality of the story.

Notes

The following abbreviations have been used for archives holding materials by Sylvia Plath:

Lilly   The Lilly Library, Indiana University, Bloomington
Mortimer   The Mortimer Rare Book Room, Smith College
MARBL   Manuscript, Archives and Rare Book Library, Emory University

Unless stated otherwise, all letters cited are by Sylvia Plath.

Introduction

1. Nancy Hargrove, *The Journey Toward Ariel: Sylvia Plath's Poems of 1956–1959* (Lund: Lund University Press, 1994).
2. Tim Kendall, *Sylvia Plath: A Critical Study* (London: Faber, 2001), 1.
3. Kathleen Connors and Sally Bayley, *Eye Rhymes: Sylvia Plath's Art of the Visual* (Oxford and New York: Oxford University Press, 2007), 1.
4. Tracy Brain, *The Other Sylvia Plath* (Harlow: Longman, 2001), 38.
5. Al Strangeways, *Sylvia Plath: The Shaping of Shadows* (Madison and Teaneck, NJ: Fairleigh Dickinson University Press and London: Associated University Presses, 1998); Robin Peel, *Writing Back: Sylvia Plath and Cold War Politics* (Madison and Teaneck, NJ: Fairleigh Dickinson University Press and London: Associated University Presses, 2002); Connors and Bayley, *Eye Rhymes*; Anita Helle, ed., *The Unraveling Archive: Essays on Sylvia Plath* (Ann Arbor, MI: University of Michigan Press, 2007); Brain, *The Other Sylvia Plath*.
6. Ted Hughes, 'Introduction', in Sylvia Plath, *Johnny Panic and the Bible of Dreams, and Other Prose Writings* (London: Faber, 1977), 12–13.
7. These are 'Mary Jane's Passport', 'A May Morning', 'Morning in the Agora', 'The Mummy's Tomb', 'Stardust' and 'Victory'. All six are held at Lilly, Plath MSS II, Box 8.
8. These are 'About a year ago I was babysitting', 'An Evening at the

Hofthizers', 'The Garden Party', 'The music wailed out from the radio'. All four are held at Mortimer.

9. Ted Hughes, 'Billy Hook and the Three Souvenirs', *Jack and Jill*, July 1958, 29.

10. The stories from 1948 are 'The Attic View', 'The Brink', 'Gramercy Park', 'Heat', 'In This Field We Wander Through', 'Sarah' and 'The Visitor'. Those from 1949 are 'Among the Shadow Throngs', 'The Dark River', A Day in June', 'East Wind', 'The Green Rock', 'Place: A Bedroom, Saturday Night in June', 'The Island' (a radio play) and 'And Summer Will Not Come Again'. Those from 1950 are 'First Date', 'The New Girl', 'Room in the World' (a play) and 'The New Zealand spinach was good that morning'. All but two of these are at Lilly, Plath MSS II Box 8. 'The New Zealand spinach was good that morning' is at Mortimer; 'And Summer Will Not Come Again' was published in *Seventeen*, August 1950, 191, 275–6.

11. Linda Wagner-Martin, *Sylvia Plath: A Literary Life*, 2nd. edn. (Basingstoke and New York: Palgrave Macmillan, 2003), 9.

12. Sylvia Plath, 'The Dark River'. Lilly, Plath MSS II, Box 8, folder 11.

13. Sylvia Plath, 'East Wind'. Lilly, Plath MSS II, Box 8, folder 12.

14. These are: from 1950, 'Den of Lions'; from 1951, 'The Perfect Setup', 'Suburban Nocturne' and 'Mary Ventura'; from 1952, 'The Latvian' (of which an earlier draft called 'The Estonian' also survives), 'Though Dynasties Pass' (of which an earlier draft called 'Brief Encounter' also survives), 'The New Day', 'Initiation' and 'Marcia Ventura and the Ninth Kingdom'; from 1953, 'Dialogue' and 'I Lied for Love'. From its content and style, the undated and incomplete story 'The English Bike' should also be included amongst the works written during this period. Plath also wrote the now lost stories, 'The Two Gods of Alice Denway', an earlier version of 'Among the Bumblebees', some time before 26 January 1953 (*J* 168), and 'The Birthday' during the academic year 1952–53 (Letter to Aurelia Plath, 8 June 1953. Lilly, Plath MSS II, Box 3). On the verso of Plath's draft for an essay on the Collected Poems of Dylan Thomas, there are two pages of a story in which the narrator, a college art student, is about to begin a relationship of some kind with her art professor, on whom all the other girls have a crush (Lilly, Plath MSS II, Box 10, folder 7). On the verso of Plath's essay, 'The Equilibrists', and on the verso of papers at MARBL discussing Hughes' interest in animal poems, there are six pages from two separate drafts of a story about a girl called Alison who watches people skating at Rockefeller Center during the Christmas holidays. An encounter takes place between a countess and a general, and the pair dance romantically on the ice. At the end of the story, the music finishes, the magic fades and Alison goes home sadly to her ordinary life (Lilly, Plath MSS II, Box 10, folder 8; MARBL, Ted Hughes Papers, 1940–1997, Box 140, 15).

15. *Seventeen*, May 1951; October 1952; January 1953.

16. *LH* 150. *Letters Home* gives the date of this letter as 'Undated; January 1955', but it can be dated more precisely. The letter is postmarked 17 January, which was a Monday, and was written the previous Saturday, which would have been 15 January. Lilly, Plath MSS II, Box 5.

17. Letter to Warren Plath, 28 July 1955. Lilly, Plath MSS II, Box 5; Letter to Aurelia Plath, 9 August 1955. Lilly, Plath MSS IV.

18. On the verso of the manuscript of Hughes' story 'The Harvesting', there are two pages of a story, and half a page of notes for the same story, which also features a character based on Richard Sassoon. The story begins with the American heroine Sheila amazed at the austere cold and lack of conveniences in her Cambridge University rooms (MARBL, Ted Hughes Papers, 1940–1997, Box 140, folder 14). I would date this story between October 1955, when Plath arrived in Cambridge, and February 1956, when she met Hughes.

19. Ted Hughes, letter to Sylvia Plath, 9 October 1956. Lilly, Plath MSS II, Box 6.

20. Sylvia Plath, 'Afternoon in Hardcastle Crags'. MARBL, Ted Hughes Papers, 1940–1997, Box 139, folder 2.

21. Letter to Aurelia Plath, 10 August 1956, Lilly, Plath MSS II, Box 6.

22. Sylvia Plath, 'Two Fat Girls on Beacon Hill'. MARBL, Ted Hughes Papers, 1940–1997, Box 140, folder 10.

23. Sylvia Plath, Poems: Lists, 1959–1963. Mortimer.

24. Ibid.

25. Sylvia Plath, 'The Mummy'. MARBL, Ted Hughes Papers, 1940–1997, Box 139, folder 34.

26. C. G. Jung, *The Development of Personality*, tr. R. F. C. Hull (New York: Pantheon, 1954), 55. Plath made four pages of reading notes on this book, now held at Mortimer, in which she copied out the entire passage quoted here.

27. Ibid., 125.

28. Ibid., 127.

29. Plath, Poems: Lists, 1959–1963. Mortimer.

30. Irralie Doel argues that the reason for this editorial change is that *My Weekly* typically preferred situations rather than images for the titles of their stories. Peter K. Steinberg and Irralie Doel, 'Sylvia Plath's "Perfect Place", The Sylvia Plath 75th Year Symposium, Oxford, 28 October 2007.

31. Anne Stevenson, *Bitter Fame: A Life of Sylvia Plath* (Boston, MA and New York: Houghton Mifflin, 1989), 206.

32. Plath, Poems: Lists, 1959–1963. Mortimer

33. Helena Annan, letter to Sylvia Plath, 19 January 1962. Mortimer.

34. *Letters of Ted Hughes*, ed. Christopher Reid (London: Faber, 2007), 90.

35. My thanks to Heather Clark, who drew my attention to six of these pages she found on the verso of Hughes' papers at MARBL.

36. Sylvia Plath, 'Runaway'. MARBL, Ted Hughes Papers 1940–1997, Box 139, folder 39.

37. Sylvia Plath, 'Nine Letters to Lynne Lawner', *Antaeus* 28 (1978), 45.

38. Aurelia Plath, 'The 1972 Edition of McCall's . . .', Draft Notes for Authors' Series Talk. Mortimer. All references in this paragraph are to this document. See also Aurelia Plath, 'For the Authors' Series Talk – Wellesley College Club, 16 March 1976'. Mortimer.

39. Letter to Ann Davidow Goodman, 27 April 1961. Mortimer.

40. See also Plath's letter to Alfred Kazin, 26 April 1961, cited in Paul

Alexander, *Rough Magic: A Biography of Sylvia Plath* (New York: Da Capo, 1991), 259.

41. *Letters of Ted Hughes*, 182.
42. Ted Hughes, 'Sylvia Plath and Her Journals', *Winter Pollen: Occasional Prose*, ed. William Scammell (London: Faber and Faber, 1994), 185.
43. Letter to James Michie, 14 November 1961. Mortimer.
44. Sylvia Plath, Personal Papers, Calendar 1962. Mortimer.
45. Letter to Olive Higgins Prouty, November 20, 1962. Mortimer.
46. Letter to Olive Higgins Prouty, 29 September 1962. Lilly, Plath MSS II, Box 6a. See also *LH* 464.
47. Ibid.; letter to Olive Higgins Prouty, 18 October 1962. Lilly, Plath MSS II, Box 6a.
48. A. Alvarez, 'My Friendship with Sylvia Plath and Ted Hughes', in conversation with Sally Bayley, *The Sylvia Plath 75th Year Symposium*, Oxford, 28 October 2007.
49. See letter to Aurelia Plath, 18 October 1962. Lilly, Plath MSS II, Box 6a.
50. Letter to Olive Higgins Prouty, 20 November 1962.
51. Judith Kroll, *Chapters in a Mythology: The Poetry of Sylvia Plath* (New York: Harper & Row, 1976), 66. See also Kroll's note on p. 229.
52. Olwyn Hughes, Corrections of Diane Middlebrook's *Her Husband*. MARBL, Olwyn Hughes Papers 1956–97, Box 2, folder 20.
53. Department of Special Collections, Stanford University, Nathaniel Tarn Papers, Box 29, folder 3.
54. Elizabeth Sigmund, 'Why It's Time to Honour Sylvia', *Devon Today*, April 2000, 34–6.
55. Letter to Olive Higgins Prouty, 22 January 1963. Lilly, Plath MSS II, Box 6a.
56. Ted Hughes, 'The Art of Poetry LXXI', *Paris Review* 134 (1995), 98.
57. Olwyn Hughes, Corrections of Diane Middlebrook's *Her Husband*. MARBL, Olwyn Hughes Papers 1956–97, Box 2, folder 20.

Chapter 1

1. Ted Hughes, 'Introduction', in Sylvia Plath, *Johnny Panic and the Bible of Dreams, and Other Prose Writings* (London: Faber, 1977), 13.
2. Elizabeth Drew, *The Modern Novel: Some Aspects of Contemporary Fiction* (New York: Harcourt Brace, 1926), 110.
3. Ibid., 116.
4. Elizabeth Drew, *The Novel: A Modern Guide to Fifteen English Masterpieces* (New York: Norton, 1963), 265-6. See also *The Enjoyment of Literature* (New York: Norton, 1935), 145.
5. Ibid., 266.
6. Drew's lecture notes on *To the Lighthouse*, in which she interprets the novel in the same metaphysical way as in *The Novel*, are held in the Elizabeth Drew Papers, Sophia Smith Collection, Smith College.
7. Virginia Woolf, *To the Lighthouse*, ed. Stella McNichol and Hermione Lee (London: Penguin [1927], 1992), 35. Plath's copy of the novel is held at MARBL. Drew, *The Novel*, 269.

8. Sylvia Plath, *Venus in the Seventh*, 64. MARBL, Ted Hughes Papers 1940–1997, Box 140, folder 11.

9. Virginia Woolf, *Mrs Dalloway*, ed. David Bradshaw (Oxford: Oxford University Press [1925], 2000), 129. Plath's copy of the novel is held at Mortimer.

10. Ibid.

11. Ibid., 26, 52.

12. As Karen Kukil points out, Elizabeth Minton fantasises the death of her brother during a scene in which she loses her mother's brooch by the sea, which derives from the scene in which Minta Doyle loses her grandmother's brooch by the sea in *To the Lighthouse*. 'Discovering Sylvia Plath and Virginia Woolf in the Archives', 18th Annual Conference on Virginia Woolf, Denver, June 2008.

13. Woolf, *To the Lighthouse*, 167.

14. Ibid., 182.

15. Woolf, *A Writer's Diary*, 145.

16. Woolf, *To the Lighthouse*, 94.

17. Ibid., 8.

18. Drew, *The Novel*, 277, 269.

19. Woolf, *To the Lighthouse*, 43.

20. Letter from Dick Norton to Sylvia Plath, 21 January 1953. Mortimer.

21. Letter from Dick Norton to Sylvia Plath, 29 January 1953. Lilly, Plath MSS II, Box 3.

22. Steven Gould Axelrod, Sylvia Plath: *The Wound and the Cure of Words* (Baltimore, MD and London: Johns Hopkins University Press, 1990), 107.

23. Virginia Woolf, *A Room of One's Own and Three Guineas*, ed. Morag Shiach (Oxford: Oxford University Press [1929, 1938], 1992), 45.

24. Ibid., 69.

25. Ibid., 117.

26. Ibid.

27. Isobel Armstrong and Alan Sinfield, '"This Drastic Split in the Functions of a Whole Woman": An Uncollected Article by Sylvia Plath', *Literature and History* 1 (1990), 77.

28. Ben Yagoda, *About Town: The* New Yorker *and the World It Made* (New York: Da Capo, 2000), 300–1. See *J* 545, 295, 327-8, 482, 487, 496, 511; *LH* 208, 249, 252, 284.

29. Thomas Leitch, 'The *New Yorker* School', *Critical and Creative Approaches to the Short Story*, ed. Noel Kaylor (Lewiston, NY: E. Mellen Press, 1997), 125.

30. Ibid., 149.

31. Ibid., 144.

32. Yagoda, *About Town*, 294.

33. Sylvia Plath, 'The Matisse Chapel'. Lilly, Plath MSS II, Box 13, folder 4.

34. Peter de Vries, 'Afternoon of a Faun', *New Yorker*, 4 February 1956, 27.

35. Peter de Vries, 'The Irony of it All', *New Yorker*, 20 October 1956, 33.

36. Robert Scholes, 'Esther Came Back Like a Retreaded Tire', *Ariel Ascending: Writings about Sylvia Plath*, ed. Paul Alexander (New York: Harper & Row, 1985), 130.

37. Charles Newman, 'Candor is the Only Wile: The Art of Sylvia Plath', *The Art of Sylvia Plath: A Symposium*, ed. Charles Newman (Bloomington, IN and London: Indiana University Press, 1970), 35; Margaret L. Shook, 'Sylvia Plath: The Poet and the College', *Sylvia Plath: The Critical Heritage*, ed. Linda W. Wagner (London and New York: Routledge, 1988), 116.

38. Linda Wagner-Martin, *Sylvia Plath: A Biography* (New York: St. Martin's Press, 1987), 186–7; Alan Sinfield, *Literature, Politics and Culture in Postwar Britain* (Oxford: Blackwell, 1989), 214–16.

39. Sylvia Plath, Notes on English 321b. Mortimer.

40. Jean Stafford et al., *Stories* (New York: Farrar, Strauss & Giroux, 1956). In this volume, Plath read 'Beatrice Trueblood's Story', 'Bad Characters', 'The Liberation' and 'In the Zoo', all first published in the *New Yorker*. Jean Stafford, *Children are Bored on Sunday* (New York: Harcourt Brace, 1953). In this volume, Plath read 'A Country Love Story' and 'The Echo and the Nemesis', first published in the *New Yorker*, and 'The Interior Castle', first published in *Partisan Review*.

41. Jean Stafford, 'The Warlock', *New Yorker*, 24 December 1955, 27–8. When Plath returned to Cambridge in January 1956 after her European vacation, there was a stack of *New Yorker* magazines waiting for her, in which she found this story. Letter to Aurelia Plath, 10 January 1956. Lilly, Plath MSS II, Box 6.

42. *The Collected Stories of Jean Stafford* (New York: Farrar, Strauss & Giroux, 2005), 403.

43. Ibid., 404.

44. Ibid., 39.

45. Stafford, 'The Warlock', 28.

46. *The Collected Stories of Jean Stafford*, 135.

47. Stafford, 'The Warlock', 28.

48. *The Collected Stories of Jean Stafford*, 186.

49. Ibid., 188.

50. Ibid., 186. See Sylvia Plath, *The Bell Jar*: early draft, Chapter 4. Mortimer.

51. Ibid., 307, 306, 309, 310.

52. Ibid., 285, 287.

53. Sylvia Townsend Warner, 'The Locum Tenens', *New Yorker*, 29 March 1958, 35.

54. Sylvia Townsend Warner, 'Shadows of Death', *New Yorker*, 30 May 1959, 25.

55. Ibid.

56. Sylvia Townsend Warner, 'A Golden Legend', *New Yorker*, 8 February 1958, 28.

57. Ibid.

58. Sylvia Townsend Warner, 'Interval for Metaphysics', *New Yorker*, 25 October 1958, 38.

59. Mavis Gallant, 'August', *New Yorker*, 29 August 1959, 38.

60. Mavis Gallant, 'Jeux d'Été', *New Yorker*, 27 July 1957, 33.

61. Mavis Gallant, 'The Moabitess', *New Yorker*, 2 November 1957, 44.

62. Mavis Gallant, 'Bernadette', *New Yorker*, 12 January 1957, 31.

63. Mavis Gallant, 'Green Water, Green Sky', *New Yorker*, 27 June 1959, 22–9; 'Travellers Must Be Content', *New Yorker*, 11 July 1959, 27–54; 'August', *New Yorker*, 29 August 1959, 26–63.
64. Gallant, 'Green Water, Green Sky', 22.
65. Gallant, 'August', 27.
66. Ibid.
67. The four most popular women's magazines throughout the 1950s were *Ladies' Home Journal*, *McCall's*, *Good Housekeeping* and, until it folded in 1957, *Woman's Home Companion*. As Nancy Walker points out, all four 'served middle-class domestic life'. *Shaping Our Mothers' World: American Women's Magazines* (Jackson, MS: University Press of Mississippi, 2000), 65. For Plath's ambition to publish women's magazine fiction, see *LH* 91, 148-9, 150, 156, 208, 259, 263, 290, 303, 312, 313, 326, 433; *J* 186, 545, 291, 366, 443, 457, 471.
68. See also letter to Aurelia Plath, 16 April 1962. Lilly, Plath MSS II, Box 6a.
69. Aurelia Plath, 'For the Authors' Series Talk – Wellesley College Club, 3/16, 1976'. Mortimer.
70. Ted Hughes, draft of Introduction to *Johnny Panic and the Bible of Dreams*. MARBL, Ted Hughes Papers, 1940–97, Box 112, folder 16.
71. *The Writer's 1954 Year Book*, 40. Mortimer.
72. Ibid.
73. Ibid., 38
74. Letter to Warren Plath, 6 July 1955. Lilly, Plath MSS II, Box 5.
75. Letter to Warren Plath, 28 July 1955. Lilly, Plath MSS II, Box 5.
76. See Kathleen Perry, 'God is Love', *Ladies' Home Journal*, February 1955, 49, 142–4; Victoria Ferguson, 'One Magic Morning', *McCall's*, April 1955, 49, 98–106; Louis Paul, 'Sister Louise Goes to Town', *McCall's*, January 1955, 38, 76–81.
77. Ann Chidester, 'The Bride's Sister', *Ladies' Home Journal*, June 1955, 88.
78. Letter to Aurelia Plath, 15 January 1955. Lilly, Plath MSS II, Box 5.
79. Hamlen Hunt, 'Marry I Must', *Ladies' Home Journal*, November 1957, 72, 110–12.
80. Sylvia Plath, 'The Smoky Blue Piano'. Lilly, Plath MSS II, Box 8, folder 17.
81. See, for example, Jean O'Connell, 'Into the Here', *Ladies' Home Journal*, July 1951, 40; Isabel Langis, 'The End of the Beautiful Friendship', *Good Housekeeping*, February 1957, 115.
82. Sylvia Plath, 'Platinum Summer'. Lilly, Plath MSS II, Box 8, folder 16.
83. Joseph Marx, 'Young Enough to Know Better', *Ladies' Home Journal*, May 1955, 55, 132-8.
84. George Sumner Albee, 'The Ugliest Woman in Town', *Ladies' Home Journal*, April 1955, 104.
85. Letter to Aurelia Plath, 18 March 1956. Lilly, Plath MSS II, Box 6.
86. Sylvia Plath, Poems: Lists, 1959–63. Mortimer.
87. Sylvia Plath, 'The Christmas Heart'. Lilly, Plath MSS II, Box 8, folder 11.
88. Plath, 'Platinum Summer'.

89. *The Tender Trap*, dir. Charles Walters, 1955. VHS, MGM / UA Home Video, 1993.
90. Viña Delmar, 'Midnight of a Bridesmaid', *Ladies' Home Journal*, March 1955, 194.
91. Ibid.
92. Sylvia Plath, 'The Laundromat Affair'. MARBL, Ted Hughes Papers 1940–1997, Box 139, folder 30.
93. Ann Ritner, 'The Heart Has its Reasons', *Ladies' Home Journal*, March 1954, 168.
94. Ibid.
95. Sylvia Plath, 'Operation Valentine'. MARBL, Ted Hughes Papers 1940–1997, Box 139, folder 35.
96. Susan Hubert , *Questions of Power: The Politics of Women's Madness Narratives* (Newark, DE: University of Delaware Press and London: Associated University Presses, 2002), 19.
97. Marilyn Yalom, *Maternity, Mortality and the Literature of Madness* (London: Pennsylvania State University Press, 1985), 10.
98. Anthony Burgess, 'Transatlantic Englishmen', *The Observer*, 27 January 1963, 22.
99. 'New Fiction', *The Times*, 24 January 1963, 13.
100. Letter from Elizabeth Lawrence to Sylvia Plath, 16 January 1963. Mortimer.
101. Patricia Blake, 'I Was Afraid to be a Woman', *Cosmopolitan*, June 1959, 57.
102. Ibid., 58.
103. Ibid.
104. Ibid.
105. Ibid., 61.
106. Eugene D. Fleming, 'Psychiatry and Beauty', *Cosmopolitan*, June 1959, 34.
107. Ibid., 33.
108. Ibid., 36.
109. Ibid.
110. Linda Wagner-Martin, *The Bell Jar, A Novel of the Fifties* (New York: Twayne, 1992), 79.
111. Tim Kendall, *Sylvia Plath: A Critical Study* (London: Faber, 2001), 57.
112. Wagner-Martin, *Sylvia Plath: A Biography*, 164.
113. Shirley Jackson, *The Road Through the Wall, Hangsaman, The Bird's Nest* (New York: Quality Paperback Book Club [1948, 1951, 1953], 1998), 351.
114. Ibid., 375.
115. Ibid.
116. Ibid., 318.
117. Ibid.
118. Ibid., 295.
119. Eddie Cohen, letter to Sylvia Plath, 4 April 1951. Lilly, Plath MSS II, Box 1.
120. *The Snake Pit*, dir. Anatole Litvak, perf. Olivia de Havilland. DVD, Twentieth-Century Fox, 1948.

121. Mary Jane Ward, *The Snake Pit* (New York: Random House, 1946), 12.
122. Ibid., 37.
123. Ibid., 89.
124. Ibid.
125. Ibid., 133.
126. Ibid., 84.
127. Ibid., 103.
128. Ibid., 272.
129. Jennifer Dawson, *The Ha-Ha* (London: Virago, 1985), 56.
130. Ibid., 67.
131. Ibid., 166.
132. Woolf, *A Room of One's Own and Three Guineas*, 134.
133. H.D., *Tribute to Freud* (Boston, MA: New Directions [1956], 1974), 116.
134. Anaïs Nin, *Under a Glass Bell, and Other Stories* (Athens, OH: Ohio University Press [1947], 1995), 13.
135. Antonia White, *Beyond the Glass* (London: Virago, 1954), 70.
136. Letter to Aurelia Plath, 2 January 1957. Lilly, Plath MSS II, Box 6.
137. *Letters of Ted Hughes*, 97.
138. Ted Hughes, 'The Art of Poetry LXXI', 95.
139. *Letters of Ted Hughes*, 53.
140. Ted Hughes, letter to Sylvia Plath, 10 October 1956. Lilly, Plath MSS II, Box 6.
141. Sylvia Plath, 'First Date'. Lilly, Plath MSS II, Box 8, folder 12.
142. Ted Hughes, letter to Sylvia Plath, 10 October 1956. Lilly, Plath MSS II, Box 6.
143. *Letters of Ted Hughes*, 72–3.
144. Ibid., 67.
145. Sylvia Plath, Notes for Poem Subjects, n.d. Mortimer.
146. Heather Clark, '"Wilful Revisionism": Rivalry and Remaking in the Early Work of Sylvia Plath and Ted Hughes', *Symbiosis* 9 (2005), 175–91. See also idem, 'Tracking the Thought-Fox: Sylvia Plath's Revision of Ted Hughes', *Journal of Modern Literature* 28 (2005), 100–12.
147. Ted Hughes, letters to Sylvia Plath, 9 October 1956; 10 October 1956. Lilly, Plath MSS II, Box 6.
148. See Tracy Brain, *The Other Sylvia Plath* (Harlow: Longman, 2001), 145–7, for an argument that the story is influenced by Virginia Woolf's 'The Legacy'.
149. Sylvia Plath, *Venus in the Seventh*, 76. MARBL, Ted Hughes Papers 1940–1997, Box 140, folder 11.
150. *Letters of Ted Hughes*, 76.
151. Sylvia Plath, Poems: Lists, 1959–1963. Mortimer.
152. See letter to Aurelia Plath, 26 December 1959. Lilly, Plath MSS II, Box 6.
153. Letter to Aurelia Plath, 16 October 1956. Lilly, Plath MSS II, Box 6.
154. *Letters of Ted Hughes*, 46.
155. Ibid., 45. See Ted Hughes, *Difficulties of a Bridegroom* (London: Faber and Faber, 1995), ix.
156. Ted Hughes, 'The Callum-Makers: A Fable'. MARBL, Ted Hughes Papers, 1940–1997, Box 87, folder 2; 'Bartholomew Pygge, Esq.', *Granta*, 4 May, 1957, 23–5.

157. Hughes, *Difficulties of a Bridegroom*, 40.
158. Sylvia Plath, 'The Invisible Man', 2–6. MARBL, Ted Hughes Papers 1940–1997, Box 139, folder 26.
159. Sylvia Plath, 'The Invisible Man', 15. Mortimer.
160. Ted Hughes, *Difficulties of a Bridegroom*, 89.
161. Ibid.

Chapter 2

1. Plath wrote the following poems on the verso of the extant drafts of *The Bell Jar*: 'Elm', 'The Rabbit Catcher', 'Pheasant', 'Among the Narcissi', 'Crossing the Water', 'An Appearance', 'The Tour', 'The Courage of Shutting Up', 'The Bee Meeting', 'Berck-Plage', 'Fever 103°', 'Waking in Winter', 'New Year on Dartmoor'. Mortimer.
2. Lynda Bundtzen, *The Other Ariel* (Amherst, MA: University of Massachusetts Press, 2001), 5–6; Susan Van Dyne, *Revising Life: Sylvia Plath's Ariel Poems* (Chapel Hill, NC: University of North Carolina Press, 1993), 102; Tracy Brain, *The Other Sylvia Plath* (Harlow: Longman, 2001), 202–7.
3. The last two stories she rewrote in January 1955 for *Mademoiselle*'s short story contest (*LH* 155). The manuscript of 'Among the Bumblebees' at MARBL was written while Plath was living at Lawrence House, from February 1954 to May 1955, and it is most likely that she wrote the story for Kazin's course in Fall 1954. The manuscript at the Lilly Library is a Smith College assignment.
4. In *Sylvia Plath: A Biography* (New York: St. Martin's Press, 1987) Linda Wagner-Martin writes that Plath wrote 'at least fifty-five new poems' for Alfred Fisher in the Spring 1955 semester (117). This would be a prodigious rate of production, however, greater even than that at which Plath wrote in the autumn of 1962, and in fact she seems to have shown Fisher some twenty poems before the semester began (*LH* 149, 151). Whilst many of these Fisher poems were written in the Spring 1955 semester, many others were written earlier, most likely throughout 1954, following her return to Smith.
5. Plath, 'Platinum Summer'. Lilly, Plath MSS II, Box 8, folder 16; Plath, 'The Smoky Blue Piano'. Lilly, Plath MSS II, Box 8, folder 17.
6. Sylvia Plath, 'Tomorrow Begins Today'. Lilly, Plath MSS II, Box 8, folder 19.
7. Nephie Christodoulides, *Out of the Cradle Endlessly Rocking: Motherhood in Sylvia Plath's Work* (New York and Amsterdam: Rodopi, 2005), 50.
8. Plath, 'The Smoky Blue Piano', 13.
9. Sylvia Plath, 'Home is Where The Heart Is'. Lilly, Plath MSS II, Box 8, folder 12.
10. Sylvia Plath, 'The Matisse Chapel'. Lilly, Plath MSS II, Box 13, folder 4.
11. Ibid.
12. Christina Britzolakis, *Sylvia Plath and the Theatre of Mourning* (Oxford: Clarendon Press, 1999), 31.

13. Sylvia Plath, *Venus in the Seventh*, 42–3, 76. MARBL, Ted Hughes Papers 1940–1997, Box 140, folder 11.
14. Ibid., 43, 73.
15. Ibid., 42.
16. Ibid., 68, 70-1.
17. Tim Kendall, *Sylvia Plath: A Critical Study* (London: Faber, 2001), 13.
18. *Letters of Ted Hughes*, 182.
19. Brain, *The Other Sylvia Plath*, 153-5.
20. Letter to James Michie, 14 November 1961. Mortimer.
21. Brain, *The Other Sylvia Plath*, 155.
22. Linda Wagner-Martin, *The Bell Jar, A Novel of the Fifties* (New York: Twayne, 1992), 82.
23. Sylvia Plath, Plan of *The Bell Jar*. Mortimer.
24. Kendall, *Sylvia Plath*, 42.
25. Christina Britzolakis describes this complexity in 'The Babysitters' as 'the ambivalence of "sisterhood"', arguing that it derives from 'the uneasy accommodations of domesticity with professional aspiration' negotiated by educated women like the speaker and addressee of the poem. *Sylvia Plath and the Theatre of Mourning*, 129.
26. Marcia Brown Stern, 'Day Off', Journal Extract, 24 July 1951. Mortimer.
27. Philip Wylie, *Generation of Vipers* (New York and Toronto: Farrar & Rinehart, 1942), ix, xiii.
28. Letter to Marcia Brown, 25 July 1952. Mortimer.
29. Kendall, *Sylvia Plath*, 91.

Chapter 3

1. Stan Smith, *Inviolable Voice: History and Twentieth Century Poetry* (Dublin: Gill & Macmillan, 1982), 200–25. See Jerome Mazzaro, 'Sylvia Plath and the Cycles of History', for the earliest version of this case.
2. Tracy Brain, *The Other Sylvia Plath* (Harlow: Longman, 2001), 36, 37.
3. Sandra Gilbert and Susan Gubar, *No Man's Land, Vol. 3: Letters from the Front* (New Haven, CT and London: Yale University Press, 1994), 297.
4. Al Strangeways, *Sylvia Plath: The Shaping of Shadows* (Madison and Teaneck, NJ: Fairleigh Dickinson University Press and London: Associated University Presses, 1998), 77-131.
5. Robin Peel, *Writing Back: Sylvia Plath's Cold War Politics* (Madison and Teaneck, NJ: Fairleigh Dickinson University Press and London: Associated University Presses, 2002); 'The Ideological Apprenticeship of Sylvia Plath', *Journal of Modern Literature* 27 (2004), 59–72; 'Body, Word and Photograph: Sylvia Plath's Cold War Collage and the Thalidomide Scandal', *Journal of American Studies* 40 (2006), 71–95.
6. Pat Macpherson, *Reflecting on The Bell Jar* (London and New York: Routledge, 1991), 1–5.
7. Richard Fried, '1950–1960', *A Companion to Twentieth Century America*, ed. Stephen J. Whitfield (Oxford and New York: Blackwell, 2004), 84.

8. Martin Halliwell, *American Culture in the 1950s* (Edinburgh: Edinburgh University Press, 2007), 11, 4.

9. Stephen J. Whitfield, *The Culture of the Cold War*, 2nd edn. (Baltimore, MD and London: Johns Hopkins University Press, 2006), 180.

10. Joanne Meyerowitz, *Not June Cleaver: Women and Gender in Postwar America, 1945–1960* (Philadelphia: Temple University Press, 1994), 4.

11. Joanne Meyerowitz, 'Beyond the Feminine Mystique: A Reassessment of Postwar Mass Culture, 1946-1958', *Not June Cleaver*, 229–62.

12. Joanne Meyerowitz, 'Sex, Gender, and the Cold War Language of Reform', *Rethinking Cold War Culture*, ed. Peter J. Kuznick and James Gilbert (Washington, DC and London: Smithsonian Institution Press, 2001), 116.

13. Linda Wagner-Martin, *Sylvia Plath: A Biography* (New York: St. Martin's Press, 1987), 19.

14. Letter to Eddie Cohen, 11 August 1950. Lilly, Plath MSS II, Box 1.

15. Harold H. Kolb, Jr., 'Mr Crockett', *Virginia Quarterly Review* 78, Spring 2002, 316.

16. Strangeways, *Sylvia Plath: The Shaping of Shadows*, 78.

17. Sylvia Plath, 'Room in the World'. Lilly, Plath MSS II, Box 8, folder 16.

18. Sylvia Plath and Perry Norton, 'Youth's Plea for World Peace', *Christian Science Monitor*, 16 March 1950, 19.

19. Langdon Hammer, 'Plath at War', *Eye Rhymes: Sylvia Plath's Art of the Visual*, ed. Kathleen Connors and Sally Bayley (Oxford and New York: Oxford University Press, 2007), 151.

20. Sylvia Plath, Résumé, 1950. Mortimer.

21. Letter to Hans-Joachim Neupert, 12 August 1950. Mortimer.

22. Eddie Cohen, Letter to Sylvia Plath, 9 September 1950. Lilly, Plath MSS II, Box 1.

23. Letter to Hans-Joachim Neupert, 24 December 1950. Mortimer. See also letter to Eddie Cohen, c. 9–14 September 1950. Lilly, Plath MSS II, Box 1.

24. Letter to Eddie Cohen, c. 9–14 September 1950. Lilly, Plath MSS II, Box 1.

25. Ibid. In 'A Vicious American Memory: Sylvia Plath's Critique of Wars, Wars, Wars', *Xchanges* 4:2 (2005), 6–7, Amanda Bradley argues that Virginia Woolf is one of Plath's precursors as a feminist critic of war.

26. Kathleen Connors, 'Living Color: The Interactive Arts of Sylvia Plath', *Eye Rhymes: Sylvia Plath's Art of the Visual*, ed. Kathleen Connors and Sally Bayley (Oxford and New York: Oxford University Press, 2007), 35.

27. Hammer, 'Plath at War', 152.

28. Letter to Warren Plath, 24 July 1952. Lilly, Plath MSS II, Box 2.

29. Letter to Aurelia Plath, 25 October 1952. Lilly, Plath MSS II, Box 3.

30. Letter to Aurelia Plath, 6 November 1952. See also letter to Warren Plath, 6 November, 1952. Lilly, Plath MSS II, Box 3.

31. Letter to Aurelia Plath, 23 February 1951. Lilly, Plath MSS II, Box 1.

32. Letter to Aurelia Plath, 11 May 1952. Lilly, Plath MSS II, Box 2.

33. Sylvia Plath, Draft of Analysis of *Mademoiselle* College Issue. Lilly, Plath MSS II, Box 12, folder 7.

34. Letter to Aurelia Plath, 6 March 1952. Lilly, Plath MSS II, Box 2.

35. See Dick Norton, letter to Sylvia Plath, February 1952. Lilly, Plath MSS II, Box 2.
36. Ellen Schrecker, *No Ivory Tower: McCarthyism and the Universities* (Oxford and New York: Oxford University Press, 1986), 194–5. See also letter to Phil McCurdy, 5 February, 1954, in which Plath refers to the event. Mortimer.
37. Letter to Phil McCurdy, n.d. [March–April 1954]. Mortimer.
38. Cyrilly Abels, Letter to Sylvia Plath, 16 March, 1954. Lilly, Plath MSS II, Box 4.
39. Letter to Aurelia Plath, 5 May, 1953. Lilly, Plath MSS II, Box 3.
40. Sylvia Plath, 'The Perfect Setup', *Seventeen*, October 1952, 102.
41. Ibid., 104.
42. Renée Curry, *White Women Writing White: H.D., Elizabeth Bishop, Sylvia Plath, and Whiteness* (Westport, CT and London: Greenwood Press, 2000), 123–68.
43. Kate A. Baldwin, 'The Radical Imaginary of *The Bell Jar*', *Novel: A Forum on Fiction* 38 (2004), 34.
44. Dorothy Wang, 'Sylvia Plath, Race, and White Womanhood', *The Sylvia Plath 75th Year Symposium at Smith College*, Smith College, 26 April, 2008.
45. Sylvia Plath, *The Bell Jar*, 239. MARBL, Ted Hughes Papers, 1940–1997, Box 139, folder 6.
46. Curry, *White Women Writing White*, 124.
47. Charles J. Ogletree, Jr., *With All Deliberate Speed: Reflections on the First Half Century of Brown v. Board of Education* (New York and London: Norton, 2004), 128.
48. Cited in Whitfield, *The Culture of the Cold War*, 21.
49. Sylvia Plath, 'Brief Encounter'. Lilly, Plath MSS II, Box 8, folder 10.
50. Sylvia Plath, 'Though Dynasties Pass'. Lilly, Plath MSS II, Box 8, folder 18.
51. Thomas Hardy, *The Complete Poems*, ed. James Gibson (Basingstoke and New York: Palgrave, 2001), 543.
52. I have relied here on three accounts of the Rosenberg case: Ronald Radosh and Joyce Milton, *The Rosenberg File*, 2nd edn. (New Haven, CT and London: Yale University Press, 1997); John F. Neville, *The Press, the Rosenbergs, and the Cold War* (Westport, CT and London: Praeger, 1995); and Walter and Miriam Schneir, *Invitation to an Inquest* (London: W. H. Allen, 1966).
53. Quoted in Paul Alexander, *Rough Magic: A Biography of Sylvia Plath* (New York: Da Capo, 1991), 113.
54. *New York Times*, 18 June 1953, 1.
55. *New York Times*, 19 June 1953, 1.
56. Sylvia Plath, *The Bell Jar*: third draft. Mortimer.
57. Pat Macpherson, *Reflecting on The Bell Jar* (London and New York: Routledge, 1991), 36.
58. Letter to Enid Epstein, 26 January 1955. Mortimer.
59. S. Ansky, *The Dybbuk, and Other Writings*, ed. David G. Roskies (New Haven, CT and London: Yale University Press, 2002).
60. Sylvia Plath, 'Suffering Angel', *New Statesman*, 7 December 1962, 829.
61. Macpherson, *Reflecting on The Bell Jar*, 29.

62. Marie Ashe, 'The Bell Jar and the Ghost of Ethel Rosenberg', *Secret Agents: The Rosenberg Case, McCarthyism and Fifties America*, ed. Marjorie Garber and Rebecca Walkowitz (New York: Routledge, 1995), 222.

63. Andrew Ross, *No Respect: Intellectuals and Popular Culture* (London and New York: 1989), 17.

64. Radosh and Milton, *The Rosenberg File*, 344.

65. J. Edgar Hoover, 'The Crime of the Century: The Case of the A-Bomb Spies', *Reader's Digest*, May 1951, 149.

66. Max Eastman, 'Why We Must Outlaw the Communist Party', *Reader's Digest*, September 1950, 42–4; J. Edgar Hoover, 'Red Spy Masters in America', *Reader's Digest*, August 1952, 83–7; Ken Jones, 'The FBI Wants You', *Reader's Digest*, February 1951, 65–8. For the anti-Communism of the *Reader's Digest*, see Marianne Russ, 'The *Reader's Digest* During the McCarthy Era', <http://list.msu.edu/cgi-bin/wa?A2=ind0209a&L=aejmc&F=&S=&P=1510>. Accessed 15 June 2007.

67. J. Edgar Hoover, *On Communism* (New York: Random House, 1969), 100.

68. 'Text of Judge Kaufman's Statement on Sentencing Bomb Spies', *The New York Times*, 6 April 1951, 10.

69. Dwight D. Eisenhower, *The White House Years: Mandate for Change, 1953–1956* (London: Heinemann, 1963), 225.

70. Radosh and Milton, *The Rosenberg File*, 280–1.

71. Ibid., 264, 102.

72. Sylvia Plath, 'Dialogue'. Lilly, Plath MSS II, Box 8, folder 11.

73. Sylvia Plath, *The Bell Jar*: early draft, Chapter 4, p. 13. Mortimer.

74. 'Guest Editor Schedule'. Lilly, Plath MSS II, Box 12, folder 7.

75. Sylvia Plath, Calendar, 1953. Lilly, Plath MSS II, Box 7, folder 5.

76. Sylvia Plath, 'B. and K. at the Claridge', *Smith Alumnae Quarterly*, November 1956, 17. See *LH* 242.

77. Baldwin, 'The Radical Imaginary of *The Bell Jar*', 30–3.

78. Plath, *The Bell Jar*: early draft, Chapter 4, p. 1.

79. J. Edgar Hoover, *Masters of Deceit: The Story of Communism in America* (London: J. M. Dent & Sons, 1958), 267.

80. See Peel, *Writing Back*, 58, and Halliwell, *American Culture in 1950s*, 189–224, for the place of Plath's collage in the history of the genre.

81. Jacqueline Rose, *The Haunting of Sylvia Plath*, 2nd edn. (London: Virago, 1996), 9–10; Peel, *Writing Back*, 58–61.

82. *Public Papers of the Presidents of the United States: Dwight D. Eisenhower, 1953* (Washington, DC: US Government Printing Office, 1960), 272.

83. 'A Push that Put Polaris Way Ahead', *Life*, 6 June 1960, 112.

84. Ibid., 113.

85. Cited in Whitfield, *The Culture of the Cold War*, 60.

86. Letter to Marcia Brown Plumer, December 1961. Mortimer.

87. Letter to Hans-Joachim Neupert, 12 August 1950.

88. *Dr. Strangelove*, dir. Stanley Kubrick, perf. Peter Sellers, 1963. DVD, Columbia Tristar, 2004.

89. Langdon Hammer, 'Plath's German', *The Sylvia Plath 75th Year Symposium at Smith College*, Smith College, 26 April 2008.

90. Hammer, 'Plath's German'. See Anita Helle, 'Reading Plath Photographs: In and Out of the Museum', *The Unraveling Archive: Essays on Sylvia Plath*, ed. Anita Helle (Ann Arbor, MI: University of Michigan Press, 2007), 187, for an analysis of this photograph.
91. Letter to Hans-Joachim Neupert, 30 May 1950. Lilly, Plath MSS II, Box 1.
92. Sylvia Plath, 1953 Calendar, Lilly, Plath MSS II Box 7, folder 5.
93. Plath's copy of this book is held at MARBL.
94. Letters to Aurelia Plath, 10 January 1960; 24 January 1960. Lilly, Plath MSS II, Box 6.
95. Letter to Aurelia Plath, 2 August 1960. Lilly, Plath MSS II, Box 6.
96. Sylvia Plath, Calendar, 1 October 1962; 4 January 1963. Mortimer.
97. Peter Orr, ed., *The Poet Speaks: Interviews with Contemporary Poets* (London: Routledge & Kegan Paul, 1966), 169.
98. Don Heinrich Tolzmann, ed., *German-Americans in the World Wars, Vol. IV: The World War Two Experience* (Munich and London: Saur, 1995-96).
99. Gordon Lameyer, *Dear Sylvia*, unpublished typescript. Lilly, Lameyer MSS.
100. Hammer, 'Plath at War', 150.

Chapter 4

1. Sylvia Plath, 'Mlle's Last Word on College, '53', *Mademoiselle*, August 1953, 235.
2. 'Mademoiselle's College Board Contest', *Mademoiselle*, August 1952, 353.
3. Neva Nelson and Janet Wagner, 'Jobiographies', *Mademoiselle*, August 1953, 252.
4. 'S^n', *Mademoiselle*, August 1953, 274.
5. Ibid.
6. Beth Bailey, *From Front Porch to Back Seat: Courtship in Twentieth-Century America* (Baltimore, MD and London: Johns Hopkins University Press, 1988), 119–20.
7. Paul Landis cites the opposing views of Walter Stokes and Albert Ellis, published in *Marriage and Family Living*, but contradicts them both. *Making the Most of Marriage* (New York: Appleton-Century-Crofts, 1955), 250. In the 1958 edition of their book, Judson and Mary Landis acknowledge Kinsey's work on premarital sex in women, but discount its relevance. *Building a Successful Marriage*, 3rd edn. (Englewood Cliffs, NJ: Prentice Hall, 1958), 213, 221.
8. Judson and Mary Landis, *Building a Successful Marriage*, 2nd edn. (New York: Prentice Hall, 1953), 138–43.
9. Paul Landis, *Making the Most of Marriage*, 264–5.
10. John Schindler, *Woman's Guide to Better Living, 52 Weeks a Year* (Engelwood Cliffs, NJ: Prentice-Hall, 1957), 206.
11. Peter Bertocci, *The Human Venture in Sex, Love and Marriage* (New York: Association Press, 1949), 50, 36, 61, 79.

12. Letter to Ann Davidow, January 1952. Mortimer.
13. Sylvia Plath, 'Den of Lions', *Seventeen*, 10 (May 1951), 144. Cf. *J* 14.
14. Plath, 'Den of Lions', 145.
15. Ibid.
16. Letter to Ann Davidow, 21 March 1952. Mortimer.
17. Sylvia Plath, *The Bell Jar*: third draft, 271. Mortimer.
18. The journal is held at Mortimer.
19. Aurelia Plath, 'Discussions on the Role of Woman and Sex', Biographical Jottings. Mortimer.
20. Margaret Culkin Banning, *The Case for Chastity* (New York and London: Harper, 1937); 'The Case for Chastity', *Reader's Digest*, 31 (August 1937), 1–10.
21. Banning, *The Case for Chastity*, 3, 13, 16, 1.
22. Ibid., 22.
23. Ibid.
24. Tim Kendall, *Sylvia Plath: A Critical Study* (London: Faber, 2001), 55.
25. Olive Higgins Prouty, letter to Aurelia Plath, 26 August 1953. Lilly, Plath MSS II, Box 4.
26. 'Sleeping Pills Missing with Wellesley Girl', *Boston Herald*, 26 August 1953. Aurelia Plath's copies of this article are at Lilly, Plath MSS II, Oversize no. 11.
27. Letter to Aurelia Plath, 28 October 1959. Lilly, Plath MSS II, Box 6.
28. Perry Norton, e-mail to author, 11 December 2009.
29. See Alex Beam, interview with Ruth Tiffany Barnhouse, 9 August 1997. Audio CD. Mortimer.
30. John Ehrenreich, ed., *The Cultural Crisis of Modern Medicine* (New York and London: Monthly Review Press, 1978), 15.
31. Irving Zola, 'Medicine as an Institution of Social Control', in ibid., 80, 81.
32. Diana Scully and Pauline Bart, 'A Funny Thing Happened on the Way to the Orifice: Women in Gynaecology Textbooks', in John Ehrenreich, *The Cultural Crisis of Modern Medicine*, 213.
33. Diana Scully, *Men Who Control Women's Health: The Miseducation of Obstetrician-Gynecologists*, 2nd edn. (New York and London: Teachers College Press, 1994), 107.
34. Scully and Bart, 'A Funny Thing', 217.
35. Thomas Jeffcoate, *Principles of Gynaecology* (London: Butterworth, 1967), 726, cited in Scully and Bart, 'A Funny Thing', 220.
36. Gena Corea, *The Hidden Malpractice: How American Medicine Treats Women as Patients and Professionals* (New York: William Morrow, 1977), 17.
37. Sylvia Plath, 'Nine Letters to Lynne Lawner', *Antaeus* 28 (1978), 50.
38. Plath, *The Bell Jar*: early draft, Chapter 3, p. 14. Mortimer.
39. Doris Haire, 'The Cultural Warping of Childbirth', in John Ehrenreich, *The Cultural Crisis of Modern Medicine*, 192.
40. Adrienne Rich, *Of Woman Born: Motherhood as Experience and Institution* (New York: Norton, 1976), 176.
41. Sylvia Plath, *The Bell Jar*: second draft, Chapter 6, p. 3. Mortimer.
42. The Boston Women's Health Book Collective, *Our Bodies, Ourselves: A Book by and for Women* (New York: Simon & Schuster, 1973), 252.

43. Haire, 'The Cultural Warping of Childbirth', 192.
44. See Donald Caton, *What a Blessing She Had Chloroform: The Medical and Social Response to the Pain of Childbirth from 1800 to the Present* (New Haven, CT: Yale University Press, 1999), 130–51.
45. See Judith Walzer Leavitt, 'Birthing and Anesthesia: The Debate over Twilight Sleep', *Signs* 6 (1980), 147–64.
46. Hanna Rion, *The Truth About Twilight Sleep* (New York: McBride, Nast & Co., 1915), 358.
47. Plath's copy of the book is held at Mortimer. She has written exclamation marks in the margin of the book next to Dick-Read's statements that 'childbirth is not a physical function' (11) and that girls tend to fall in love with one 'semi-divine individual' (7). She marks numerous passages on fear as the mother's main cause of pain in delivery and underlines all the sub-headings in Chapter V on the things that intensify this pain. Chapter IX, on diet, is heavily underlined.
48. Sylvia Plath, 'Nine Letters to Lynne Lawner', 50.
49. Letter to Marcia Brown Plumer, 8 February 1960. Mortimer.
50. Plath, 'Nine Letters to Lynne Lawner', 50. See also *LH* 374; Letter to Marcia Brown Plumer, 1 April 1960. Mortimer.
51. Plath, *The Bell Jar*: early draft, Chapter 3, p. 15. Mortimer.
52. Corea, *The Hidden Malpractice*, 16.
53. Scully, *Men Who Control Women's Health*, 138.
54. Ibid., 120.
55. Nancy Hunter Steiner, *A Closer Look at Ariel: A Memory of Sylvia Plath* (Toronto: Popular Library, 1973), 91.
56. Ibid., 92.
57. Maria Farland, 'Sylvia Plath's Anti-Psychiatry', *Minnesota Review* 55-7 (2002): 245–56.
58. Phyllis Chesler, *Women and Madness* (New York: Doubleday, 1972), 61.
59. Ibid., 62, 63.
60. Phyllis Chesler, *Women and Madness*, 2nd edn. (Basingstoke and New York: Palgrave, 2005), 177–8.
61. Chesler, *Women and Madness*, 65.
62. Ibid., 66.
63. Ibid., 67.
64. Inge Broverman et al., 'Sex Role Stereotypes and Clinical Judgements of Mental Health', *Journal of Consulting and Clinical Psychology*, 34 (1970), 1.
65. Ibid., 5.
66. Ibid., 4.
67. Carol Warren, *Madwives: Schizophrenic Women in the 1950s* (New Brunswick, NJ and London: Rutgers University Press, 1987), 106.
68. Ibid.
69. Ibid., 171.
70. Shirley Angrist et al., 'Rehospitalization of Female Mental Patients', *Archives of American Psychiatry* 4 (1961), 363–70.
71. Chesler, *Women and Madness*, 96.
72. Jeffrey Geller and Maxine Harris, ed., *Women of the Asylum: Voices from Behind the Walls, 1840–1945* (New York: Anchor, 1994), 285.

73. Janet Frame, *Faces in the Water* (New York: George Braziller, 1961), 40, 15.

74. R. D. Laing and A. Esterson, *Sanity, Madness and the Family: Families of Schizophrenics*, 2nd edn. (New York: Basic Books, 1971), 150, 162.

75. Chesler, *Women and Madness*, 256, 255.

76. Elaine Showalter, *The Female Malady: Women, Madness and English Culture, 1830–1980* (London and New York: Penguin, 1985), 212.

77. Warren, *Madwives*, 65.

78. Charlotte Perkins Gilman, 'Why I Wrote the Yellow Wall-Paper', *The Yellow Wall-Paper*, ed. Dale Bauer (Boston, MA and New York: Bedford/ St. Martins [1892], 1998), 347.

79. Warren, *Madwives*, 54, 144, 176.

80. Jane Ussher, *Women's Madness: Misogyny or Mental Illness?* (Amherst, MA: University of Massachusetts Press, 1991), 167.

81. Sylvia Plath, *The Bell Jar*: outline of chapters. Mortimer.

82. Sylvia Plath, *The Bell Jar*: third draft, 196–7. Mortimer.

83. 'Fine Art in Signature Fabrics Give New Inspiration to American Fashions', *Harper's Bazaar*, January 1953, 21–4; Jerry Gilden, Advertisement, *Harper's Bazaar*, May 1953, 45.

84. Deborah Nelson compares Plath's and Anne Sexton's views of the 'necessarily confessional relationship of women to their doctors' with the Supreme Court decision in *Roe v. Wade* ten years later: 'The privacy of the doctor's office is rhetorical: it depends upon the woman's facility with language, on her ability to argue convincingly for the autonomy only the doctor can give her'. *Pursuing Privacy in Cold War America* (New York: Columbia University Press, 2002), 106.

85. See Warren, *Madwives*, 129; Leonard Roy Frank, 'The Electroshock Quotationary', *Ethical Human Psychology and Psychiatry* 8 (2006), 157–8.

86. See Peter Breggin, *Brain-Disabling Treatments in Psychiatry: Drugs, Electroshock and the Role of the FDA* (New York: Springer, 1997), 142–4; Bonnie Burstow, 'Electroshock as a Form of Violence Against Women', *Violence Against Women* 12 (2006), 379–81.

87. Linda Wagner-Martin, *Sylvia Plath: A Biography* (New York: St. Martin's Press, 1987), 112. This effect of ECT was distressing to Ernest Hemingway, when he received the treatment in 1960. A. E. Hotchner recalls his comment, 'What is the sense of ruining my head and erasing my memory, which is my capital, and putting me out of business? It was a brilliant cure, but we lost the patient.' *Papa Hemingway: A Personal Memoir* (New York: Random House, 1966), 280. Bonnie Burstow cites the testimony of an electroshock survivor to the Toronto Board of Health in 1984: 'I was . . . studying playwriting. As anybody knows, the kind of creative writing that you do . . . depends strongly on what you are made up of, on what your past memories are . . . I can't write any more . . . Since the shock treatment, I'm missing between eight and fifteen years of memory and skills'. 'Electroshock', 380.

88. Frank, 'The Electroshock Quotationary', 159.

89. Ibid.

90. Quoted in Paul Alexander, *Rough Magic: A Biography of Sylvia Plath* (New York and London: Viking, 1991), 129.

91. Ibid., 130.
92. Frank, 'The Electroshock Quotationary', 157–77.
93. Showalter, *The Female Malady*, 210.
94. Mary Jane Ward, *The Snake Pit* (New York: Random House, 1946), 43.
95. Gordon Lameyer, *Dear Sylvia*. Lilly, Lameyer MSS.
96. Quoted in Alex Beam, *Gracefully Insane: The Rise and Fall of America's Premier Mental Hospital* (New York: Public Affairs, 2001), 155. See also Beuscher's comments in her interview with Karen Maroda, 'Sylvia and Ruth', *salon.com*, 2004. <http://archive.salon.com/books/feature/2004/11/29/plath_therapist>. Accessed 24 July 2007.
97. Ollie Mae Bozarth, 'Shock: The Gentleman's Way to Beat up a Woman', *Madness Network News*, June 1976, 27.
98. Burstow, 'Electroshock', 379.
99. 'Billions of Dollars for Prettiness', *Life*, 24 December 1956, 121.
100. Bernice Peck, 'It Ought to be Taught', *Mademoiselle*, August 1955, 276.
101. Schindler, *Woman's Guide to Better Living*, 173.
102. Naomi Wolf, *The Beauty Myth: How Images of Beauty are Used Against Women* (New York: William Morrow, 1991), 10–11.
103. Bailey, *From Front Porch to Back Seat*, 35–41.
104. 'How to be Marriageable', *Ladies' Home Journal*, March 1954, 46.
105. Bailey, *From Front Porch to Back Seat*, 43.
106. Polly Weaver, 'Pursuit of Learning and the Undaily Male', *Mademoiselle*, January 1958, 81.
107. Ibid.
108. Jhan and June Robbins, '129 Ways to Get a Husband', *McCall's*, May 1958, 28.
109. Judith Chase Churchill, 'What Do You Know About Marriage?', *Woman's Home Companion*, September 1950, 42.
110. Jhan and June Robbins, '129 Ways to Get a Husband', 90.
111. *Voices and Visions, Program 9: Sylvia Plath*. VHS, New York Center for Visual History, 1988.
112. Aurelia Plath, 'Discussions on the Role of Woman and Sex'. Mortimer.
113. Jhan and June Robbins, '129 Ways to Get a Husband', 90.
114. Weaver, 'Pursuit of Learning', 81.
115. Howard Mumford Jones, 'Have College Women Let Us Down?', *Mademoiselle*, January 1952, 128.
116. 'Have College Women Let Us Down? An Answer by Loretta Valtz, Radcliffe, '52', *Mademoiselle*, March 1952, 30.
117. Helen Beal Woodward, 'The White-Collar Girl . . . And How She Grew', *Mademoiselle*, January 1952, 153.
118. Jane Whitbread and Vivien Cadden, 'Dating and Marriage', *Mademoiselle*, August 1954, 331.
119. Russell Lynes, 'What Has Succeeded Success?', *Mademoiselle*, September 1954, 161.
120. Ibid., 165.
121. Adlai Stevenson, 'A Purpose for Modern Woman', *Woman's Home Companion*, September 1955, 30.
122. Plath, 'Nine Letters to Lynne Lawner', 32.

123. Nancy Hunter Steiner, *A Closer Look at Ariel: A Memory of Sylvia Plath* (New York: Harper's Magazine Press, 1973), 81.

124. Stevenson, 'A Purpose for Modern Woman', 30.

125. Barbara Ehrenreich and Deirdre English, *For Her Own Good: Two Centuries of the Experts' Advice to Women*, 2nd. edn. (New York: Anchor, 2005), 26–30, 342.

126. Letter to Ann Davidow, 12 September 1951. Mortimer.

127. Letter to Aurelia Plath, 10 February 1955. Lilly, Plath MSS II, Box 5.

128. Letter to Enid Epstein, 26 January 1955. Mortimer.

129. Herb Graffis, 'The *Esquire* Girl, 1951 Model', *Esquire*, January 1951, 54.

130. See also letters to Aurelia Plath, 14 January 1957; 7 May 1957; 16 September 1960. Lilly, Plath MSS II, Box 6.

131. Schindler, *Woman's Guide to Better Living*, 23.

132. Letter to Aurelia Plath, 11 May 1960. Lilly, Plath MSS II, Box 6.

133. Benjamin Spock, 'Why I'm Rewriting My Baby Book', *Ladies' Home Journal*, September 1957, 22.

134. Robert Coughlan, 'Changing Roles in Modern Marriage', *Life*, 24 December 1956, 109, 110.

135. Dick Emmons, 'How to Help Your Husband Get Ahead (If He Doesn't Already Have One)', *Saturday Evening Post*, 20 March 1954, 42.

136. David Riesman, 'The Found Generation', *American Scholar*, 25 (1956), 431.

137. Benita Eisler, *Private Lives: Men and Women of the Fifties* (New York and London: Franklin Watts, 1986), 293.

138. Cited in Riesman, 'The Found Generation', 432, 431.

139. Linda Wagner-Martin, *Sylvia Plath: A Literary Life*, 2nd. edn. (Basingstoke and New York: Palgrave Macmillan, 2003), 116.

140. Susan R. Van Dyne, *Revising Life: Sylvia Plath's Ariel Poems* (Chapel Hill, NC and London: University of North Carolina Press, 1993), 123.

141. Judith Kroll, *Chapters in a Mythology: The Poetry of Sylvia Plath*, 2nd edn. (Stroud: Sutton Publishing, 2007), 193.

142. Sandra Gilbert and Susan Gubar, *No Man's Land, Vol. 3: Letters from the Front* (New Haven, CT and London: Yale University Press, 1994), 298–302.

143. Christina Britzolakis, *Sylvia Plath and the Theatre of Mourning* (Oxford: Clarendon Press, 1999), 185.

144. See also letter to Aurelia Plath, 6 May 1956. Lilly, Plath MSS II, Box 6; *LH* 253.

145. Letter to Aurelia Plath, 6 May 1956. Lilly, Plath MSS II, Box 6.

146. Letters to Aurelia Plath, 29 November 1956; 2 January 1957. Lilly, Plath MSS II, Box 6.

147. Letters to Aurelia Plath, 18 January 1960; 2 February 1960. Lilly, Plath MSS II, Box 6.

148. Letter to Aurelia Plath, 7 February 1960. Lilly, Plath MSS II, Box 6.

149. Letters to Aurelia Plath, 12 March 1962; 4 May 1962. Lilly, Plath MSS II, Box 6a.

150. Letter to Olive Higgins Prouty, 20 November 1962. Lilly, Plath MSS II, Box 6a.

151. Letter to Marcia Brown Plumer, 21 March 1956. Mortimer.

152. Isobel Armstrong and Alan Sinfield, '"This Drastic Split in the Functions of a Whole Woman": An Uncollected Article by Sylvia Plath', *Literature and History* 1:1 (1990), 77.
153. Sylvia Plath, *The Bell Jar*: early draft, Chapter 4, p. 8. Mortimer.

Chapter 5

1. Sylvia Plath, 'Coincidentally Yours'. Typescript notes. Lilly, Plath MSS II, Box, folder 11.
2. Letter to Aurelia Plath, 24 January 1960. Lilly, Plath MSS II, Box 6.
3. Letter to Aurelia Plath, 7 February 1962. Lilly, Plath MSS II, Box 6a; Letter to Aurelia Plath, 8 December 1962. Mortimer.
4. Letter to Aurelia Plath, 10 March 1960. Lilly, Plath MSS II, Box 6.
5. Letter to Aurelia Plath, 29 December 1961. Lilly, Plath MSS II, Box 6a; *LH* 438, 455.
6. Christina Britzolakis, *Sylvia Plath and the Theatre of Mourning* (Oxford: Clarendon Press, 1999), 18.
7. Marsha Bryant, 'Ariel's Kitchen: Plath, *Ladies' Home Journal*, and the Domestic Surreal', *The Unraveling Archive: Essays on Sylvia Plath*, ed. Anita Helle (Ann Arbor. MI: University of Michigan Press, 2007), 218.
8. Linda Wagner-Martin, *Sylvia Plath: A Literary Life*, 2nd edn. (Basingstoke and New York: Palgrave Macmillan, 2003), 17.
9. Linda Wagner-Martin asserts that the 'The Christmas Heart' was written first and that 'In the Mountains' was written 'the next year' (*Sylvia Plath: A Literary Life*, 19). Although the manuscript of 'The Christmas Heart' is not dated, this reference from Plath's letters, along with the absence of any references to the story in her journals and letters between December 1952 and June 1953, when it would have to have been written if it were the first story, make it clear that 'In the Mountains' was the first story and that 'The Christmas Heart' is the revision, done in 1955.
10. Letter to Aurelia Plath, 18 March 1956. Lilly, Plath MSS II, Box 6.
11. Sylvia Plath, 'The Christmas Heart'. Lilly, Plath MSS II, Box 8, folder 11.
12. Anne Stevenson, *Bitter Fame: A Life of Sylvia Plath* (Boston, MA and New York: Houghton Mifflin, 1989), 206.
13. Letter to Aurelia Plath, 27 January 1961. Lilly, Plath MSS II, Box 6a.
14. Stevenson, *Bitter Fame*, 205.
15. Tracy Brain, *The Other Sylvia Plath* (Harlow: Longman, 2001), 53.
16. Letter from Helena Annan to Sylvia Plath, 19 January 1962. Mortimer.
17. Peter K. Steinberg, '"I Should Be Loving This": Sylvia Plath's "The Perfect Place" and *The Bell Jar*', *Plath Profiles* 1 (2008), 253–62.
18. Brain, *The Other Sylvia Plath*, 91–105.
19. Sylvia Plath, 'The Perfect Place', *My Weekly*, 28 October 1961, 6.
20. Ibid.
21. Ibid.
22. Ibid.
23. Sylvia Plath, 'A Winter's Tale'. Mortimer.
24. Plath, 'The Perfect Place', 4.

25. Ibid., 5.
26. Plath, 'A Winter's Tale'.
27. Plath, 'The Perfect Place', 4.
28. Sylvia Plath, 'Shadow Girl'. Mortimer.
29. Plath, 'The Perfect Place', 5.
30. Sylvia Plath, 'The Visitor'. Lilly, Plath MSS II, Box 8, folder 19.
31. Betty Friedan, *The Feminine Mystique* (New York and London: Norton, 1963), 33–68.
32. Sylvia Plath, 'Home is Where the Heart Is'. Lilly, Plath MSS II, Box 8, folder 12.
33. Kathy Newman, 'True Lies: *True Story Magazine* and Working-Class Consumption in Postwar America', *Minnesota Review* 55–7 (2002), 232.
34. Plath, 'I Lied for Love'. Lilly, Plath MSS II, Box 8, folder 13.
35. Marsha Bryant, 'Plath, Domesticity and the Art of Advertising', *College Literature* 29:3 (2002), 20–1.
36. Nephie Christodoulides, *Out of the Cradle Endlessly Rocking: Motherhood in Sylvia Plath's Work* (Amsterdam and New York: Rodopi, 2005), 32.
37. Aurelia Plath, letter to Carol and Ted Hughes, 2 July 1972. Lilly, Plath MSS II, Box 6a.
38. Sylvia Plath, 'Platinum Summer'. Lilly, Plath MSS, Box 8, folder 16.
39. Dawn Crowell Norman, 'Journal Beauty Workshop', *Ladies' Home Journal*, September 1952, 157.
40. Plath, 'Platinum Summer'.
41. *Good Housekeeping*, January 1945, 9.
42. *Good Housekeeping*, August 1955, 125; October 1955, 89.
43. *Ladies' Home Journal*, November 1952, 34.
44. *Seventeen*, July 1950, 75.
45. *Vogue*, January 1950, 153; *Vogue*, 1 February 1950, 197.
46. *Ladies' Home Journal*, January 1950, 153.
47. Dawn Crowell Norman, 'Personality Brush-Up . . . in Three Acts', *Ladies' Home Journal*, February 1949, 141.
48. Norman, 'Journal Beauty Workshop', 156–7.
49. Britzolakis, *Sylvia Plath and the Theatre of Mourning*, 39.
50. Dick Norton, letter to Sylvia Plath, 26 November 1952. Lilly, Plath MSS II. Box 3.
51. See *J* 107; letter to Ann Davidow, 5 March 1951. Mortimer.
52. Letter to Ann Davidow, January 1952. Mortimer.
53. Sylvia Plath, 'Sunday at the Mintons', Typescript with holograph corrections. Lilly, Plath MSS II, Box 8, folder 18.
54. Ibid., 12.
55. Sally Bayley, 'Sylvia Plath and the Costume of Femininity', *Eye Rhymes: Sylvia Plath's Art of the Visual*, ed. Kathleen Connors and Sally Bayley (Oxford: Oxford University Press, 2007), 194.
56. Sylvia Plath, Draft Analysis of the *Mademoiselle* College Issue. Lilly, Plath MSS II, Box 12, folder 7.
57. Margaret Mead, *Male and Female* (New York: W. Morrow, 1949), 331, 344.

58. R. A. Norton, 'Individualism and Sylvia Plath: An Analysis and Synthesis'. Mortimer.
59. Tracy Brain, 'Dangerous Confessions: The Problem of Reading Sylvia Plath Biographically', *Modern Confessional Writing: New Critical Essays*, ed. Jo Gill (London and New York: Routledge, 2006), 19.
60. *Letters of Ted Hughes*, 151. See *LH* 349-50.
61. Letters to Aurelia Plath, 20 July 1959; 28 July 1959. Lilly, Plath MSS II, Box 6. *Letters of Ted Hughes*, 150–1.
62. Letter to Aurelia Plath, 28 July 1959. Lilly, Plath MSS II, Box 6.
63. Lucas Myers, 'Ah Youth . . . Ted Hughes and Sylvia Plath at Cambridge and After', *Grand Street*, 98.
64. Sylvia Plath, Notes for Poem Subjects, n.d. Mortimer.
65. Sylvia Plath, 'The Fifty-Ninth Bear', Typescript with holograph corrections. Mortimer.

Bibliography

Works by Sylvia Plath

In addition to the works cited in the List of Abbreviations, I have consulted the
following works by Sylvia Plath:

'And Summer Will Not Come Again', *Seventeen* 9, August 1950, 191, 275–6.
'B. and K. at the Claridge', *Smith Alumnae Quarterly*, November 1956,
16–17.
'Den of Lions', *Seventeen* 10, May 1951, 127, 144–5.
Interview with Peter Orr, *The Poet Speaks: Interviews with Contemporary
Poets*, ed. Peter Orr (London: Routledge & Kegan Paul, 1966), 167–72.
'Letters from Sylvia', ed. Gordon Lameyer, *Smith Alumnae Quarterly*, February
1976, 3–10.
'Mlle's Last Word on College, '53', *Mademoiselle*, August 1953, 235.
'Nine Letters to Lynne Lawner', *Antaeus* 28 (1978), 31–51.
'The Perfect Place', *My Weekly*, 28 October 1961, 3–7, 31.
'The Perfect Setup', *Seventeen*, October 1952, 76, 100–4.
'Suffering Angel', Review of *Lord Byron's Wife*, *New Statesman*, 7 December
1962, 828–9.
(with Perry Norton), 'Youth's Plea for World Peace', *Christian Science Monitor*,
16 March 1950, 19.

I have consulted the archives of Plath's work at the Lilly Library, Indiana
University, Bloomington; the Mortimer Rare Book Room, Smith College; and
the Manuscript, Archives, and Rare Book Library, Emory University.

Literary and Cultural Sources

S. Ansky, *The Dybbuk, and Other Writings*, ed. David G. Roskies (New Haven,
CT and London: Yale University Press, 2002).
Margaret Culkin Banning, *The Case for Chastity* (New York and London:
Harper, 1937).
Peter Bertocci, *The Human Venture in Sex, Love and Marriage* (New York:
Association Press, 1949).

Patricia Blake, 'I Was Afraid to Be a Woman', *Cosmopolitan*, June 1959, 57–61.

Jennifer Dawson, *The Ha-Ha* (London: Virago [1961], 1985)

Peter de Vries, 'Afternoon of a Faun', *New Yorker*, 4 February 1956, 27–32.

Peter de Vries, 'The Irony of It All', *New Yorker*, 20 October 1956, 33–7.

Dr. Strangelove, or: How I Learned to Stop Worrying and Love the Bomb, dir. Stanley Kubrick, perf. Peter Sellers, 1963. DVD, Columbia Tristar, 2004.

Dick Emmons, 'How to Help Your Husband Get Ahead (If He Doesn't Already Have One)', *Saturday Evening Post*, 20 March 1954, 42.

Eugene D. Fleming, 'Psychiatry and Beauty', *Cosmopolitan*, June 1959, 31–6.

Janet Frame, *Faces in the Water* (New York: George Braziller, 1961).

Mavis Gallant, 'Bernadette', *New Yorker*, 12 January 1957, 24–34.

Mavis Gallant, 'An Emergency Case', *New Yorker*, 16 February 1957, 34–6.

Mavis Gallant, 'Jeux d'Été', *New Yorker*, 27 July 1957, 30–4.

Mavis Gallant, 'The Moabitess', *New Yorker*, 2 November 1957, 42–6.

Mavis Gallant, 'Green Water, Green Sky', *New Yorker*, 27 June 1959, 22–9.

Mavis Gallant, 'Travellers Must Be Content', *New Yorker*, 11 July 1959, 27–54.

Mavis Gallant, 'August', *New Yorker*, 29 August 1959, 26–63.

Mavis Gallant, *Green Water, Green Sky* (London: Bloomsbury [1959], 1995).

Charlotte Perkins Gilman, *The Yellow Wall-Paper*, ed. Dale Bauer (Boston, MA and New York: Bedford/St. Martins, Press [1892], 1998).

H.D., *Tribute to Freud* (Boston, MA: New Directions [1956], 1974).

Herb Graffis, 'The *Esquire* Girl, 1951 Model', *Esquire*, January 1951, 54. 210–14.

'Have College Women Let Us Down? An Answer by Loretta Valtz, Radcliffe, '52', *Mademoiselle*, March 1952, 30, 34.

J. Edgar Hoover, 'The Crime of the Century: The Case of the A-Bomb Spies', *Reader's Digest*, May 1951, 149–68.

J. Edgar Hoover, *Masters of Deceit: The Story of Communism in America* (London: J. M. Dent & Sons, 1958).

'How Feminine Are You to Men?', *Woman's Home Companion*, May 1946, 34.

'How to Be Marriageable', *Ladies Home Journal*, March 1954, 46–9; April 1954, 48–9; May 1954, 54–5; June 1954, 50–1.

Ted Hughes, 'Bartholomew Pygge, Esq.', *Granta*, May 4, 1957, 23–5.

Ted Hughes, 'Billy Hook and the Three Souvenirs', *Jack and Jill*, July 1958, 26–32.

Ted Hughes, 'The Caning', *Texas Quarterly* III:4, Winter 1960, 27–37.

Ted Hughes, 'Miss Mambrett and the Wet Cellar', *Texas Quarterly* IV:3, Autumn 1961, 46–55.

Ted Hughes, *Difficulties of a Bridegroom* (London: Faber and Faber, 1995).

Shirley Jackson, *The Road Through the Wall, Hangsaman, The Bird's Nest* (New York: Quality Paperback Book Club [1948, 1951, 1954], 1998).

Howard Mumford Jones, 'Have College Women Let Us Down?', *Mademoiselle*, January 1952, 128.

Life, Special Issue on The American Woman, 24 December 1956.

Russell Lynes, 'What Has Succeeded Success?', *Mademoiselle*, September 1954, 101, 161–5.

Mary McCarthy, *The Group* (New York: Harcourt, Brace & World, 1963).

Anaïs Nin, *Under a Glass Bell, and Other Stories* (Athens, OH: Ohio University Press [1947], 1995).

Dawn Crowell Norman, 'Personality Brush-Up . . . in Three Acts', *Ladies' Home Journal*, February 1949, 141.

Dawn Crowell Norman, 'Journal Beauty Workshop', *Ladies' Home Journal*, September 1952, 156–7.

Bernice Peck, 'It Ought to Be Taught', *Mademoiselle*, August 1955, 276.

Jhan and June Robbins, '129 Ways to Get a Husband', *McCall's*, May 1958, 28, 90–2.

John Schindler, *Woman's Guide to Better Living, 52 Weeks a Year* (Engelwood Cliffs, NJ: Prentice-Hall, 1957).

The Snake Pit, dir. Anatole Litvak, perf. Olivia de Havilland. DVD, Twentieth-Century Fox, 1948.

Benjamin Spock, 'Why I'm Rewriting My Baby Book', *Ladies' Home Journal*, September 1957, 22, 25–8.

Jean Stafford, 'The Warlock', *New Yorker*, 24 December 1955, 25–44.

Jean Stafford, *The Collected Stories of Jean Stafford* (New York: Farrar, Strauss & Giroux, 2005).

Adlai Stevenson, 'A Purpose for Modern Woman', *Woman's Home Companion*, September 1955, 29–31.

The Tender Trap, dir. Charles Walters, perf. Frank Sinatra, Debbie Reynolds, 1955. VHS, MGM / UA Home Video, 1993.

Mary Jane Ward, *The Snake Pit* (New York: Random House, 1946).

Sylvia Townsend Warner, 'Wild Wales', *New Yorker*, 28 December 1957, 22–6.

Sylvia Townsend Warner, 'A Golden Legend', *New Yorker*, 8 February 1958, 28–30.

Sylvia Townsend Warner, 'The Locum Tenens', *New Yorker*, 29 March 1958, 32–8.

Sylvia Townsend Warner, 'Interval for Metaphysics', *New Yorker*, 25 October 1958, 38–40.

Sylvia Townsend Warner, 'A Question of Disposal', *New Yorker*, 15 August 1959, 26–31.

Sylvia Townsend Warner, 'The Fifth of November', *New Yorker*, 14 November 1959, 48–51.

Sylvia Townsend Warner, 'Shadows of Death', *New Yorker*, 30 May 1959, 23–6.

Polly Weaver, 'Pursuit of Learning and the Undaily Male', *Mademoiselle*, January 1958, 81–4, 123.

Jane Whitbread and Vivien Cadden, 'Dating and Marriage', *Mademoiselle*, August 1954, 245, 330–41.

Antonia White, *Beyond the Glass* (London: Virago, 1954).

Helen Beal Woodward, 'The White-Collar Girl . . . And How She Grew', *Mademoiselle*, January 1952, 100, 151–3.

Virginia Woolf, *A Writer's Diary*, ed. Leonard Woolf (San Diego: Harcourt, 1953).

Virginia Woolf, *To the Lighthouse*, ed. Stella McNichol and Hermione Lee (London: Penguin [1927], 1992).

Virginia Woolf, *A Room of One's Own and Three Guineas*, ed. Morag Shiach (Oxford: Oxford University Press [1929, 1938], 1992).

Virginia Woolf, *Mrs Dalloway*, ed. David Bradshaw (Oxford: Oxford University Press [1925], 2000).

Philip Wylie, *Generation of Vipers* (New York and Toronto: Farrar and Rinehart, 1942).

Critical and Historical Sources

Paul Alexander, *Rough Magic: A Biography of Sylvia Plath* (New York: Da Capo, 1991).

Shirley Angrist et al., 'Rehospitalization of Female Mental Patients', *Archives of American Psychiatry* 4 (1961), 363–70.

Isobel Armstrong and Alan Sinfield, '"This Drastic Split in the Functions of a Whole Woman": An Uncollected Article by Sylvia Plath', *Literature and History* 1 (1990), 75–9.

Marie Ashe, '*The Bell Jar* and the Ghost of Ethel Rosenberg', *Secret Agents: The Rosenberg Case, McCarthyism and Fifties America*, ed. Marjorie Garber and Rebecca L. Walkowitz (New York: Routledge, 1995), 215–31.

Steven Gould Axelrod, *Sylvia Plath: The Wound and the Cure of Words* (Baltimore, MD and London: Johns Hopkins University Press, 1990).

Beth Bailey, *From Front Porch to Back Seat: Courtship in Twentieth-Century America* (Baltimore, MD and London: Johns Hopkins University Press, 1988).

Kate A. Baldwin, 'The Radical Imaginary of *The Bell Jar*', *Novel: A Forum on Fiction* 38 (2004), 21–40.

Sally Bayley, '"I Have Your Head on My Wall": Sylvia Plath and the Rhetoric of Cold War America', *European Journal of American Culture* 25 (2006), 155–71.

Sally Bayley, 'Sylvia Plath and the Costume of Femininity', *Eye Rhymes: Sylvia Plath's Art of the Visual*, ed. Kathleen Connors and Sally Bayley (Oxford: Oxford University Press, 2007), 183–204.

Alex Beam, *Gracefully Insane: The Rise and Fall of America's Premier Mental Hospital* (New York: Public Affairs, 2001).

Diane S. Bonds, 'The Separative Self in Sylvia Plath's *The Bell Jar*', *Women's Studies* 18 (1990), 49–64.

The Boston Women's Health Book Collective, *Our Bodies, Ourselves: A Book by and for Women* (New York: Simon & Schuster, 1973).

Marilyn Boyer, 'The Disabled Body as a Metaphor for Language in Sylvia Plath's *The Bell Jar*', *Women's Studies* 33 (2004), 199–223.

Ollie Mae Bozarth, 'Shock: The Gentleman's Way to Beat up a Woman', *Madness Network News*, June 1976, 27.

Amanda J. Bradley, 'A Vicious American Memory: Sylvia Plath's Feminist Critique of Wars, Wars, Wars', *XChanges* 4 (2005).

Tracy Brain, *The Other Sylvia Plath* (Harlow: Longman, 2001).

Tracy Brain, 'Dangerous Confessions: The Problem of Reading Sylvia Plath Biographically', *Modern Confessional Writing: New Essays*, ed. Jo Gill (London and New York, Routledge, 2006), 11–32.

Peter Breggin, *Brain-Disabling Treatments in Psychiatry: Drugs, Electroshock and the Role of the FDA* (New York: Springer, 1997).

Wini Breines, *Young, White and Miserable: Growing up Female in the Fifties* (Chicago and London: University of Chicago Press, 1992).

Inge Broverman et al., 'Sex Role Stereotypes and Clinical Judgements of Mental Health', *Journal of Consulting and Clinical Psychology*, 34 (1970), 1–7.

Marsha Bryant, 'Plath, Domesticity and the Art of Advertising', *College Literature* 29 (2002), 17–34.

Marsha Bryant, 'Ariel's Kitchen: Plath, *Ladies' Home Journal* and the Domestic Surreal', *The Unraveling Archive: Essays on Sylvia Plath*, ed. Anita Helle (Ann Arbor, MI: University of Michigan Press, 2007), 211–37.

Christina Britzolakis, *Sylvia Plath and the Theatre of Mourning* (Oxford: Clarendon Press, 1999).

E. Miller Budick, 'The Feminist Discourse of Sylvia Plath's *The Bell Jar*', *College English* 49 (1987), 872–85.

Lynda K. Bundtzen, *The Other Ariel* (Stroud: Sutton Publishing, 2001).

Anthony Burgess, 'Transatlantic Englishmen', *The Observer*, 27 January 1963, 22.

Bonnie Burstow, 'Electroshock as a Form of Violence Against Women', *Violence Against Women* 12 (2006), 372–92.

Donald Caton, *What a Blessing She Had Chloroform: The Medical and Social Response to the Pain of Childbirth from 1800 to the Present* (New Haven, CT: Yale University Press, 1999).

Phyllis Chesler, *Women and Madness*, 2nd edn. (Basingstoke and New York: Palgrave, 2005).

Nephie Christodoulides, *Out of the Cradle Endlessly Rocking: Motherhood in Sylvia Plath's Work* (New York and Amsterdam: Rodopi, 2005).

Heather Clark, 'Tracking the Thought Fox: Sylvia Plath's Revision of Ted Hughes', *Journal of Modern Literature* 28 (2005), 100–12.

Heather Clark, '"Wilful Revisionism": Rivalry and Remaking in the Early Work of Sylvia Plath and Ted Hughes', *Symbiosis* 9 (2005), 175–91.

Kathleen Connors, 'Living Color: The Interactive Arts of Sylvia Plath', *Eye Rhymes: Sylvia Plath's Art of the Visual*, ed. Kathleen Connors and Sally Bayley (Oxford and New York: Oxford University Press, 2007), 1–144.

Stephanie Coontz, *The Way We Never Were: American Families and the Nostalgia Trap*, 2nd edn. (New York: Basic Books, 2000).

Gena Corea, *The Hidden Malpractice: How American Medicine Treats Women as Patients and Professionals* (New York: William Morrow, 1977).

Susan Coyle, 'Images of Madness and Retrieval: An Exploration of Metaphor in *The Bell Jar*', *Studies in American Fiction* 12 (1984), 161–74.

Renée Curry, *White Women Writing White: H.D., Elizabeth Bishop, Sylvia Plath, and Whiteness* (Westport, CT and London: Greenwood Press, 2000).

Susan J. Douglas, *Where the Girls Are: Growing up Female with the Mass Media* (New York: Three Rivers Press, 1994).

Elizabeth Drew, *The Modern Novel: Some Aspects of Contemporary Fiction* (New York: Harcourt Brace, 1926).

Elizabeth Drew, *The Enjoyment of Literature* (New York: Norton, 1935).

Elizabeth Drew, *The Novel: A Modern Guide to Fifteen English Masterpieces* (New York: Norton, 1963).

Barbara Ehrenreich and Deirdre English, *For Her Own Good: Two Centuries of the Experts' Advice to Women*, 2nd edn. (New York: Anchor Books, 2005).

John Ehrenreich (ed.), *The Cultural Crisis of Modern Medicine* (New York and London: Monthly Review Press, 1978).

Benita Eisler, *Private Lives: Men and Women of the Fifties* (New York and London: Franklin Watts, 1986).

Stephen C. Enniss and Karen V. Kukil, 'No Other Appetite': *Sylvia Plath, Ted Hughes, and the Blood Jet of Poetry* (New York: The Grolier Club, 2005).

Maria Farland, 'Sylvia Plath's Anti-Psychiatry', *Minnesota Review* 55–7 (2002), 245–56.

Leonard Roy Frank, 'The Electroshock Quotationary', *Ethical Human Psychology and Psychiatry* 8 (2006), 157–77.

Betty Friedan, *The Feminine Mystique* (London and New York: Norton, 1963).

Jeffrey Geller and Maxine Harris (eds.), *Women of the Asylum: Voices from Behind the Walls, 1840–1945* (New York: Anchor, 1994).

Sandra Gilbert and Susan Gubar, *No Man's Land, Vol. 3: Letters from the Front* (New Haven, CT and London: Yale University Press, 1994).

Martin Halliwell, *American Culture in the 1950s* (Edinburgh: Edinburgh University Press, 2007).

Langdon Hammer, 'Plath at War', *Eye Rhymes: Sylvia Plath's Art of the Visual*, ed. Kathleen Connors and Sally Bayley (Oxford and New York: Oxford University Press, 2007), 145–57.

Langdon Hammer, 'Plath's German', *The Sylvia Plath 75th Year Symposium at Smith College*, Smith College, 26 April 2008.

Nancy Hargrove, *The Journey Toward Ariel: Sylvia Plath's Poems of 1956–1959* (Lund: Lund University Press, 1994).

Anita Helle (ed.) *The Unraveling Archive: Essays on Sylvia Plath* (Ann Arbor, MI: University of Michigan Press, 2007).

Susan Hubert, *Questions of Power: The Politics of Women's Madness Narratives* (Newark, DE: University of Delaware Press; London: Associated University Presses, 2002).

Ted Hughes, *Letters of Ted Hughes*, ed. Christopher Reid (London: Faber and Faber, 2007).

Ted Hughes, 'Introduction', in Sylvia Plath, *Johnny Panic and the Bible of Dreams, and Other Prose Writings* (London: Faber, 1977), 11–20.

Ted Hughes, *Winter Pollen: Occasional Prose*, ed. William Scammell (London: Faber and Faber, 1994).

Ted Hughes, 'The Art of Poetry LXXI', *Paris Review* 134 (1995), 55–94.

C. G. Jung, *The Development of Personality*, tr. R.F.C. Hull (New York: Pantheon, 1954).

Tim Kendall, *Sylvia Plath: A Critical Study* (London: Faber, 2001).

Harold H. Kolb, Jr., 'Mr Crockett', *Virginia Quarterly Review* 78, Spring 2002, 312–23.

Judith Kroll, *Chapters in a Mythology: The Poetry of Sylvia Plath*, 2nd edn. (Stroud: Sutton Publishing, 2007).

Karen V. Kukil, 'Discovering Sylvia Plath and Virginia Woolf in the Archives', 18th Annual Conference on Virginia Woolf, University of Denver, 21 June 2008.

R. D. Laing and A. Esterson, *Sanity, Madness and the Family: Families of Schizophrenics*, 2nd edn. (New York: Basic Books, 1971).

Judith Walzer Leavitt, 'Birthing and Anesthesia: The Debate over Twilight Sleep', *Signs* 6 (1980), 147–64.

Thomas M. Leitch, 'The *New Yorker* School', *Critical and Creative Approaches to the Short Story*, ed. Noel Kaylor (Lewiston, NY: Edwin Mellen Press, 1997), 123–49.

Garry M. Leonard, '"The Woman is Perfected. Her Dead Body Wears the Smile of Accomplishment": Sylvia Plath and *Mademoiselle* Magazine', *College Literature* 19 (1992), 60–82.

Pat Macpherson, *Reflecting on The Bell Jar* (London and New York: Routledge, 1991).

Janet Malcolm, *The Silent Woman: Sylvia Plath and Ted Hughes* (New York: Random House, 1993).

Karen Maroda, 'Sylvia and Ruth', *salon.com*, 2004. <http://archive.salon.com/books/feature/2004/11/29/plath_therapist>. Accessed 24 July 2007.

Elaine Martin, 'Mothers, Madness, and the Middle Class in *The Bell Jar* and *Les mots pour le dire*', *French-American Review* 5 (1981), 24–47.

Elaine Tyler May, *Homeward Bound: American Families in the Cold War Era* (New York: Basic Books, 1988).

Jerome Mazzaro, 'Sylvia Plath and the Cycles of History', *Sylvia Plath: New Views on the Poetry*, ed. Gary Lane (Baltimore, MD and London: Johns Hopkins University Press, 1979), 218–40.

Margaret Mead, *Male and Female* (New York: W. Morrow, 1949).

Joanne Meyerowitz, 'Beyond the Feminine Mystique: A Reassessment of Postwar Mass Culture, 1946–1958', *Not June Cleaver: Women and Gender in Postwar America, 1945–1960*, ed. Joanne Meyerowitz (Philadelphia: Temple University Press, 1994), 229–62.

Joanne Meyerowitz, 'Sex, Gender, and the Cold War Language of Reform', *Rethinking Cold War Culture*, ed. Peter J. Kuznick and James Gilbert (Washington, DC and London: Smithsonian Institution Press, 2001), 106–23.

Diane Middlebrook, *Her Husband: Ted Hughes and Sylvia Plath – A Marriage* (London and New York: Penguin, 2003).

Douglas T. Miller and Marion Nowak, *The Fifties: The Way We Really Were* (Garden City, NY: Doubleday, 1977).

Eva Moskowitz, '"It's Good to Blow Your Top": Women's Magazines and a Discourse of Discontent, 1945–1965', *Journal of Women's History* 8 (1996), 66–98.

Deborah Nelson, *Pursuing Privacy in Cold War America* (New York: Columbia University Press, 2002).

John F. Neville, *The Press, the Rosenbergs, and the Cold War* (Westport, CT and London: Praeger, 1995).

'New Fiction', *The Times*, 24 January 1963, 13.

Charles Newman, 'Candor is the Only Wile: The Art of Sylvia Plath', *The Art of Sylvia Plath: A Symposium*, ed. Charles Newman (Bloomington, IN and London: Indiana University Press, 1970), 21–55.

Kathy M. Newman, 'True Lies: *True Story Magazine* and Working-Class Consumption in Postwar America', *Minnesota Review* 55–7 (2002), 223–44.

Charles J. Ogletree, Jr., *With All Deliberate Speed: Reflections on the First Half*

Century of Brown v. Board of Education (New York and London: Norton, 2004).

Robin Peel, 'The Bell Jar Manuscripts, Two January 1962 Poems, "Elm," and Ariel', *Journal of Modern Literature* 23 (2000), 441–54.

Robin Peel, *Writing Back: Sylvia Plath's Cold War Politics* (Madison and Teaneck, NJ: Fairleigh Dickinson University Press and London: Associated University Presses, 2002).

Robin Peel, 'The Ideological Apprenticeship of Sylvia Plath', *Journal of Modern Literature* 27 (2004), 59–72.

Robin Peel, 'Body, Word and Photograph: Sylvia Plath's Cold War Collage and the Thalidomide Scandal', *Journal of American Studies* 40 (2006), 71–95.

Ronald Radosh and Joyce Milton, *The Rosenberg File*, 2nd edn. (New Haven, CT and London: Yale University Press, 1997).

Adrienne Rich, *Of Woman Born: Motherhood as Experience and Institution* (New York: Norton, 1976).

David Riesman, 'The Found Generation', *American Scholar*, 25 (1956), 421–36.

Neil Roberts, 'The Common Text of Sylvia Plath and Ted Hughes', *Symbiosis* 7 (2003), 157–73.

Jacqueline Rose, *The Haunting of Sylvia Plath*, 2nd edn. (London: Virago, 1996).

Andrew Ross, *No Respect: Intellectuals and Popular Culture* (London and New York: 1989).

Marianne Russ, 'The Reader's Digest During the McCarthy Era', <http://list.msu.edu/cgi-bin/wa?A2=ind0209a&L=aejmc&F=&S=&P=1510>. Accessed 15 June 2007.

Walter and Miriam Schneir, *Invitation to an Inquest* (London: W. H. Allen, 1966).

Robert Scholes, 'Esther Came Back Like a Retreaded Tire', *Ariel Ascending: Writings about Sylvia Plath*, ed. Paul Alexander (New York: Harper & Row, 1985), 130–3.

Ellen Schrecker, *No Ivory Tower: McCarthyism and the Universities* (Oxford and New York: Oxford University Press, 1986).

Diana Scully, *Men Who Control Women's Health: The Miseducation of Obstetrician-Gynecologists*, 2nd edn. (New York and London: Teachers College Press, 1994).

Margaret L. Shook, 'Sylvia Plath: The Poet and the College', *Sylvia Plath: The Critical Heritage*, ed. Linda W. Wagner (London and New York: Routledge, 1988), 114–24.

Elaine Showalter, *The Female Malady: Women, Madness and English Culture, 1830–1980* (London and New York: Penguin, 1985).

Alan Sinfield, *Literature, Politics and Culture in Postwar Britain* (Oxford: Blackwell, 1989).

Stan Smith, *Inviolable Voice: History and Twentieth Century Poetry* (Dublin: Gill & Macmillan 1992).

Pamela St. Clair, 'In Search of the Self: Virginia's Woolf's Shadow across Sylvia Plath's Page', *Woolf in the Real World: Selected Papers from the Thirteenth International Conference on Virginia Woolf*, ed. Karen V. Kukil (Clemson, SC: Clemson University Digital Press, 2003).

Pamela St. Clair and Amanda Golden (ed.), *Virginia Woolf Miscellany* 71, Spring/Summer 2007, special issue on Virginia Woolf and Sylvia Plath.

Peter K. Steinberg, '"I Should Be Loving This": Sylvia Plath's "The Perfect Place" and *The Bell Jar*', *Plath Profiles* 1 (2008), 253–62.

Peter K. Steinberg and Irralie Doel, 'Sylvia Plath's "Perfect Place"', *The Sylvia Plath 75th Year Symposium*, Oxford, 28 October 2007.

Nancy Hunter Steiner, *A Closer Look at Ariel: A Memory of Sylvia Plath* (Toronto: Popular Library, 1973).

Anne Stevenson, *Bitter Fame: A Life of Sylvia Plath* (Boston, MA and New York: Houghton Mifflin, 1989).

Al Strangeways, *Sylvia Plath: The Shaping of Shadows* (Madison and Teaneck, NJ: Fairleigh Dickinson University Press and London: Associated University Presses, 1998).

Don Heinrich Tolzmann (ed.), *German-Americans in the World Wars, Vol. IV: The World War Two Experience* (Munich and London: Saur, 1995–96).

Jane Ussher, *Women's Madness: Misogyny or Mental Illness?* (Amherst, MA: University of Massachusetts Press, 1991).

Susan Van Dyne, *Revising Life: Sylvia Plath's Ariel Poems* (Chapel Hill, NC: University of North Carolina Press, 1993).

Voices and Visions, Program 9: Sylvia Plath. VHS, New York Center for Visual History, 1988.

Linda W. Wagner, 'Plath's "Ladies' Home Journal" Syndrome, *Journal of American Culture* 7 (1984), 32–8.

Linda Wagner-Martin, *Sylvia Plath: A Biography* (New York: St. Martin's Press, 1987).

Linda Wagner-Martin, *The Bell Jar, A Novel of the Fifties* (New York: Twayne, 1992).

Linda Wagner-Martin, *Sylvia Plath: A Literary Life*, 2nd edn. (Basingstoke and New York: Palgrave Macmillan, 2003).

Nancy A. Walker, *Shaping Our Mothers' World: American Women's Magazines* (Jackson, MS: University Press of Mississippi, 2000).

Dorothy Wang, 'Sylvia Plath, Race, and White Womanhood', *The Sylvia Plath 75th Year Symposium at Smith College*, Smith College, 26 April 2008.

Carol Warren, *Madwives: Schizophrenic Women in the 1950s* (New Brunswick, NJ and London: Rutgers University Press, 1987).

Stephen J. Whitfield (ed.), *A Companion to Twentieth Century America* (Oxford and New York: Blackwell, 2004).

Stephen J. Whitfield, *The Culture of the Cold War*, 2nd edn. (Baltimore, MD and London: Johns Hopkins University Press, 2006).

Ben Yagoda, *About Town: The* New Yorker *and the World It Made* (New York: Da Capo, 2000).

Marilyn Yalom, *Maternity, Mortality and the Literature of Madness* (London: Pennsylvania State University Press, 1985).

Index